Praise for *Essential XML* Quick Reference

"I think it is a wonderfully clear and concise summary of a great deal of key XML material. I expect it to find a well-thumbed home on my bookshelf."

—Mary Holstege, PhD,
XML Architect, mathling.com, and W3C XML Schema Working Group Member

"This book is a unique collection of reference material on the most relevant XML-related standards, which takes the important W3C recommendations and puts them all in context. Something that definitely needs to be on every XML developer's desk!"

—Alexander Falk,
President and CEO of Altova, Inc. - The XML Spy Company

"*Essential XML Quick Reference* proves that Aaron Skonnard and Martin Gudgin can distill the essence of a very large, complicated topic like XML into easy to understand, bite-sized pieces. It's an invaluable asset!"

—Brad Wilson,
Principal Software Architect, Quality Software Development

"*Essential XML Quick Reference* is one of the few printed references I would actually buy."

—Don Box,
Series Editor, The DevelopMentor Series

"The full specification is quite verbose. Having the pocket reference makes life simpler when it comes to the 'What was the name of that element again?' or 'What were the order of the parameters to that function?' type questions. When I need a quick, concise, answer, I don't want to have to thumb through hundreds of pages before getting the answer I need. This book is a very welcome, often relied upon, addition to my developer tool belt."

—Drew Marsh,
Senior Architect, Mimeo.com, Inc.

Essential XML
Quick Reference

The DevelopMentor Series—Essential Reading for the Serious Developer

Books in the DevelopMentor Series:

- **Teach from the bottom up.** Before you can learn "how to" you must learn "how it works." Understanding how and why a technology works the way it does builds the problem-solving skills essential for developing great software.

- **Back theory with code.** Analogies and abstractions are great, but the real test is "does the code work?" Sample code is provided to illustrate all the concepts covered.

- **Tell the story.** Software concepts do not exist in arid isolation. They weave a story, and the best stories are created by a community of developers learning from their experiences and finding the best way to share their knowledge with their colleagues. DevelopMentor's technical team has developed its knowledge on real-world development projects in order to bring you the stories you need to truly understand software.

- **Give concise, valuable information.** The DevelopMentor Series writing style is geared toward serious developers. The books are clear and concise, and make core concepts immediately accessible. At the same time, the material is dense and rich with insight. A second reading is often a totally different—and equally valuable—experience from the first reading.

Titles in the Series:

**Watch for future titles in the DevelopMentor Series
and the Microsoft .NET Development Series.**

Essential XML
Quick Reference

A Programmer's Reference to XML, XPath, XSLT, XML Schema, SOAP, and More

Aaron Skonnard
Martin Gudgin

✦✦ Addison-Wesley

Boston • San Francisco • New York • Toronto • Montreal
London • Munich • Paris • Madrid
Capetown • Sydney • Tokyo • Singapore • Mexico City

Many of the designations used by manufacturers and sellers to distinguish their products are claimed as trademarks. Where those designations appear in this book, and Addison-Wesley, Inc., was aware of a trademark claim, the designations have been printed in initial capital letters or in all capitals.

The publisher offers discounts on this book when ordered in quantity for special sales. For more information, please contact

U.S. Corporate and Government Sales
(800) 382-3419
corpsales@pearsontechgroup.com

For sales outside of the U.S., please contact:

International Sales
(317) 581-3793
international@pearsontechgroup.com

Visit AW on the Web: *www.awprofessional.com*

Library of Congress Cataloging-in-Publication Data

Skonnard, Aaron
    Essential XML Quick Reference : a programmer's reference to XML, XPath, XSLT,
    XML Schema, SOAP, and more / Aaron Skonnard, Martin Gudgin.
        p. cm. — (The DevelopMentor series)
    ISBN 0-201-74095-8
    1. XML (Document markup language) I. Gudgin, Martin. II. Title. III. Series.

QA76.76.H94 S59 2001
005.7'2—d21   2001034105

Text printed on recycled and acid-free paper.

ISBN 0201740958

6 7 8 9 1011 ML   07 06 05 04

6th Printing   February 2004

Aaron's dedication:
To my son Nathan, for the glimpse of heaven that you brought to my life

Martin's dedication:
To Matthew and Sam, with love

Chapter Contents

Detailed Contents

List of Acronyms

ASP	Active Server Pages
API	Application Programming Interface
BOM	Byte Order Mark
CR	Carriage Return
CSS	Cascading Style Sheets
COM	Component Object Model
UTC	Coordinated Universal Time
DOM	Document Object Model
DTD	Document Type Definition
XML	Extensible Markup Language
XSL	Extensible Stylesheet Language
HTML	HyperText Markup Language
HTTP	HyperText Transfer Protocol
IDL	Interface Definition Language
ISO	International Standards Organization
IETF	Internet Engineering Task Force
JDK	Java Development Kit
JSP	Java Server Pages
LF	Line Feed
MIME	Multipurpose Internet Mail Extensions

NCName	Non-colonized Name
OMG	Object Management Group
QName	Qualified Name
RPC	Remote Procedure Call
RFC	Request For Comments
SAX	Simple API for XML
SOAP	Simple Object Access Protocol
SQL	Strutured Query Language
UTF	Unicode Transformation Format
UML	Unified Modelling Language
URI	Uniform Resource Identifier
URL	Uniform Resource Locator
URN	Uniform Resource Name
UCS	Universal Character Set
VB	Visual Basic
WD	Working Draft
W3C	World Wide Web Consortium
XInclude	XML Inclusions
Infoset	XML Information Set
XLink	XML Linking Language
XPointer	XML Pointer Language
XSLT	XSL Transformations

Preface

This book is for anyone working with today's mainstream XML technologies. It was specifically designed to serve as a handy but thorough quick reference that answers the most common XML-related technical questions.

It goes beyond the traditional pocket reference design by providing *complete* coverage of each topic along with plenty of meaningful examples. Each chapter provides a brief introduction, which is followed by the detailed reference information. This approach assumes the reader has a basic understanding of the given topic.

The detailed outline (at the beginning), index (in the back), bleeding tabs (along the side), and the page headers/footers were designed to help readers quickly find answers to their questions.

Acknowledgments

Special thanks to all of the reviewers for their thoughtful comments and detailed work, which has vastly improved this book. In particular, thanks to Mary Holstege, Mark Fussell, Chris Lovett, Amit Misra, Alexander Falk, Reyes Ponce, Gary Bushey, Drew Marsh, Brad Wilson, Robert Brunner, Greg Hack, Dan Sullivan, Scott Bloom, Ranjiv Sharma, Tim Ewald, Stuart Halloway, and Don Box. Another special thanks to Kristin Erickson, Stephane Thomas, and Patrick Peterson for their outstanding editorial support throughout the project as well as to the rest of the production staff at Addison-Wesley whose hard work turned our vision into reality. We couldn't have done it without you.

We also thank our families and friends who have contributed in countless non-technical ways. We couldn't have done it without you either.

Chapter 1
XML 1.0 and Namespaces

XML 1.0 and Namespaces in XML provide a tag-based syntax for structuring data and applying markups to documents. Documents that conform to XML 1.0 and Namespaces in XML specifications may be made up of a variety of syntactic constructs such as elements, namespace declarations, attributes, processing instructions, comments, and text. This chapter provides a description of each of the structural elements in XML along with their syntax.

1.1 Elements

```
<tagname></tagname>
<tagname/>
<tagname>children</tagname>
```

Elements typically make up the majority of the content of an XML document. Every XML document has exactly one top-level element, known as the *document element*. Elements have a name and may also have children. These children may themselves be elements or may be processing instructions, comments, CDATA sections, or characters. The children of an element are ordered. Elements may also be annotated with attributes. The attributes of an element are unordered. An element may also have namespace declarations associated with it. The namespace declarations of an element are unordered.

Elements are serialized as a pair of tags: an open tag and a close tag. The syntax for an open tag is the less-than character (<) immediately followed by the name of the element, also known as the *tagname*, followed by the greater-than character (>). The syntax for a close tag is the character sequence </ immediately followed by the tagname, followed by the greater-than character. The children of an element are serialized between the open and close tags of their parent. In cases when an element has no children, the element is said to be *empty*. A shorthand syntax may be used for empty elements consisting of the less-than character immediately followed by the tagname, followed by the character sequence />.

XML does not define any element names; rather, it allows the designer of an XML document to choose what names will be used. Element names in XML are case sensitive and must begin with a letter or an underscore (_). The initial character may be followed by any number of letters, digits, periods (.), hyphens (-), underscores, or colons (:). However, because colons are used as part of the syntax for namespaces in XML, they should not be used except as described by that specification (see Section 1.2). Element names that begin with the character sequence xml, or any recapitalization thereof, are reserved by the XML specification for future use.

Examples

An element with children

```
<Person>
  <name>Martin</name>
  <age>33</age>
</Person>
```

An element with a tagname of `Person`. The element has children with tagnames of `name` and `age`. Both of these child elements have text content.

An empty element

```
<Paid></Paid>
```

An empty element with a tagname of `Paid`

Empty element shorthand

```
<Paid/>
```

An empty element with a tagname of `Paid` using the shorthand syntax

1.2   Elements, namespaces, and namespace declarations

```
<prefix:localname xmlns:prefix='namespace URI'/>
<prefix:localname xmlns:prefix='namespace URI'></
    prefix:localname/>
<prefix:localname xmlns:prefix='namespace URI'>children</
    prefix:localname/>
```

Because XML allows designers to chose their own tagnames, it is possible that two or more designers may choose the same tagnames for some or all of their elements. XML namespaces provide a way to distinguish deterministically between XML elements that have the same local name but are, in fact, from different vocabularies. This is done by associating an element with a namespace. A namespace acts as a scope for all elements associated with it. Namespaces themselves also have names. A namespace name is a uniform resource identifier (URI). Such a URI serves as a unique string and need not be able to be dereferenced. The namespace name and the local name of the element together form a globally unique name known as a *qualified name*.

Namespace declarations appear inside an element start tag and are used to map a namespace name to another, typically shorter, string known as a *namespace prefix*. The syntax for a namespace declaration is `xmlns:prefix='URI'`. It is also possible to map a namespace name to no prefix using a default namespace declaration. The syntax for a default namespace declaration is `xmlns='URI'`. In both cases, the URI may appear in single quotes (`'`) or double quotes (`"`). Only one default namespace declaration may appear on an element. Any number of nondefault namespace declarations may appear on an element, provided they all have different prefix parts. It is legal, although not particularly useful, to map the same URI to more than one prefix.

All namespace declarations have a scope—that is, a set of elements to which they may apply. A namespace declaration is in scope for the element on which it is declared and all of that element's descendants. The in-scope mapping of a given prefix to a namespace name can be overridden by providing a new mapping for that prefix on a descendant element. The in-scope default namespace can be overridden by providing a new default namespace declaration on a descendant element.

The names of all elements in a document that conforms to the Namespaces in the XML specification are QNames. Syntactically, all QNames have a local name and an optional prefix. Both the local name and the prefix are NCNames. An NCName is a name without a colon in it. The syntax for an element with a prefix is the prefix, followed by a colon, followed by the local name. The namespace of an element with a given prefix is the namespace specified by the in-scope namespace declaration for that prefix. It is an error if no such namespace declaration is in scope. The namespace of unprefixed elements is the namespace specified by the in-scope default namespace declaration, if any. If no default namespace declaration is in scope, then such elements are not in any namespace. Elements not in any namespace are known as *unqualified elements*. The namespace name of unqualified elements is the empty string "". If a default namespace declaration is in scope and an unqualified element is required, the default namespace declaration can be masked by providing a namespace declaration of the form `xmlns=''` on the element.

Examples

Qualified and unqualified elements

```
<pre:Person xmlns:pre='urn:example-org:People' >
  <name>Martin</name>
  <age>33</age>
</pre:Person>
```

An element with a local name of `Person` and a prefix of `pre` that is mapped to the namespace name `urn:example-org:People`. The element has children with local names of `name` and `age`. Both of these child elements are unqualified; that is, they are not in any namespace.

Qualified and unqualified elements using a default namespace declaration

```
<Person xmlns='urn:example-org:People' >
  <name xmlns=''>Martin</name>
  <age xmlns=''>33</age>
</Person>
```

An element with a local name of `Person` and no prefix. The element is in the namespace `urn:example-org:People` by virtue of an in-scope default namespace declaration for that URI. The element has children with local names of `name` and `age`. Both of these child elements are unqualified; that is, they are not in any namespace. This example is equivalent to the previous example.

Qualified elements

```
<pre:Person xmlns:pre='urn:example-org:People' >
  <pre:name>Martin</pre:name>
  <pre:age>33</pre:age>
</pre:Person>
```

An element with a local name of `Person` and a prefix of `pre` that is mapped to the namespace URI `urn:example-org:People`. The element has children with local names of `name` and `age`. Both of these child elements also have a prefix of `pre` and are in the `urn:example-org:People` namespace.

Qualified elements using a default namespace declaration

```
<Person xmlns='urn:example-org:People' >
  <name>Martin</name>
  <age>33</age>
</Person>
```

An element with a local name of `Person` and no prefix. The element is in the namespace `urn:example-org:People` by virtue of an in-scope default namespace declaration for that URI. The element has children with local names of `name` and `age`. Both of these child elements are also in the `urn:example-org:People` namespace. This example is equivalent to the previous example.

1.3 Attributes

```
name='value'
name="value"
```

Elements can be annotated with attributes. Attributes can be used to encode actual data or to provide metadata about an element—that is, provide extra information about the content of the element on which they appear. The attributes for a given element are serialized inside the start tag for that element. Attributes appear as name/value pairs separated by an equal sign (=). Attribute names have the same construction rules as element names. Attribute values are textual in nature and must appear either in single quotes or double quotes. An element may have any number of attributes, but they must all have different names.

Examples

Data attributes

```
<Person name='Martin' age='33' />
```

A person represented using attributes rather than child elements

Metadata attributes

```
<age base='16' units='years' >20</age>
<age base="10" units="years" >32</age>
```

Some elements with metadata attributes

1.4 Attributes and namespaces

```
prefix:localname='value'
prefix:localname="value"
```

Attribute names are QNames. The namespace of an attribute with a given prefix is the namespace specified by the in-scope namespace declaration for that prefix. It is an error if no such namespace declaration is in scope. Unprefixed attributes are not in any namespace even if a default namespace declaration is in scope.

Examples

Qualified attributes

```
<Person xmlns='urn:example-org:People'
        xmlns:b='urn:example-org:People:base'
        xmlns:u='urn:example-org:units' >
  <name>Martin</name>
  <age b:base='10' u:units='years' >33</age>
</Person>
```

An attribute with a local name of base in the namespace `urn:example-org:People:base` and an attribute with a local name of units in the namespace `urn:example-org:units`

Unqualified attributes

```
<Person xmlns='urn:example-org:People' >
  <name>Martin</name>
  <age base='10' units='years' >33</age>
</Person>
```

Attributes that are in no namespace, even though a default namespace declaration is in scope

1.5 Processing instructions

```
<?target data?>
```

Processing instructions are used to provide information to the application processing an XML document. Such information may include instructions on how to process the document, how to display the document, and so forth. Processing instructions can appear as children of elements. They can also appear as top-level constructs (children of the document) either before or after the document element.

Processing instructions are composed of two parts: the target or name of the processing instruction and the data or information. The syntax takes the form `<?target data?>`. The target follows the same construction rules as for element and attribute names. Apart from the termination character sequence (`?>`), all markup is ignored in processing instruction content. Processing instructions defined by organizations other than the World Wide Web Consortium (W3C) may not have targets that begin with the character sequence `xml` or any recapitalization thereof.

Namespace declarations do not apply to processing instructions. Thus, creating targets that are guaranteed to be unique is problematic.

Example
Processing instructions

```
<?display table-view?>
<?sort alpha-ascending?>
<?textinfo whitespace is allowed ?>
<?elementnames <fred>, <bert>, <harry> ?>
```

Various processing instructions

1.6   Comments

```
<!-- comment text -->
```

XML supports comments that are used to provide information to humans about the actual XML content. They are not used to encode actual data. Comments can appear as children of elements. They can also appear as top-level constructs (children of the document) either before or after the document element.

Comments begin with the character sequence `<!--` and end with the character sequence `-->`. The text of the comment is serialized between the start and the end sequences. The character sequence `--` may not appear inside a comment. Other markup characters such as less than, greater than, and ampersand (&), may appear inside comments but are not treated as markup. Thus, entity references that appear inside comments are not expanded.

Examples

Legal comments

```
<!-- This is a comment about how to open ( <![CDATA[ ) and
    close ( ]]> ) CDATA sections -->
<!-- I really like having elements called <fred> in my
    markup languages -->
<!-- Comments can contain all sorts of character literals
    including &, <, >, ' and". -->
<!-- If entities are used inside comments ( &lt; for
    example ) they are not expanded. -->
```

Some syntactically legal comments

Illegal comments

```
<!-- Comments cannot contain the -- character sequence -->
<!-- Comments cannot end with a hyphen --->
<!-- Comments cannot <!-- be nested --> -->
```

Some syntactically illegal comments

1.7   Whitespace

Whitespace characters in XML are space, tab, carriage return, and line feed characters. XML requires that whitespace be used to separate attributes and namespace declarations from each other and from the element tagname. Whitespace is also required between the target and data portion of a processing instruction and between the text portion of a comment and the closing comment character sequence (-->) if that text ends with a hyphen (-). XML allows whitespace inside element content, attribute values, processing instruction data, and comment text. Whitespace is also allowed between an attribute name and the equal character and between the equal character and the attribute value. The same is true for namespace declarations. Whitespace is allowed between the tagname of an open or close tag and the ending character sequence for that tag. Whitespace is not allowed between the opening less-than character and the element tagname or between the prefix, colon, and local name of an element or attribute. Nor is it allowed between the start processing instruction character sequence <? and the target.

Examples

Legal use of whitespace

```
<pre:Vehicle xmlns:pre='urn:example-org:Transport'
    type='car' >
  <seats> 4 </seats>
  <colour> White </colour>
  <engine>
    <petrol />
    <capacity units='cc' >1598</capacity>
  </engine >
</pre:Vehicle >
```

Whitespace used in various places in an XML document: between the tagname, namespace declaration, attribute, and closing greater-than character on the top-level element start tag, between each element, in the character content of the `seats` and `colour` elements, between the tagname and the `/>` sequence of the `petrol` element, between the tagname and the closing greater-than character of the end tag for the `engine` element and the top-level element.

Illegal use of whitespace

```
<pre   :Vehicle xmlns:pre='urn:example-org:Transport'
    type='car'>
  < seats>4</ seats>
</pre:Vehicle>
```

Whitespace used incorrectly in various places in an XML document: between `pre` and `:Vehicle` in the start tag of the top-level element, between `xmlns:` and `pre` of the namespace declaration of the top-level element, between the opening less-than character and `seats` in the start tag of the child element, and between `</` and `seats` in the end tag of the child element.

1.8 Prohibited character literals

```
&lt;
&amp;
&gt;
&apos;
&quot;
```

Certain characters cause problems when used as element content or inside attribute values. Specifically, the less-than character cannot appear either as a child of an element or inside an attribute value because it is interpreted as the start of an element. The same restrictions apply to the ampersand because it is used to indicate the start of an entity reference. If the less-than or ampersand characters need to be encoded as element children or inside an attribute value, then a character entity must be used. Entities begin with an ampersand and end with a semicolon (;). Between the two, the name of the entity appears. The entity for the less-than character is < the entity for the ampersand is &.

The apostrophe (') and quote characters (") may also need to be encoded as entities when used in attribute values. If the delimiter for the attribute value is the apostrophe, then the quote character is legal but the apostrophe character is not, because it would signal the end of the attribute value. If an apostrophe is needed, the character entity ' must be used. Similarly, if a quote character is needed in an attribute value that is delimited by quotes, then the character entity " must be used.

A fifth character reference is also provided for the greater-than character. Although strictly speaking such characters seldom need to be "escaped," many people prefer to "escape" them for consistency with the less-than character.

Examples

Built-in entity in element content

```
<IceCream>
  <name>Cherry Garcia</name>
  <manufacturer>Ben &amp; Jerry</manufacturer>
</IceCream>
```

Use of the built-in entity & inside element content

Built-in entity in attribute content

```
<sayhello word='&apos;Hi&apos;' />
```

Use of the built-in entity ' inside attribute content

1.9 CDATA sections

```
<![CDATA[ text content possibly containing literal < or &
characters ]]>
```

CDATA sections can be used to "block escape" literal text when replacing prohibited characters with entity references is undesirable. CDATA sections can appear inside element content and allow < and & character literals to appear. A CDATA section begins with the character sequence <![CDATA[and ends with the character sequence]]>. Between the two character sequences, an XML processor ignores all markup characters such as <, >, and &. The only markup an XML processor recognizes inside a CDATA section is the closing character sequence]]>. The character sequence that ends a CDATA section]]> must not appear inside the element content. Instead, the closing greater-than character must be escaped using the appropriate entity >. CDATA sections cannot be nested.

Example

CDATA section

```
<sometext>
<![CDATA[ They're saying "x < y" & that  "z > y" so I guess
that means that z > x ]]>
</sometext>
```

Use of literal less-than characters in a CDATA section

1.10 The XML declaration

```
<?xml version='1.0' encoding='character encoding'
standalone='yes|no'?>
```

XML documents can contain an XML declaration that if present, must be the first construct in the document. An XML declaration is made up of as many as three name/value pairs, syntactically identical to attributes. The three attributes are a mandatory version attribute and optional encoding and standalone attributes. The order of these attributes within an XML declaration is fixed.

The XML declaration begins with the character sequence <?xml and ends with the character sequence ?>. Note that although this syntax is identical to that for processing instructions, the XML declaration is not considered to be a processing instruction. All XML declarations have a version attribute with a value that must be 1.0.

The character encoding used for the document content can be specified through the encoding attribute. XML documents are inherently Unicode, even when stored in a non-Unicode character encoding. The XML recommendation defines several possible values for the encoding attribute. For example, UTF-8, UTF-16, ISO-10646-UCS-2, and ISO-10646-UCS-4 all refer to Unicode/ISO-10646 encodings, whereas ISO-8859-1 and ISO-8859-2 refer to 8-bit Latin character encodings. Encodings for other character sets including Chinese, Japanese, and Korean characters are also supported. It is recommended that encodings be referred to using the encoding names registered with the Internet Assigned Numbers Authority (IANA).

All XML processors are required to be able to process documents encoded using UTF-8 or UTF-16, with or without an XML declaration. The encoding of UTF-8- and UTF-16-encoded documents is detected using the Unicode byte-order-mark. The XML declaration is mandatory if the encoding of the document is anything other than UTF-8 or UTF-16. In practice, this means that documents encoded using US-ASCII can also omit the XML declaration because US-ASCII overlaps entirely with UTF-8.

Only one encoding can be used for an entire XML document. It is not possible to "redefine" the encoding part of the way through. If data in different encodings needs to be represented, then external entities should be used.

If an XML document can be read with no reference to external sources, it is said to be a *stand-alone document*. Such documents can be annotated with a standalone attribute with a value of yes in the XML declaration. If an XML document requires external sources to be resolved to parse correctly and/or to construct the entire data tree (for example, a document with references to external general entities), then it is not a stand-alone document. Such documents may be marked standalone='no', but because this is the default, such an annotation rarely appears in XML documents.

Example

XML declarations

```
<?xml version='1.0' ?>
<?xml version='1.0' encoding='US-ASCII' ?>
<?xml version='1.0' encoding='US-ASCII' standalone='yes' ?>
<?xml version='1.0' encoding='UTF-8' ?>
<?xml version='1.0' encoding='UTF-16' ?>
<?xml version='1.0' encoding='ISO-10646-UCS-2' ?>
<?xml version='1.0' encoding='ISO-8859-1' ?>
<?xml version='1.0' encoding='Shift-JIS' ?>
```

1.11 Character references

```
&#DecimalUnicodeValue;
&#xHexadecimalUnicodeValue;
```

Many character encodings cannot natively represent the full range of ISO-10646 characters. When an XML document contains characters that cannot be represented natively in the chosen encoding, then these nonrepresentable characters must be written as character references. Character references begin with the character sequence &# followed by the ISO-10646 value of the character to be written in either decimal or hexadecimal form. If the character value is represented in hexadecimal form, then it must be preceded by an x. Character references end with ;.

Character references can only be used for attribute and element content. Nonrepresentable characters appearing as part of element or attribute names or as part of processing instructions or comments cannot be written using character references; rather, a more suitable encoding must be used instead.

Example

Character references

```
<?xml version='1.0' encoding='US-ASCII' ?>
<Personne occupation='&#xe9;tudiant' >
  <nom>Martin</nom>
  <langue>Fran&#231;ais</langue>
</Personne>
```

Character references appearing in element and attribute content

1.12 Well-formed XML

All XML must be well formed. A well-formed XML document is one in which, in addition to all the constructs being syntactically correct, there is exactly one top-level element, all open tags have a corresponding close tag or use the empty element shorthand syntax, and all tags are correctly nested (that is, close tags do not overlap). In addition, all the attributes of an element must have different names. If attributes are namespace qualified then the combination of namespace name and local name must be different. Similarly, all the namespace declarations of an element must be for different prefixes. All namespace prefixes used must have a corresponding namespace declaration that is in scope.

Examples

Well-formed XML

```
<?xml version='1.0' encoding='UTF-8' ?>
<p:Person xmlns:p='urn:example-org:People' >
  <name>Martin</name>
  <!-- Young and spritely -->
  <age>33</age>
  <height units='inches' >64</height>
</p:Person>
```

A well-formed XML document

XML that is not well formed

```
<?xml version='1.0' encoding='UTF-8' ?>
<p:Person>
  <name>Martin</name>
  <age value='33' >A young <b><i>and</b></i> spritely
    person</age>
  <height units='inches' units='in'>64</height>
  <weight xmlns:x1='urn:example-org:People'
    xmlns:x2='urn:example-org:People'
    x1:units='stone' x2:units='shekels' >10</weight>
</p:Person>
<p:Person/>
```

An XML document that is not well formed because it has two top-level elements, the <b> and <i> tags inside the age element overlap, the height element has duplicate unqualified attribute names, the weight element has duplicate qualified attribute names, and the namespace prefix p is not in scope

1.13 References

Extensible Markup Language (XML) 1.0 (Second Edition).
Available at http://www.w3.org/TR/REC-xml. Tim Bray et al. October, 2000.

Namespaces in XML.
Available at http:// www.w3.org/TR/REC-xml/-names. Tim Bray et al. 1998, 2000.

Chapter 2
Document Type Definitions

Document type definitions (DTDs) serve two general purposes. They provide the syntax for describing/constraining the logical structure of a document, and composing a logical document from physical entities. Element/attribute declarations are used to deal with the former, and entity/notation declarations are used to accomplish the latter.

2.1 Introduction to DTDs

DTDs contain several types of declarations including DOCTYPE, ENTITY, NOTA-TION, ELEMENT, and ATTLIST. ENTITY and NOTATION declarations are used to compose the logical structure of the document, whereas ELEMENT and ATTLIST declarations are used to describe/constrain the details of the resulting logical structure (for example, what elements are allowed as children of a person element, and so on). In addition to these declarations, DTDs may also contain comments and processing instructions.

The rest of this chapter defines the details of each type of declaration and provides examples of each.

2.2 DOCTYPE

```
<!DOCTYPE ... >
```

The DOCTYPE declaration is the container for all other DTD declarations. It's placed at the top of an XML document to associate the given document with a set of declarations. The name of the DOCTYPE must be the same as the name of the document's root element. DOCTYPE is not used in external DTDs, but rather in XML document instances that contain or reference a DTD.

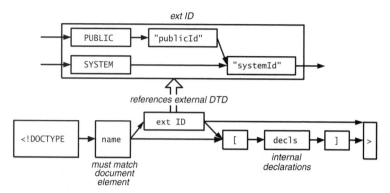

Figure 2-1 DOCTYPE syntax.

DOCTYPE may contain internal declarations (referred to as the *internal DTD subset*), may refer to declarations in external files (referred to as the *external DTD subset*), or may use a combination of both techniques. Figure 2-1 illustrates the DOCTYPE syntax for each approach.

The following subsections outline the syntax for each technique.

2.2.1 Internal declarations

```
<!DOCTYPE name [
  <!-- insert declarations here -->
]>
```

Description

The simplest way to define a DTD is through internal declarations. In this case, all declarations are simply placed between the open/close square brackets. The obvious downside to this approach is that you can't reuse the declarations across different XML document instances.

Example

Using internal declarations

```
<!DOCTYPE person [
  <!-- internal subset -->
  <!ELEMENT person (name, age)>
  <!ELEMENT name (#PCDATA)>
```

```
   <!ELEMENT age (#PCDATA)>
]>
<person>
   <name>Billy Bob</name>
   <age>33</age>
</person>
```

2.2.2 External declarations

```
<!DOCTYPE name PUBLIC "publicId" "systemId">
```

```
<!DOCTYPE name SYSTEM "systemId">
```

Description

DOCTYPE can also contain a reference to an external resource containing the declarations. This type of declaration is useful because it allows you to reuse the declarations in multiple document instances. The DOCTYPE declaration references the external resource through public and system identifiers.

A system identifier is a URI that identifies the location of the resource; a public identifier is a location-independent identifier. Processors can use the public identifier to determine how to retrieve the physical resource if necessary. As an example, some processors are built to recognize certain public identifiers to avoid ever having to dereference their associated system identifiers. This allows processors to cache a set of well-known entities for better performance.

The PUBLIC token identifies a public identifier followed by a backup system identifier. If you don't wish to use a public identifier, simply use the SYSTEM token followed by the system identifier.

Examples

Using external declarations (public identifier)

```
<!-- person.dtd -->
<!ELEMENT person (name, age)>
<!ELEMENT name (#PCDATA)>
<!ELEMENT age (#PCDATA)>

<!-- person.xml -->
<!DOCTYPE person PUBLIC
```

```
"uuid:d2d19398-4be3-4928-a0fc-26d572a19f39"
"http://www.develop.com/people/person.dtd">
<person>
  <name>Billy Bob</name>
  <age>33</age>
</person>
```

Using external declarations (system identifier)

```
<!-- person.dtd -->
<!ELEMENT person (name, age)>
<!ELEMENT name (#PCDATA)>
<!ELEMENT age (#PCDATA)>

<!-- person.xml -->
<!DOCTYPE person SYSTEM "person.dtd">
<person>
  <name>Billy Bob</name>
  <age>33</age>
</person>
```

2.2.3 Internal and external declarations

```
<!DOCTYPE name PUBLIC "publicId" "systemId" [
  <!-- insert declarations here -->
]>

<!DOCTYPE name SYSTEM "systemId" [
  <!-- insert declarations here -->
]>
```

Description

A DOCTYPE declaration can also use both the internal and external declarations. This is useful when you've decided to use external declarations but you need to extend them further or override certain external declarations. (Note: only ENTITY and ATTLIST declarations may be overridden.) See Section 2.5 for an example of overriding ENTITY declarations.

Example

Using both internal and external declarations

```
<!-- globals.dtd -->
<!ELEMENT name (#PCDATA)>
<!ELEMENT age (#PCDATA)>

<!-- person.xml -->
<!DOCTYPE person SYSTEM "globals.dtd" [
  <!ELEMENT person (name, age)>
]>
<person>
  <name>Billy Bob</name>
  <age>33</age>
</person>
```

2.3   ELEMENT

```
<!ELEMENT name content-model>
```

An ELEMENT declaration defines an element of the specified name with the specified content model. The content model defines the element's allowed children. A content model can consist of a keyword ANY/EMPTY or a child group definition enclosed within parentheses. Parentheses may be nested to create additional groups within groups.

Content model basics

Syntax	Description
ANY	Any child is allowed within the element.
EMPTY	No children are allowed within the element.
(#PCDATA)	Only text is allowed within the element.
(child1,child2,...)	Only the specified children in the order given are allowed within the element.
(child1|child2|...)	Only one of the specified children is allowed within the element.

There is also a set of occurrence modifiers that can be used to control how many times a particular child or group occurs in the content model.

Occurrence modifiers

Syntax	Description
	No modifier means the child or child group must appear exactly once at the specified location (except in a choice content model).
*	Annotated child or child group may appear zero or more times at the specified location.
+	Annotated child or child group may appear one or more times at the specified location.
?	Annotated child or child group may appear zero or one time at the specified location.

A mixed content model is a special declaration that allows a mixture of text and child elements in any order. Mixed content models must use the following syntax:

```
<!ELEMENT name (#PCDATA | child1 | child2 | ...)*>
```

Examples

Element and text content models

```
<!-- person.dtd -->
<!ELEMENT person (name, age, children?)>
<!ELEMENT name (fname, (mi|mname)?, lname)?>
<!ELEMENT fname (#PCDATA)>
<!ELEMENT lname (#PCDATA)>
<!ELEMENT mi (#PCDATA)>
<!ELEMENT mname (#PCDATA)>
<!ELEMENT age (#PCDATA)>
<!ELEMENT children (person*)>
```

```
<!-- person.xml -->
<!DOCTYPE person SYSTEM "person.dtd">
<person>
  <name>
    <fname>Billy</fname>
    <lname>Smith</lname>
  </name>
  <age>43</age>
  <children>
    <person>
      <name/>
      <age>0.1</age>
```

```
      </person>
      <person>
        <name>
          <fname>Jill</fname>
          <mi>J</mi>
          <lname>Smith</lname>
        </name>
        <age>21</age>
      </person>
    </children>
  </person>
```

Mixed content model

```
<!-- p.dtd -->
<!ELEMENT p (#PCDATA | b | i)*>
<!ELEMENT b (#PCDATA)>
<!ELEMENT i (#PCDATA)>

<!-- p.xml -->
<!DOCTYPE p SYSTEM "p.dtd">
<p>This <i>is</i> an <b>example</b> of <i>mixed</i>
<i>content</i><b>!</b></p>
```

2.4 ATTLIST

```
<!ATTLIST eName aName1 aType default
                aName2 aType default ...>
```

An ATTLIST declaration defines the set of attributes that is allowed on a given element. Each attribute in the set has a name, type, and default declaration. The following sections describe attribute types and default declarations.

Attribute types

Attribute types make it possible to constrain the attribute value in different ways. See the following list of type identifiers for details.

Type	Description
CDATA	Arbitrary character data
ID	A name that is unique within the document

Type	Description
IDREF	A reference to an ID value in the document
IDREFS	A space-delimited list of IDREF values
ENTITY	The name of an unparsed entity declared in the DTD
ENTITIES	A space-delimited list of ENTITY values
NMTOKEN	A valid XML name (see Chapter 1)
NMTOKENS	A space-delimited list of NMTOKEN values

Default declarations

After the attribute type, you must specify either a default value for the attribute or a keyword that specifies whether it is required.

Declaration	Description
"value"	Default value for attribute. If the attribute is not explicitly used on the given element, it will still exist in the logical document with the specified default value.
#REQUIRED	Attribute is required on the given element.
#IMPLIED	Attribute is optional on the given element.
#FIXED "value"	Attribute always has the specified fixed value. It may be used on the given element but it must have the specified fixed value. If the attribute is not explicitly used on the given element, it will still exist in the logical document with the specified fixed value.

Attribute enumerations

```
<!ATTLIST eName aName (token1 | token2 | token3 | ...)>
<!ATTLIST eName aName NOTATION (token1 | token2 | token3 |
    ...)>
```

It's also possible to define an attribute as an enumeration of tokens. The tokens may be of type NMTOKEN or NOTATION. In either case, the attribute value must be one of the specified enumerated values.

Examples

Using attribute types

```
<!-- emp.dtd -->
<!ELEMENT employees (employee*)>
<!ELEMENT employee (#PCDATA)>
```

```
<!ATTLIST employee
         name CDATA #REQUIRED
         species NMTOKEN #FIXED "human"
         id ID #REQUIRED
         mgr IDREF #IMPLIED
         manage IDREFS #IMPLIED>

<!-- emp.xml -->
<!DOCTYPE employees SYSTEM "emp.dtd">
<employees>
  <employee name="Billy Bob" id="e100" manage="e101 e102"/>
  <employee name="Jesse Jim" id="e101" mgr="e100"/>
  <employee name="Sarah Sas" id="e102" mgr="e100"
     manage="e103" species="human"/>
  <employee name="Nikki Nak" id="e103" mgr="e102"/>
  <employee name="Peter Pan" id="e104"/>
</employees>
```

Using attribute enumerations

```
<!-- emp.dtd -->
<!ELEMENT employee (address)>
<!-- NMTOKEN enumeration -->
<!ATTLIST employee
         title (president|vice-pres|secretary|sales)
         #REQUIRED>
<!ELEMENT address (#PCDATA)>
<!-- NOTATION enumeration -->
<!ATTLIST address
         format NOTATION (cs|lf) "cs">
<!NOTATION cs PUBLIC "urn:addresses:comma-separated">
<!NOTATION lf PUBLIC "urn:addresses:line-breaks">

<!-- emp.xml -->
<!DOCTYPE employee SYSTEM "emp.dtd">
<employee title='vice-pres'>
  <!-- notation informs consuming application how to
       process element content -->
  <address format='cs'>1927 N 52 E, Layton, UT, 84041
    </address>
</employee>
```

2.5 ENTITY

```
<!ENTITY ... >
```

Entities are the most atomic unit of information in XML. Entities are used to construct logical XML documents (as well as DTDs) from physical resources. An XML document that contains a DOCTYPE declaration is known as the *document entity*. There are several other types of entities, each of which is declared using an ENTITY declaration. A given entity is either general or parameter, internal or external, and parsed or unparsed:

General versus parameter entities

General	Entity may only be referenced in an XML document (not the DTD).
Parameter	Entity may only be referenced in a DTD (not the XML document).

Internal versus external entities

Internal	Entity value defined inline.
External	Entity value contained in an external resource.

Parsed versus unparsed entities

Parsed	Entity value parsed by a processor as XML/DTD content.
Unparsed	Entity value not parsed by XML processor.

All of these are declared using an ENTITY declaration. Figure 2–2 illustrates how the syntax varies for each type:

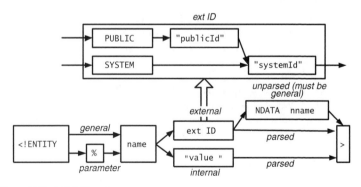

Figure 2–2   ENTITY syntax.

As you can see from Figure 2–2, unparsed entities are always general and exter-nal whereas parameter/internal entities are always parsed. In reality, there are only five distinct entity types (besides the document entity), each of which is defined in more detail in the following subsections. Note that although the syntax for external entities only shows using a system identifier, public identifiers may also be used as shown in Figure 2–2.

Distinct entity types

Syntax	Description
`<!ENTITY % name "value">`	Internal parameter
`<!ENTITY % name SYSTEM "systemId">`	External parameter
`<!ENTITY name "value">`	Internal general
`<!ENTITY name SYSTEM "systemId">`	External parsed general
`<!ENTITY name SYSTEM "systemId" NDATA nname>`	Unparsed

The previous syntax is for declaring entities. Once an entity has been declared, it can be used in either the DTD (parameter) or the XML document (general) through an entity reference. The following table shows the syntax for entity references:

Entity references

Syntax	Description
`&name;`	General
`%name;`	Parameter
Name is used as the value of an attribute of type `ENTITY` or `ENTITIES` (see Section 2.4)	Unparsed

2.5.1 Internal parameter entities

`<!ENTITY % name "value">`

Description

Internal parameter entities are used to parameterize portions of the DTD (for example, other declarations) or they can contain one or more complete declara-tions. Internal parameter entities are always parsed. A reference to an internal parameter entity (`%name;`) is replaced with the parsed content.

Parameter entities may not be referenced within other declarations in the internal subset but they may be used in place of a complete declaration. This does not apply to the external subset, however, in which parameter entities may also be referenced within other declarations. Parameter entities may be referenced within ELEMENT, ATTRIBUTE, NOTATION, and even other ENTITY declarations. It's common to override parameter entities defined in the external subset with declarations in the internal subset (see the following example).

When parameter entity references are expanded, they are enlarged by attaching one leading and trailing space character to the entity value, except when parameter entities are referenced within other entity values. As a result, parameter entity references may not be used as part of a name (because XML names may not contain whitespace) as shown here:

```
<!ELEMENT %prefix;:person (child1, child2)> <!-- illegal -->
```

But they may be used to parameterize a complete name, as shown here:

```
<!ELEMENT %completeName; (child1, child2)> <!-- legal -->
```

Examples

Parameter entities in the internal subset

```
<!DOCTYPE person [
  <!ELEMENT person (name)>
  <!ENTITY % nameDecl "<!ELEMENT name (#PCDATA)>">
  <!-- parameter entity expands to
       complete declaration -->
  %nameDecl;
]>
<person><name>Billy Bob</name></person>
```

Parameter entities in the external subset

```
<!-- person.dtd -->
<!ENTITY % person-content "name, age">
<!ELEMENT person (%person-content;)>
<!ELEMENT name (#PCDATA)>
<!ELEMENT age (#PCDATA)>

<!-- person1.xml -->
<!DOCTYPE person SYSTEM "person.dtd">
```

```
<person>
   <name>Billy Bob</name>
   <age>33</age>
</person>
```

```
<!-- person2.xml -->
<!DOCTYPE person SYSTEM "person.dtd" [
   <!-- change person's content model -->
   <!ENTITY % person-content "age, name">
]>
<person>
   <age>33</age>
   <name>Billy Bob</name>
</person>
```

This example illustrates how the **person** element's content model can be specified through the **person-content** parameter entity.

Parameterizing an external DTD with respect to namespace prefixes

```
<!-- person.dtd -->
<!ENTITY % prefix "p">
<!ENTITY % personName "%prefix;:person">
<!ENTITY % nameName "%prefix;:name">
<!ENTITY % ageName "%prefix;:age">
<!ENTITY % xmlnsPerson "xmlns:%prefix;">
<!ELEMENT %personName; (%nameName;, %ageName;)>
<!ATTLIST %personName;
          %xmlnsPerson; CDATA #REQUIRED>
<!ELEMENT %nameName; (#PCDATA)>
<!ELEMENT %ageName; (#PCDATA)>
```

```
<!-- person1.xml -->
<!DOCTYPE p:person SYSTEM "person.dtd">
<p:person xmlns:p='urn:person:demo'>
   <p:name>Billy Bob</p:name>
   <p:age>33</p:age>
</p:person>
```

```
<!-- person2.xml -->
<!DOCTYPE x:person SYSTEM "person.dtd" [
   <!-- override the prefix to be 'x' -->
```

```
<!ENTITY % prefix "x">
]>
<x:person xmlns:x='urn:person:demo'>
  <x:name>Billy Bob</x:name>
  <x:age>33</x:age>
</x:person>
```

This external DTD was designed for a person document that uses namespace prefixes. Because the actual namespace prefix used doesn't matter, it has been defined as a parameter entity that is then used to construct the other names used in the DTD. By default, the prefix is expected to be `'p'`. However, a given instance document can override its value by providing a new declaration for the prefix parameter entity.

2.5.2 External parameter entities

```
<!ENTITY % name PUBLIC "publicId" "systemId">
```

```
<!ENTITY % name SYSTEM "systemId">
```

Description

External parameter entities are used to include declarations from external resources. External parameter entities are always parsed. A reference to an external parameter entity (%name;) is replaced with the parsed content. The restrictions on where internal parameter entity references are used also apply to external parameter entity references (see previous section for more details).

Example

Using external parameter entities

```
<!-- person-decls.dtd -->
<!ELEMENT person (name, age)>
<!ELEMENT name (#PCDATA)>
<!ELEMENT age (#PCDATA)>

<!-- person.xml -->
<!DOCTYPE person [
  <!ENTITY % decls SYSTEM "person-decls.dtd">
  %decls;
```

```
]>
<person>
  <name>Billy Bob</name>
  <age>33</age>
</person>
```

This example uses an external parsed entity (`decls`) to include the set of declarations that are contained in `person-decls.dtd`.

2.5.3 Internal general entities

```
<!ENTITY name "value">
```

Description

Internal general entities always contain parsed XML content. The parsed content is placed in the logical XML document everywhere it's referenced (`&name;`).

Example

Using internal general entities

```
<!DOCTYPE person [
  <!ENTITY n "<fname>Billy</fname><lname>Smith</lname>">
  <!ENTITY a "<age>33</age>">
]>
<person>
  <name>&n;</name>
  &a;
</person>
```

The resulting logical document could be serialized as follows:

```
<person>
  <name>
    <fname>Billy</fname>
    <lname>Smith</lname>
  </name>
  <age>33</age>
</person>
```

2.5.4 External general parsed entities

```
<!ENTITY name PUBLIC "publicId" "systemId">

<!ENTITY name SYSTEM "systemId">
```

Description

External general parsed entities are used the same way as internal general entities except for the fact that they aren't defined inline. They always contain parsed XML content that becomes part of the logical XML document wherever it's referenced (&name;).

Example

Using external general parsed entities

```
<!DOCTYPE person [
  <!ENTITY n SYSTEM "name.xml">
  <!ENTITY a SYSTEM "age.xml">
]>
<person>
  <name>&n;</name>
  &a;
</person>
```

The result of this example would be the same as the previous example, assuming that the `name.xml` and `age.xml` files contain the same content as the inline definitions used in the previous example. Notice that `name.xml` wouldn't be a well-formed XML document (although it is a well-formed external entity), but the resulting document is indeed well-formed.

2.5.5 Unparsed entities

```
<!ENTITY name PUBLIC "publicId" "systemId" NDATA nname>

<!ENTITY name SYSTEM "systemId" NDATA nname>
```

Description

Unparsed entities make it possible to attach arbitrary binary resources to an XML document. Unparsed entities are always general and external. They simply point to a resource via the resource's public or system identifier. It's up to the consuming application to dereference and process the resource at the appropriate time. Because unparsed entities can reference any binary resource, applications require additional information to determine the resource's type. The notation name (nname) provides exactly this type of information (see Section 2.6 for more details).

Because unparsed entities don't contain XML content, they aren't referenced the same way as other general entities (&name;), but rather through an attribute of type ENTITY/ENTITIES.

Example

Using unparsed entities

```
<!DOCTYPE person [
  <!ELEMENT person (#PCDATA)>
  <!ATTLIST person photo ENTITY #REQUIRED>
  <!ENTITY imgEntity SYSTEM "aaron.gif" NDATA pic>
  <!NOTATION pic PUBLIC "urn:mime:img/gif">
]>
<person photo='imgEntity'>Aaron</person>
```

2.6 NOTATION

```
<!NOTATION name PUBLIC "publicId">
```

```
<!NOTATION name PUBLIC "publicId" "systemId">
```

```
<!NOTATION name SYSTEM "systemId">
```

Notation declarations associate a name with a type identifier, which can be either a public or a system identifier. The actual type identifiers are application specific, although it's common to see MIME types used within public identifiers. Unparsed entities are associated with notation names to associate type with the referenced binary resource.

Example

Using NOTATIONs with unparsed entities

```
<!DOCTYPE person [
  <!-- person declarations -->
```

```
<!ELEMENT person (#PCDATA)>
<!ATTLIST person bio ENTITY #REQUIRED>
<!ENTITY bioEntity SYSTEM "aaron.htm" NDATA html>
<!NOTATION html PUBLIC "urn:mime:text/html">
]>
<person bio="bioEntity">Aaron</person>
```

2.7   INCLUDE and IGNORE

```
<![INCLUDE[
  ...
]]>
<![IGNORE[
  ...
]]>
```

There are two conditional statements, INCLUDE and IGNORE, that may be used to control what declarations are processed as part of the DTD at a given point in time. Declarations within INCLUDE blocks are included in the DTD whereas declarations within IGNORE blocks are ignored. When used in conjunction with a parameter entity, it's possible for instance documents to control what sections of the DTD are included or ignored (see the following example).

Example

Using INCLUDE and IGNORE

```
<!-- person.dtd -->
<!ENTITY % v1 'INCLUDE' >
<!ENTITY % v2 'IGNORE' >

<![%v1;[
<!ELEMENT person (fname, lname, age)>
]]>
<![%v2;[
<!ELEMENT person (name, age)>
<!ELEMENT name (fname, lname)>
]]>

<!-- person-v1.xml -->
<!DOCTYPE person SYSTEM "person.dtd">
```

```
<person>
  <fname>Billy</fname>
  <lname>Bob</lname>
  <age>33</age>
</person>

<!-- person-v2.xml -->
<DOCTYPE person SYSTEM "person.dtd" [
  <!-- toggle values for v2 content model -->
  <!ENTITY % v1 'IGNORE'>
  <!ENTITY % v2 'INCLUDE'>
]>
<person>
  <name>
    <fname>Billy</fname>
    <lname>Bob</lname>
  </name>
  <age>33</age>
</person>
```

This example allows users to switch easily between `person` content models by changing the values of the `v1/v2` parameter entities.

2.8   References

Extensible Markup Language (XML) 1.0 (Second Edition) Recommendation.
Available at *http://www.w3.org/TR/REC-xml*. Tim Bray et al. October 2000.

Tim Bray's Annotated XML 1.0 Specification.
Available at *http://www.xml.com/axml/testaxml.htm*.

XML Information Set.
Available at *http://www.w3.org/TR/xml-infoset*.

Chapter 3
XPath 1.0

The XML Path Language version 1.0 (XPath) defines the W3C-sanctioned syntax for addressing parts of an XML document. XPath expressions are evaluated against a document's logical tree structure to identify a set of nodes (for example, elements, attributes, text, and so on).

This layer of abstraction shields developers from the complexity of a document's physical structure and greatly simplifies processing. After a brief introduction, this chapter presents the syntax for building XPath expressions.

3.1   Introduction to XPath

XPath defines a *tree model* against which all expressions are evaluated. The XPath tree model codifies the logical structure of an XML document, which has since been formally defined as the XML Information Set (Infoset). Figure 3–1 illustrates the XPath tree model.

Most XPath expressions identify a set of nodes in the tree. For example, the following XPath expression identifies the two `price` elements:

```
/invoice/item/price
```

This type of expression is called a *location path*. Location path expressions look like file system paths only they navigate through the XPath tree model to identify a set of nodes (known as a `node-set`).

Because XPath is an abstract language, it can be used in many environments. It's heavily used throughout XSL Transformations (XSLT) to identify nodes in the input document (see Chapter 5 for details). It's also used in most Document Object Model (DOM) implementations for richer querying capabilities. The following JavaScript illustrates how XPath can be used with Microsoft's MSXML 3.0 DOM implementation:

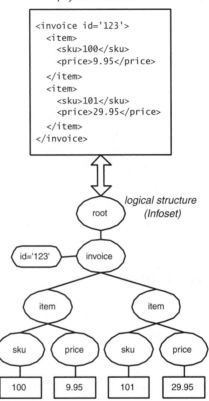

physical document

```
<invoice id='123'>
  <item>
    <sku>100</sku>
    <price>9.95</price>
  </item>
  <item>
    <sku>101</sku>
    <price>29.95</price>
  </item>
</invoice>
```

Figure 3–1 XPath tree model.

```
var nl = doc.selectNodes("/invoice/item/price");
for (i=0; i<nl.length; i++) {
    ... // process price element here
}
```

This code could be rewritten in a variety of languages using a variety of XML processors. XPath is even used in some of today's modern data access technologies to expose the underlying data store as XML to consumers. Remember that XPath expressions simply define how to traverse a logical XML structure to identify a node-set, but where the logical structure actually comes from is an implementation detail.

By default, XPath traverses the tree in *document order*. Document order is the order in which the nodes would appear in a serialized XML document, as illustrated in Figure 3–2. In some cases, however, it's necessary to traverse nodes in *reverse document order*, which is simply the reverse of the order shown in Figure 3–2 (more on this later).

In addition to `node-sets`, XPath supports three other data types: `booleans`, `numbers`, and `strings`. XPath defines how `node-sets` are both coerced and compared with each of these types.

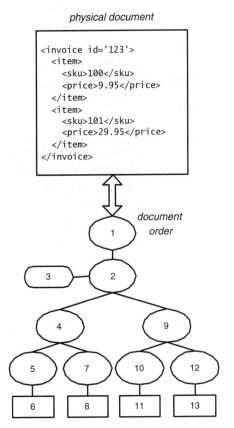

physical document

```
<invoice id='123'>
  <item>
    <sku>100</sku>
    <price>9.95</price>
  </item>
  <item>
    <sku>101</sku>
    <price>29.95</price>
  </item>
</invoice>
```

document order

Figure 3–2   Document order.

XPath type system

Data type	Description
node-set	A collection of nodes without duplicates
boolean	true or false
number	A floating point number (see IEEE 754 standard)
string	A sequence of UCS characters

Every XPath expression yields an object of one of these types. One can explicitly coerce an object to another type through the boolean(), number(), or string() function. Objects are also implicitly coerced when necessary (for example, when you pass a node-set to a function that expects a string).

To convert/compare node-sets to objects of other types, nodes from XPath's tree model need to be mapped back to a string. XPath defines how to evaluate a node's *string-value* for this purpose.

Node string-value

Node type	String-value
Root	Concatenation of all descendant text nodes
Element	Concatenation of all descendant text nodes
Attribute	Normalized attribute value
Text	Character data
Processing instruction	Character data following the processing instruction target
Comment	Character data within comment delimiters
Namespace	Namespace URI

Figure 3–3 illustrates the string-value of each node in the sample invoice document shown earlier.

Mapping nodes back to strings makes it easy to convert/compare them with other objects. It also makes it possible to build a wide variety of other expressions.

The following summarizes the types of expressions supported by XPath. The operators used to build these expressions are shown in order of increasing precedence (top to bottom, left to right). As usual, parentheses may be used to control precedence explicitly.

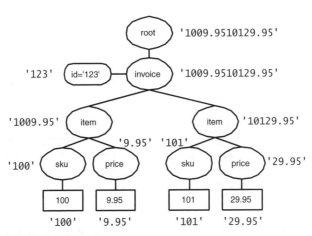

Figure 3-3   Node string-values.

XPath expressions and operators

Expression type	Operators
Location paths	/, //, |
Boolean expressions	or, and
Equality expressions	=, !=
Relational expressions	<=, <, >=, >
Numerical expressions	+, –, div, mod, *, – (unary)

The rest of this chapter covers the details of each expression type along with XPath's function library.

3.2   Location path expressions

`/step/step/step/... | step/step/...`

A location path expression yields a `node-set`. Location paths can be absolute or relative. Absolute location paths begin with a forward slash (/) whereas relative location paths do not. A location path consists of one or more *location steps*, each separated by a forward slash.

XPath defines two terms—*context node-set* and *context node*—to help describe how the location path evaluation process works. The context `node-set` is defined as the current set of nodes that has been identified up to a given point in the expression. The context node is defined as the current node being processed.

The location steps are evaluated in order (left to right) one at a time. Each location step is evaluated against the nodes in the context `node-set`. If the location path is absolute, the original context `node-set` consists of the root node; otherwise, it consists of the current context node (what this means depends on where the expression is being used).

The first location step is then evaluated with each node in the context `node-set` serving as the context node. The resulting `node-set`s are then "unioned" into a new `node-set`, which becomes the context `node-set` for the next step. This process continues for each location step in the path. The `node-set` produced by the final location step is the result of the expression.

Location paths may be "unioned" together through the | operator. The combination of the two `node-set`s excluding duplicates is the result of the union.

Examples

`/invoice/item`	Identifies the child `item` elements of the root `invoice` element.
`item/sku`	Identifies the child `sku` elements of the context node's child `item` elements.
`sku	price	desc`	Identifies the context node's child `sku`, `price`, and `desc` elements.

3.2.1 Location steps

`axis::node-test[predicate1][predicate2][...]`

Description

A location step identifies a new `node-set` relative to the context `node-set`. The location step is evaluated against each node in the context `node-set`, and the union of the resulting `node-set`s becomes the context `node-set` for the next step. Location steps consist of an *axis* identifier, a *node test*, and zero or more *predicate*s (see Figure 3–4). For more information on axes, node tests, and predicates, see the following sections.

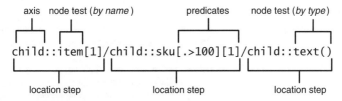

Figure 3–4   Location step syntax.

XPath

3.2.2 Axis

Description

XPath defines several axes, each of which identifies a set of nodes relative to the context node.

Axis descriptions

Axis	Description
self	Identifies the context node.
child	Default axis. Identifies the children of the context node. When the axis is omitted, the child is assumed.
parent	Identifies the parent of the context node.
descendant	Identifies the descendants of the context node. A descendant is a child, a grandchild, a great-grandchild, and so on. *Warning*: descendant typically requires the processor to search the entire tree below the context node.
descendant-or-self	Identifies the context node and the descendant axis.
ancestor	Identifies the ancestors of the context node. The ancestors of the context node consist of the parent, the grandparent, the great-grandparent, and so on.
ancestor-or-self	Identifies the context node and the ancestor axis.
following	Identifies all nodes that are after the context node in document order, excluding descendants, attributes, and namespace nodes (for example, all start tags that come after the context node's end tag). *Warning*: following typically requires the processor to search the entire document after the context node (excluding descendants).
following-sibling	Identifies the siblings of the context node from the following axis.

Axis	Description
preceding	Identifies all nodes that are before the context node in document order, excluding ancestors, attributes, and namespace nodes (for example, all end tags that come before the context node's start tag). *Warning:* preceding typically requires the processor to search the entire document before the context node (excluding ancestors).
preceding-sibling	Identifies the siblings of the context node from the preceding axis.
attribute	Identifies the attributes of the context node.
namespace	Identifies the namespace nodes of the context node.

Each axis has a direction and a principal node type. The direction of an axis is either forward or reverse. Forward axes traverse nodes in document order whereas reverse axes traverse nodes in reverse document order. The axis direction is significant when locating nodes by position. For example, the first child element is the first child element in document order. The first ancestor element, however, is the first ancestor element in reverse document order, which is the ancestor element nearest the context node.

When identifying nodes by name or the * wildcard, only nodes of the axis' principal node type are considered. For example, child::foo identifies the child foo elements whereas attribute::foo identifies the attribute nodes named foo. Likewise, the expression child::* only identifies the child element nodes (child text, comment, or processing instruction nodes are not identified).

Axis direction and principle node type

Axis	Direction	Principle node type
self	Not applicable	Element
child	Forward	Element
parent	Not applicable	Element
descendant	Forward	Element
descendant-or-self	Forward	Element
ancestor	Reverse	Element
ancestor-or-self	Reverse	Element
following	Forward	Element
following-sibling	Forward	Element
preceding	Reverse	Element

Axis	Direction	Principle node type
preceding-sibling	Reverse	Element
attribute	Not applicable	Attribute
namespace	Not applicable	Namespace

Figure 3–5 illustrates the group of nodes identified by each axis, assuming E is the context node.

XPath

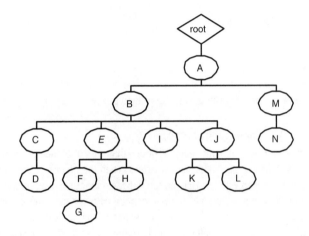

Axis	Nodes (relative to E)
self	E
parent	B
child	F,H
descendant	F,G,H
descendant-or-self	E,F,G,H
ancestor	B,A,root
ancestor-or-self	E,B,A,root
preceding	D,C
preceding-sibling	C
following	I,J,K,L,M,N
following-sibling	I,J

Figure 3–5   XPath axes.

Examples

/child::invoice/child::customer	Identifies the child customer elements of the root invoice element.
child::item/attribute::id	Identifies the id attribute of each of the context node's child item elements.
preceding::sku	Identifies the sku elements that come before the context node.

3.2.3 Node test

Description

Nodes tests are used to identify nodes within an axis. If a node test evaluates to true for a given node, it remains in the node-set; otherwise, it's removed. Node tests can be performed by name or by type.

3.2.3.1 Node test by name

When performing name tests, all nodes that are not of the specified axis' principal node type are automatically discarded. Then the names of the remaining nodes are compared with the QName (prefix:local name) specified in the location step. The QName is expanded to a *namespace name* (local name + namespace URI), which is then compared with the namespace name of each node in question. If the namespace names match, the node remains in the set; otherwise, it's discarded.

In order for an XPath processor to expand a QName into a namespace name, it needs access to namespace bindings. Hence, XPath processors need to provide a mechanism for establishing namespace bindings that will be used while evaluating expressions. In XSLT, this can be accomplished through a standard XML 1.0 namespace declaration (in the XSLT document). In the DOM, however, extra implementation-specific configuration is required. The following line of code illustrates the approach taken by Microsoft's MSXML version 3.0 DOM implementation:

```
doc.setProperty("SelectionNamespaces",
  "xmlns:i='urn: example:ns1' xmlns:x='urn: example:n2'
  xmlns:x='urn:invoice:ids'");
```

Every XPath processor should provide an equivalent mechanism for establishing namespace bindings. The prefixes used in node tests can then be resolved against these bindings when the processor compares names.

Name tests that do not include a prefix (for example, `child::foo`) identify nodes that belong to no namespace (default namespaces never come into play).

The name wildcard (`*`) can also be used to identify all nodes of the axis' principal node type. This wildcard can also be used in conjunction with a namespace prefix (for example, `child::f:*`) to identify all nodes (of the axis' principal node type) from a given namespace.

Name test	Description
QName	`true` for all nodes that have the specified expanded namespace name and are of the axis' principal node type
*	`true` for all nodes of the axis' principal node type

Examples

`child::i:item`	Assuming i is mapped to `urn:example-org:invoices` for these examples, this step identifies the child `item` elements in the `urn:example-org:invoices` namespace.
`child::i:*`	Identifies all `child` elements from the `urn:example-org:invoices` namespace.
`/child::sku`	Identifies the child `sku` elements that belong to no namespace.
`/child::i:invoice/attribute::id`	Identifies the `id` attribute (from no namespace) of the root invoice element from the `urn:example-org:invoices` namespace.
`/descendant::price`	Identifies all `price` elements in the document from no namespace.

3.2.3.2 Node test by type

A node test by type is `true` if the node in question is of the type specified. XPath defines several node type identifiers for use in node tests.

Type identifier	Description
text()	Identifies text nodes.
comment()	Identifies comment nodes.
processing-instruction(target?)	Identifies processing instruction nodes that match the (optionally) specified target string.
node()	Identifies all nodes in an axis regardless of type.

Examples

child::text()	Identifies the child text nodes.
/child::invoice/child::comment()	Identifies the child comment nodes of the root invoice element.
/child::invoice/child::node()	Identifies all child nodes (regardless of type) of the root invoice element.
/child::processing-instruction('xsl-stylesheet')	Identifies the root node's child processing instruction node with a target of 'xsl-stylesheet'.

3.2.4 Predicate

Description

Predicates are placed inside square brackets [...] at the end of a location step (see location step syntax described earlier). A predicate filters a node-set to produce a new node-set. For each node in the node-set to be filtered, the predicate expression is evaluated with that node as the context node and the result is coerced to a boolean. If the result is **true**, the node remains in the node-set; otherwise, it's removed. The predicate expression can be any basic expression (see Section 3.3 on basic expressions).

Examples

child::item[position()=1]	Returns the first child item element (same as item[1]; see the following section).

`child::invoice[child::item][2]`	Returns the second child `invoice` element that has at least one child `item` element.
`descendant::sku[attribute::id > 100]`	Identifies the descendant `sku` elements that have an `id` attribute greater than 100.

XPath

3.2.5 Location path abbreviations

Description

XPath defines several abbreviations that can be used when building location path expressions. This facilitates building compact expressions that can be used in URI fragment identifiers (for example, XPointer) and XML attribute values (for example, XLink). The syntactical constructs that may be abbreviated are as follows, along with their corresponding abbreviation.

Verbose form	Abbreviation
`child::`	omitted
`attribute::`	@
`self::node()`	.
`parent::node()`	..
`/descendant-or-self::node()/`	//
`[position()=number]`	[number]

Examples

`/child::reviews/child::review`	`/reviews/review`
`child::review/attribute::id`	`review/@id`
`self::node()/descendant-or-self::node()/child::book`	`.//book`
`parent::node()/child::review[position()=1]`	`../review[1]`

3.3 Basic expressions

In addition to location path expressions, there are several other basic expression constructs including boolean, equality, relational, and numerical. These expressions may be used in any situation in which the resulting object isn't required to be a node-set. They are commonly used within XPath predicates as well as various XSLT constructs (for example, if/when statements). The details of these expression types are described in the following subsections.

3.3.1 Boolean expressions

Operators: or, and

XPath supports standard and/or boolean expressions. Each operand is evaluated and coerced to a boolean (as if by calling the **boolean** function) before evaluation.

Examples

/invoice/item or /invoice/foo	Returns true (assuming there are at least child item elements under the root invoice element).
item[sku and price]	Identifies the child item elements that have both sku and price child elements.
item[(sku < 100) or (price > 50.0)]	Identifies the child item elements that have either a price child element with a value less than 100 or a sku child element with a value greater than 50.

3.3.2 Equality expressions

Operators: =, !=

Equality expressions test two objects for equality. When one of the objects is a node-set, the definition of equality is far from intuitive. Two node-sets are equal if there is at least one node in each node-set with string-values that are equal. But at the same time, two node-sets are unequal if there is at least one node in each node-set with string-values that are unequal. This makes it possible (and actually quite common) to have two objects that are both equal and unequal at the same time (assuming one is a `node-set`). The following summarizes how `node-set` equality is determined for each object type:

Node-set equality/inequality

Type	Description
node-set	Two `node-set`s are equal if there is at least one node in each `node-set` with string-values that are equal. Two `node-set`s are unequal if there is at least one node in each `node-set` with string-values that are unequal.
number	A `node-set` equals a `number` if it contains a node with a string-value converted to a number that matches the `number` in question. A `node-set` is not equal to a `number` if it contains a node with a string-value converted to a `number` that does not equal the `number` in question.
string	A `node-set` equals a `string` if it contains a node with a string-value that matches the `string` in question. A `node-set` is not equal to a `string` if it contains a node with a string-value that does not equal the `string` in question.
boolean	A `node-set` equals a `boolean` if the result of converting the `node-set` to a `boolean` is the same as the `boolean` value in question. A `node-set` does not equal a `boolean` if the result of converting the `node-set` to a `boolean` is not the same as the `boolean` value in question.

Examples

`price = 3.95`	`true` if there is at least one child `price` element with a string-value that equals `3.95`.
`price != 3.95`	`true` if there is at least one child `price` element with a string-value that does not equal `3.95`.
`not(price = 3.95)`	`true` if there is not a single child `price` element with a string value that equals `3.95`.
`not(price != 3.95)`	`true` if all child `price` elements have a string-value equal to `3.95`.
`/descendant::invoice[@id = 100]`	Identifies all `invoice` elements that have an `id` attribute equal to `100`.

`sku != preceding::sku`	Returns `true` if there is at least one child `sku` element with a string-value that does not equal that of one of the preceding `sku` elements. (Note: This is not the same as `not(sku = preceding::sku)`. See next example.)
`not(sku = preceding::sku)`	Returns `true` if there is not a single child `sku` element with a string-value that equals that of one of the preceding `sku` elements. (Note: This is not the same as `sku != preceding::sku`. See previous example.)
`/descendant::sku[not(. = preceding::sku)]`	Identifies the descendant `sku` elements with string-values that do not equal those of one of the preceding `sku` elements. This expression only identifies the first `sku` with a given value; all other `sku` elements with the same value are excluded from the result `node-set` (like doing a SELECT DISTINCT in SQL). Note: Using `!=` does not return the same result (see previous examples).

If neither of the objects is a `node-set` and the operands are of different types, implicit coercions happen according to type precedence. Objects of lower type precedence are always coerced into an object of the other type before evaluating equality.

Equality type precedence (not involving `node-set`s)	Type
1 (highest)	`boolean`
2	`number`
3	`string`

Examples

`true() = "foo"`	true (foo coerced to `true`)
`true() != 1.32`	false (1.32 coerced to `true`)
`"1.2" = 1.2`	true (1.2 coerced to 1.2)

3.3.3 Relational expressions

Operators: `<=, <, >=, >`

Relational expressions make it possible to compare two objects. Relational expressions are evaluated by converting both operands to `numbers`, which are then compared. If one of the operands is a `node-set`, the numerical value of each node in the set is compared against the other operand as described for equality expressions. In this case, the comparison is true if there is at least one node in the `node-set` with a numerical value that makes the comparison true.

Examples

`price <= 100`	`true` if there is at least one child `price` element with a numerical value that is less than or equal to 100.
`/descendant::item[price <= 100]`	Identifies all `item` elements that have a child `price` element with a numerical value that is less than or equal to 100.
`price > preceding::price`	`true` if there is a child `price` element with a numerical value that is greater than one of the preceding `price` elements.
`/descendant::item[price > preceding::price]`	Identifies all `item` elements for which the numerical value of one child `price` element is greater than at least one of the preceding `price` elements.

3.3.4 Numerical expressions

Operators: `+, -, div, mod, *, -` (unary)

Numerical expressions make it possible to perform basic arithmetic operations on numbers. Each operand is evaluated and coerced to a number (as if by calling the `number` function) before evaluation. The operators shown above are listed in order of increasing precedence, left to right.

Examples

`2 + 3.5 * 2`	9.0
`5 div 2.0 - '1.0'`	1.5
`5 mod -2`	1
`-5 mod 2`	-1
`item[(price mod 2) = 0]`	Identifies the child `item` elements that have an even `price`.

3.4 Core Function Library

XPath defines a core function library that all implementations are required to support. There are three functions available for explicitly converting between the XPath data types: `string()`, `number()`, and `boolean()`. (Note: You cannot coerce a `string`, `number`, or `boolean` to a `node-set`.) If a function expects an argument of a specific type and an object of a different type is used, it's implicitly coerced to the expected type as if by calling the appropriate coercion function.

All of the functions in the core library belong to no namespace, so their names don't require a namespace prefix. XPath implementations may augment the core library with proprietary extension functions. When this is the case, the extension function names must be qualified with a namespace prefix. The following summarizes the functions in the core function library.

Node-set function	**Description**
`id`	Identifies nodes by ID.
`lang`	Checks the context node for the specified language.
`last`	Returns the size of the context `node-set`.
`local-name`	Returns the local name of a node.
`name`	Returns the QName of a node.
`namespace-uri`	Returns the namespace URI of a node.
`position`	Returns the index of the context node in the context `node-set`.

Boolean function	Description
boolean	Converts an object to a boolean.
false	Returns false.
not	Returns the logical not of the argument.
true	Returns true.

Number function	Description
ceiling	Rounds up to the next integer.
count	Returns the number of nodes in a node-set.
floor	Rounds down to the next integer.
number	Converts an object to a number.
round	Rounds to the nearest integer.
sum	Totals of a list of numbers.

String function	Description
concat	Concatenates multiple strings.
contains	Determines if a string contains a substring.
normalize-space	Strips leading/trailing whitespace from a string.
starts-with	Determines if a string starts with a substring.
string	Converts an object to a string.
string-length	Returns the length of a string.
substring	Returns a substring identified by position.
substring-after	Returns the substring after a specified string.
substring-before	Returns the substring before a specified string.
translate	Translates letters in a string.

Each function is described in the following subsections in alphabetical order.

3.4.1 boolean

```
boolean boolean(object)
```

Description

boolean converts its argument into a boolean. The conversion details depend on the type of argument object.

Type	Description
node-set	Returns `true` if the `node-set` is nonempty; `false` otherwise.
string	Returns `true` if the string length is nonzero; `false` otherwise.
number	Returns `true` if the number is nonzero (not negative zero, positive zero, or NaN [`not a number`]).
other	Is converted to a `boolean` in a way that is dependent on that type.

Examples

`boolean(*/item)`	Returns `true` if there is at least one grandchild `item` element; false otherwise.
`boolean(string(customer))`	Returns `true` if the string-value of the first child `customer` element is nonempty.
`boolean(sum(price))`	Returns `true` if the sum of the child `price` elements is nonzero.

3.4.2 ceiling

`number ceiling(number)`

Description

`ceiling` returns the smallest integer that is not less than the argument.

Examples

`ceiling(43.6)`	44
`ceiling('43.6')`	44
`ceiling(-2.5)`	-2
`ceiling(sum(price) div count(price))`	Returns the rounded-up average price of the child `price` elements.
`ceiling(item/price)`	Returns the rounded-up `price` of the first child `item` element.

3.4.3 concat

```
string concat(string, string, string*)
```

Description

concat returns the concatenation of its arguments.

Examples

concat('hello',' world')	'hello world'
concat('number(not(', false(), '())) = ', 1)	'number(not(false())) = 1'
concat(fname, ' ', mi, '. ', lname)	Returns 'Fred' 'B' and 'Smith', assuming the child fname, mi, and lname elements contain 'Fred', 'B', and 'Smith', respectively.

3.4.4 contains

```
boolean contains(string, string)
```

Description

contains returns true if the first string contains the second string.

Examples

contains('network', 'two')	true.
contains(title, 'XML')	true if the first child title element contains 'XML'; false otherwise.
contains(price, 5)	true if the first child price element contains the number 5; false other- wise.
contains('so true!!!', true())	true (true() is coerced to true).

3.4.5 count

```
number count(node-set)
```

Description

count returns the number of nodes in the argument node-set.

Examples

count(item)	Returns the number of child item elements.
count(descendant::* | text())	Returns the total number of descendant elements and child text nodes.
invoice[count(item) > 3]	Returns the child invoice elements that have more than three child item elements.

3.4.6 false

```
boolean false()
```

Description

Returns false.

Examples

false()	false
string(false())	'false'
number(false())	0

3.4.7 floor

```
number floor(number)
```

Description

floor returns the largest integer that is not greater than the argument.

Examples

floor(43.6)	43
floor('43.6')	43
floor(-2.5)	-3
floor(item/price)	Returns the rounded-down price of the first child item element.

3.4.8 id

node-set id(object)

Description

id returns a node-set that is identified through unique IDs (requires DTD or schema that leverages unique ID types). The exact behavior of id depends on the type of argument object.

Type	Description
node-set	The id function is applied to the string-value of each node in the argument node-set. The union of the resulting node-sets is returned.
other	The argument is first converted to a string, which is then split into a whitespace-separated list of tokens. The resulting node-set contains the element nodes that have a unique ID equal to one of the tokens in the list.

Examples

id('isbn-0201709147')	Returns the element with a unique ID of isbn-0201709147.
id('isbn-0201709147 isbn-0201604426 isbn-0201379368')	Returns the three elements with the specified unique IDs.
id(book/@similarBooks)	Returns the elements that are referred to by the child book's similarBook attribute (for example, <book similarBooks='b1 b2'/>).

3.4.9 lang

```
boolean lang(string)
```

Description

lang returns a boolean indicating whether the language specified by the argument string is the same as (or a sublanguage of) the language of the context node, which is specified via the xml:lang attribute. If the context node has no xml:lang attribute, it inherits the language of the nearest ancestor element that does have the xml:lang attribute. If no ancestor has an xml:lang attribute, false is returned. The language string comparisons are case insensitive and they ignore language suffixes identified by '-'.

Examples

lang('en')	Returns true if the language of the context node is 'en' or a sublanguage of 'en' (for example, 'en-us').
desc[lang('en')]	Returns all child desc elements that have a language of 'en' or is a sublanguage of 'en' (for example, 'en-us').

3.4.10 last

```
number last()
```

Description

last returns a number equal to the size of the context node-set.

Examples

invoice/item[last() > 3]	Returns the child item elements of the child invoice elements that have more than three child item elements.
invoice/item[last()=position()]	Returns the last item element of each child invoice element.

3.4.11 `local-name`

`string local-name(node-set?)`

Description

`local-name` returns the local name of the node in the argument `node-set` that is first in document order. If the argument `node-set` is empty or has no local name, an empty `string` is returned. If the argument is omitted, it defaults to a `node-set` with the context node as its only member.

Examples

`local-name(..)`	Returns the local name of the context node's parent.
`descendant::*[local-name()='price']`	Returns all `descendant` elements that have a local name of `'price'`.

3.4.12 `name`

`string name(node-set?)`

Description

`name` returns the QName of the node in the argument `node-set` that is first in document order. If the argument `node-set` is empty or has no local name, an empty `string` is returned. If the argument is omitted, it defaults to a `node-set` with the context node as its only member.

Examples

`name(*)`	Returns the QName of the first child element.
`descendant::*[name() = 'dm:author'`]	Returns all `descendant` elements that have a QName of `'dm:author'`.

3.4.13 namespace-uri

`string namespace-uri(node-set?)`

Description

`namespace-uri` returns the namespace URI of the node in the argument `node-set` that is first in document order. If the argument `node-set` is empty or has no namespace URI, an empty `string` is returned. If the argument is omitted, it defaults to a `node-set` with the context node as its only member.

Examples

`namespace-uri(../..)`	Returns the namespace URI of the context node's grandparent.
`descendant::*[local-name() = 'price' and namespace- uri() = 'urn:invoices']`	Returns all `descendant` elements that have a local name of `'price'` and a namespace URI of `'urn:invoices.'`

3.4.14 normalize-space

`string normalize-space(string?)`

Description

`normalize-space` returns the argument `string` with whitespace normalized. Normalization consists of stripping all leading/trailing whitespace as well as replacing embedded whitespace sequences with a single space character. Whitespace characters are defined as spaces, tabs, CR, and LF. If the argument is omitted, it defaults to the string-value of the context node.

Examples

`normalize-space( ' hello    world ')`	`'hello world'`
`normalize-space(desc)`	Returns the normalized string-value of the first child `desc` element.
`normalize-space()`	Returns the normalized string-value of the context node.

3.4.15 not

`boolean not(boolean)`

Description

`not` returns `true` if the argument is `false`; `false` otherwise.

Examples

`not(true())`	`false`
`not(price)`	Returns `false` if the context node has child `price` elements; `true` otherwise.
`item/price[not( position() = last() )]`	Returns the `price` elements that are not the last child of their parent `item` element.

3.4.16 number

`number number(object?)`

Description

`number` converts its argument into a `number`. The conversion details depend on the type of argument object.

Type	Description
`node-set`	The `node-set` is first converted to a `string` (per the string function); then the resulting `string` is converted to a `number` according to the rules for `string` (see next entry).
`string`	Converted to an IEEE 754 floating point number (see the IEEE 754 standard for more details). If the argument string does not represent a number, `NaN` is returned.
`boolean`	`true` is converted to 1, `false` to zero.
`other`	Converted to a `number` in a way that is dependent on that type.

Examples

`number('33.3')`	`33.3`
`number(true())`	`1`

`number('xml')`	NaN
`number(price)`	Returns the numerical value of the string-value of the first child `price` element.

3.4.17 position

`number position()`

Description

`position` returns the index of the context node in the context **node-set** (1 based).

Examples

`item[position()=1]`	Returns the first child `item` element.
`price[position()=last() ]`	Returns the last child `price` element.

3.4.18 round

`number round(number)`

Description

`round` returns the integer that is closest to the argument number. If two **numbers** match this criterion, the bigger **number** (closest to positive infinity) is returned. If the argument is less than zero but greater than or equal to `-0.5`, negative zero is returned. If the argument is not a number (**NaN**), positive infinity, negative infinity, positive zero, or negative zero, it simply returns the same value passed in.

Examples

`round(1.5)`	2
`round(10 div 3)`	3
`round(price)`	Returns the rounded-off value of the first child `price` element.

3.4.19 `starts-with`

`boolean starts-with(string, string)`

Description

`starts-with` returns `true` if the first `string` starts with the second `string`.

Examples

`starts-with('$12.05', '$')`	Returns `true`.
`starts-with(title, 'Essential')`	Returns `true` if the first child `title` element starts with `'Essential'`; `false` otherwise.
`starts-with(price, 5)`	Returns `true` if the first child `price` element starts with the number 5; `false` otherwise.
`starts-with('true/false', true())`	Returns `true`.

3.4.20 `string`

`string string(object?)`

Description

`string` converts its argument into a `string`. The conversion details depend on the type of argument object. If the argument is omitted, it defaults to a `node-set` with the context node as its only member.

Type	Description
`node-set`	The string-value of the node in the `node-set` that is first in document order. If the `node-set` is empty, an empty `string` is returned.
`boolean`	`true` is converted to the `string 'true'` and `false` is converted to `'false'`.
`number`	The number is represented in decimal form preceded with a minus symbol (-) if the number is negative. A decimal point is not included for integer values. If the number is NaN, the `string 'NaN'` is returned. If the number is positive or negative zero, the `string '0'` is returned. If the number is positive infinity, the `string 'Infinity'` is returned. If the number is negative infinity, the `string '-Infinity'` is returned.
`other`	Is converted to a `string` in a way that is dependent on that type.

Examples

`string(true())`	`'true'`
`string(-100.23)`	`'-100.23'`
`string(/foo/bar)`	Returns the string-value of the root `foo` element's first child `bar` element.

3.4.21 string-length

`number string-length(string?)`

Description

`string-length` returns the number of characters in the string. If the argument is omitted, it defaults to the string-value of the context node.

Examples

`string-length('XML')`	3
`string-length(customer)`	Returns the length of the string-value of the first child `customer` element.

3.4.22 substring

`string substring(string, number, number?)`

Description

`substring` returns the substring of the first argument starting at the 1-based position specified by the second argument with the length specified by the third argument. If the third argument is omitted, it returns the substring starting at the position specified by the second argument to the end of the string.

Examples

`substring('goodbye',4,2)`	`'db'`
`substring('goodbye',5)`	`'bye'`

`concat(substring(lastname, 1,6),'.gif')`	Returns a file name, which is the concatenation of the first six letters of the `lastname` child element with '`.gif`' (for example, '`skonna.gif`').

3.4.23 substring-after

`string substring-after(string, string)`

Description

`substring-after` returns the substring of the first `string` that follows the first occurrence of the second `string`. If the first `string` doesn't contain the second `string`, an empty `string` is returned.

Examples

`substring-after('dm:invoice', ':')`	'`invoice`'
`substring-after('1972-10-30', '-')`	'`10-30`'
`substring-after(filename, '.')`	Returns the `filename` element's file extension (for example, `.gif`).

3.4.24 substring-before

`string substring-before(string, string)`

Description

`substring-before` returns the substring of the first `string` that precedes the first occurrence of the `string` string. If the first `string` doesn't contain the second `string`, an empty `string` is returned.

Examples

`substring-before('dm:invoice', ':')`	'`dm`'
`substring-before('1972-10-30', '-')`	'`1972`'
`substring-before(filename, '.')`	Returns the `filename` element's value excluding the extension.

3.4.25 `sum`

`number sum(node-set)`

Description

`sum` converts the string-value of each node in the argument `node-set` to a number and then calculates the total.

Examples

sum example	Description
`sum(/items/i)`	Returns `9.0`, assuming the following XML document: `<items> <i>1.0</i><i>3.0</i><i>5.0</i> </items>`.
`sum(/items/i) div count(items/i)`	Returns `3.0`, (assuming the previous document).

3.4.26 `translate`

`string translate(string, string, string)`

Description

`translate` returns the first argument `string` with occurrences of the characters in the second argument `string` replaced by the character at the corresponding position in the third argument `string`. If there is a character in the second argument `string` that doesn't have a replacement character in the corresponding position of the third argument `string` (because the second argument `string` is longer), all occurrences of that character are removed.

Examples

`translate('10-30-1972', '-', '/')`	`'10/30/1972'`
`translate('skonnard', 'kosadrn', 'oxb')`	`'box'`

3.4.27 true

`boolean true()`

Description

Returns `true`.

Examples

`true()`	`true`
`string(true())`	`'true'`
`number(true())`	`1`

3.5 References

XML Path Language (XPath) Version 1.0 Recommendation.
Available at *http://www.w3.org/TR/xpath*.

IEEE 754.
http://standards.ieee.org/reading/ieee/stdpublic/description/busarch/754-1985_des.html

Chapter 4
XPointer, XInclude, and XML Base

The XML Pointer Language (XPointer) version 1.0 defines syntax for using fragment identifiers with XML resources. This makes it possible to extend XPath to support interdocument (as opposed to just intradocument) addressing. XPointer also provides a more flexible syntax for addressing portions of an XML document that are not addressable in XPath (for example, points and ranges).

XML Inclusions (XInclude) version 1.0 defines the syntax for general-purpose XML-based inclusions. XInclude functionality is similar to that provided by external entities or `#include` in C++. The difference is that XInclude works at the Infoset level rather than during preprocessing. XInclude leverages URI references as well as XPointer fragments to identify resources for inclusion.

When multiple XML resources are used to build a logical XML document, questions arise when resolving relative URIs. XML Base defines this process along with a syntax for explicitly controlling the base URI of elements in a document.

The rest of this chapter presents the syntax for these three specifications: XPointer, XInclude, and XML Base. At the time of writing, these three specifications were still under development at the W3C. See Section 4.4 for the version of each specification used in this chapter.

4.1 XPointer version 1.0

An XPointer expression is attached to a URI reference as a fragment identifier. The context of an XPointer expression is always initialized to the root node of the identified XML resource. XPointer provides three types of expressions: full XPointers, bare names, and child sequences.

4.1.1 Full XPointers

`uri-reference#scheme(expression)scheme(expression)...`

Description

Full XPointers consist of one or more XPointer parts, optionally separated by whitespace (see Figure 4–1).

Scheme name	Description
`xpointer(xptr-expr)`	XPointer expression provides access to nodes in an XML document as well as arbitrary non-node locations (based on XPath).
`xmlns(prefix=nsURI)`	Expression defines a namespace declaration in scope for the fragment parts to the right. In the event that more than one `xmlns` part to the left of an `xpointer` part specifies the same prefix, the rightmost one of these is used for that `xpointer` part.

Each XPointer part starts with a scheme name and is followed by a scheme-specific expression. When the scheme is `xpointer`, the contained expression is based on XPath with XPointer-specific extensions. When the scheme is `xmlns`, the contained expression contains a namespace declaration. There are no other schemes defined at this time, but this is an extensibility point for the future.

XPointer expressions are evaluated from left to right in order. Evaluation stops once a fragment part successfully identifies a portion of the resource. If a fragment part fails or does not identify anything, the next fragment part is evaluated, and so on. If the processor doesn't recognize the scheme or if there is something about the expression that causes it to fail, the processor moves on to the next fragment part.

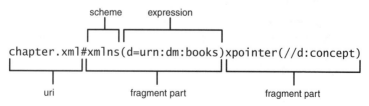

Figure 4–1 Full XPointer example.

Examples

Simple full XPointer expression

```
xslt.xml#xpointer(/descendant::concept[@id='template'])
```

Identifies the `concept` elements in `xslt.xml` that belong to no namespace and that have an `id` attribute equal to `'template'`.

Full XPointer expression with namespaces

```
xslt.xml#xmlns(d=urn:example:dm1)xmlns(d=urn:example:dm2)
   xmlns(x=urn:ids-r-us)xpointer(//
      d:concept[@x:id='template'])
```

Identifies the `concept` elements in `xslt.xml` that belong to the `urn:example:dm2` namespace and that have an `id` attribute from the `urn:ids-r-us` namespace equal to `'template'`.

Full XPointer expression with multiple XPointer parts

```
xslt.xml#xpointer(id('template'))xpointer(//
   *[@id='template'])
```

Identifies the `concept` elements in `xslt.xml` that have an attribute of type ID equal to `'template'`. If the DTD/schema isn't available, the first fragment part fails and the second is evaluated, which simply identifies all elements with an `id` attribute equal to `'template'`.

4.1.2 Bare names

```
uri-reference#bare-name
```

Description

An XPointer bare name is simply an abbreviation for the following full XPointer expression that leverages the XPath `id` function: `xpointer(id(bare-name))`.

Example

Equivalent expressions

```
xslt.xml#xpointer(id('prod1'))
xslt.xml#prod1
```

These expressions are equivalent. The first is a full XPointer expression whereas the second is an XPointer bare name.

4.1.3 Child sequences

```
uri-reference#(bare-name | /1)/n/n/n/n...
```

Description

A child sequence is a simplified addressing syntax that locates an element by stepwise navigation using a sequence of integers separated by forward slashes (/). Each integer n locates the nth child element of the previously located element. This is equivalent to an XPath location step of the form *[n]. The first item in the child sequence can be either a bare name (see previous section) or the string '/1', which identifies the document element.

Example

Equivalent expressions

```
xslt.xml#xpointer(/*[1]/*[2]/*[7]/*[3]/*[2])
xslt.xml#/1/2/7/3/2
xslt.xml#section7/3/2
```

All of these expressions are equivalent. The first is a full XPointer expression that uses XPath. The second is the equivalent XPointer child sequence. The third expression uses a bare name to identify the seventh child of the second child of the document element by ID followed by a relative child sequence.

4.1.4 XPointer extensions to XPath

Description

In XPath, location path expressions produce node-sets. XPointer, on the other hand, is capable of identifying portions of a document that cannot be modeled with XPath node-sets. As a result, XPointer generalizes XPath's notion of node and node-set with location and location-set. XPointer locations consist of points, ranges, and XPath nodes. XPointer location-sets are a collection of locations.

Definitions

point

A point location identifies a container node along with an index to its child data. If the node can have children (for example, element nodes), the index refers to a position within the child node's collection (called a *node-point*). If the node cannot have children (for example, text nodes), the index refers to an offset within the node's character data (called a *character-point*). The following describes how various XPath-isms are evaluated for a point location:

Concept	Description
expanded name	None
string-value	Empty
axes	The child, descendant, attribute, and namespace axes are empty. The self axis contains the point itself whereas the parent axis contains the node-point's container node. The ancestor axis contains the node-point's container node and its ancestors. A node-point's siblings are the children of the container node that are before or after the node-point while a character point doesn't have any siblings.

range

A range location consists of two points: a start point and an end point. Everything within these two points (in document order) is part of the range location. The following describes how various XPath-isms are evaluated for a range location:

Concept	Description
expanded name	None
string-value	If the points are both character-points and the container nodes of the points are the same, then the string-value consists of the characters between the two points. Otherwise, the string-value consists of the characters that are in text nodes between the two points.
axes	The axes of a range location are the axes of its start point.

4.1.5 XPointer node tests

Description

XPointer extends the XPath node type identifiers (to account for point and range locations) for performing node tests by type.

Node test (by type)	Description
point()	Identifies locations of type point.
range()	Identifies locations of type range.

Example

Identifying the points in a range

```
xpointer(range(//intro)/point)())
```

4.1.6 XPointer function library

Description

XPointer adds several functions to the XPath core function library that must be supported by XPointer implementations. These additional functions support working with point and range locations in XPointer expressions. Like the XPath functions, the XPointer functions don't belong to a namespace, so their names don't need to be qualified with a namespace prefix. XPointer processors may extend this library by using namespace-qualified function names.

4.1.6.1 end-point

```
location-set end-point(location-set)
```

Description

For each location in the argument location-set, **end-point** adds a location of type point to the resulting location-set. The end point of a location is evaluated according to location type as follows:

Type	Description
point	Same as the point
range	The end point of the range

Type	Description
`attribute, namespace`	Error
`root, element`	The container node is the same as the node in question. The index is the number of child nodes.
`text, comment, processing instruction`	The container node is the same as the node in question. The index is the length of the node's string-value.

Example

Identifying the end point of a range

```
xpointer(end-point(id('section1')/range-to(//summary)))
```

XPointer

4.1.6.2 here

```
location-set here()
```

Description

The `here` function returns a location-set with a single location, which represents the node that contains the XPointer expression being evaluated.

Examples

Identifying the element containing the expression

```
xpointer(here())
```

Identifying an ancestor of the containing element

```
xpointer(here()/ancestor::chapter[1])
```

4.1.6.3 origin

```
location-set origin()
```

Description

The `origin` function enables addressing relative to out-of-line links such as defined in XLink. This allows XPointers to be used in applications to express relative locations when links do not reside directly at one of their end points. The function returns a location-set with a single member, which locates the element from which a user or program initiated traversal of the link.

Examples

Identifying the origin element that linked to this document

```
xpointer(origin())
```

Identifying the descendants of the origin element

```
xpointer(origin()/descendant::node())
```

4.1.6.4 range

```
location-set range(location-set)
```

Description

The range function returns ranges representing the covering range of the locations in the argument location-set. The covering range of a location is determined based on location type as follows:

Type	Description
range	Identical to the range
attribute/namespace	The container node of the start point and the end point of the covering range is the attribute or namespace location, the index of the start point of the covering range is zero, and the index of the end point of the covering range is the length of the string-value of the attribute or namespace location.
root node	The container node of the start point and the end point of the covering range is the root node, the index of the start point of the covering range is zero, and the index of the end point of the covering range is the number of children of the root location.
point	The start and end points of the covering range are the point itself.
other	The container node of the start point and the end point of the covering range is the parent of the location, the index of the start point of the covering range is the number of preceding sibling nodes of the location, and the index of the end point is one greater than the index of the starting point.

Examples

Identifying the covering range of each intro element

```
xpointer(range(//intro))
```

Identifying the covering range of each id attribute

```
xpointer(range(//intro/@id))
```

4.1.6.5 range-inside

```
location-set range-inside(location-set)
```

Description

The `range-inside` function returns ranges covering the contents of the locations in the argument location-set.

Examples

Identifying ranges that span the children of each intro element

```
xpointer(range-inside(//intro))
```

Identifying ranges that span the text within the intro elements

```
xpointer(range-inside(//intro/text()))
```

4.1.6.6 range-to

```
location-set range-to(expression)
```

Description

`range-to` returns a location-set consisting of zero or more ranges. The start point of each range is that of the context location whereas the end point is that of the location found by evaluating the expression with respect to the context location.

Examples

Identifying a range between two points

```
xpointer(id('section1')/range-to(id('section2')))
```

Identifying a set of ranges

```
xpointer(//intro/range-to(section[1])
```

Identifies a set of ranges, where each range starts from an `intro` element to its first child `section` element.

4.1.6.7 `start-point`

```
location-set start-point(location-set)
```

Description

For each location in the argument location-set, `start-point` adds a location of type `point` to the resulting location-set. The start point of a location is evaluated according to location type as follows:

Type	Description
`point`	Same as the point
`range`	The start point of the range
`attribute, namespace`	Error
`root, element, text, comment, processing instruction`	The container node is the same as the node in question. The index is zero.

Example

Identifying the start point of a range

```
xpointer(start-point(//intro/range-to(section[1])))
```

4.1.6.8 `string-range`

```
location-set string-range(location-set, string, number?,
    number?)
```

Description

For each location in the `location-set` argument, `string-range` returns a set of string ranges within the location's string-value. The string-value of the location is searched for substrings that match the `string` argument, and the resulting `location-set` will contain a range location for each nonoverlapping match, beginning with the offset (relative to the start of the match) specified by the third argument (default = 1) and spanning the number of characters specified by the fourth argument (default is the length of the matched string).

Examples

Identifying the third occurrence of '*Infoset*' *in* intro *elements*

```
xpointer(string-range(//intro,'Infoset')[3])
```

Identifying a set of string ranges

```
xpointer(string-range(//intro, 'Infoset', 3, 2))
```

Identifies a set of string ranges spanning the substring 'fos' within all occurrences of 'Infoset' in intro elements.

4.2 XInclude

XInclude provides an alternative to external general entities that uses normal XML syntax and that works at the Infoset level, not the serialized entity level. XInclude is the moral equivalent of the EntityReference node type from the DOM, because it exists solely as a placeholder for the content that it references. An XInclude-aware processor will silently replace the XInclude reference with the content that it references. This is similar to the way entity references are expanded, the difference being that XInclude processing occurs after parsing, not during parsing.

As an example, if elements in the included document belong to no namespace, they will still belong to no namespace even if the including document has a default namespace declaration on the root element. Again, XInclude defines how to merge the Infosets of both documents after parsing has taken place.

The XInclude namespace only consists of a single element, include, which can be used in conjunction with any other namespace.

Namespace

http://www.w3.org/1999/XML/xinclude

4.2.1 include

```
<xinc:include href='url reference' parse='xml|text'
    xmlns:xinc='http://www.w3.org/1999/XML/xinclude'/>
```

Description

A placeholder element for the resource referenced by the `href` attribute. The `parse` attribute specifies the type of resource.

Attributes

Syntax	Description
`href='URI reference'`	The `href` attribute contains a URI reference to the included content.
`parse='(xml|text)'`	The attribute is an enumerated value of either `xml` (default) or `text`, indicating how the referenced data is to be included. `xml` causes the referenced data to be interpreted as XML (à la parsed entities), and the referenced Infoset is merged at this location. `text` indicates that the referenced data should be included as a single text node.

Example

Using XInclude to merge documents

```
<!-- intro.txt -->
The XML Pointer Language (XPointer) 1.0 defines
syntax for using fragment identifiers with XML
resources.
```

```
<!-- xptr-refs.xml -->
<references>
  <reference>
    <desc>XML Pointer Language Version 1.0</desc>
    <uri>http://www.w3.org/TR/xptr</uri>
  </reference>
</references>
```

```
<!-- chapter.xml -->
<chapter xmlns='http://www.develop.com/exmlref'
  xmlns:xinc='http://www.w3.org/1999/XML/xinclude'>
  <title><xinc:include href='
    xptr-refs.xml#xpointer(//desc/text())'/></title>
  <intro>
    <xinc:include href='intro.txt' parse='text'/>
  </intro>
  <xinc:include href='xptr-refs.xml'/>
</chapter>
```

The logical resulting document could be serialized as follows:

```
<chapter xmlns='http://www.develop.com/exmlref'>
  <title>XML Pointer Language Version 1.0</title>
  <intro>
The XML Pointer Language (XPointer) 1.0 defines
syntax for using fragment identifiers with XML
resources.
  </intro>
  <references xmlns=''>
    <reference>
      <desc>XML Pointer Language Version 1.0</desc>
      <uri>http://www.w3.org/TR/xptr</uri>
    </reference>
  </references>
</chapter>
```

XML Base

4.3 XML Base

When multiple XML resources are used to build a logical XML document (for example, via external entities, XInclude, and so on), questions arise about how to resolve relative URIs. XML Base defines this process along with a syntax for explicitly controlling the base URI of elements in a document.

By default, relative URIs found in a document are resolved relative to the original entity's base URI. For example, an entity located at `http://www.develop.com/exmlref/xptr.xml` will have a base URI of `http://www.develop.com/exmlref/`. All relative URIs found in that entity will be resolved relative to its base URI. Because this may not always be desirable, XML Base provides the `xml:base` attribute for explicitly overriding the base URI of any element in a document.

4.3.1 `xml:base`

`xml:base='URI reference'`

Description

The `xml:base` attribute allows an element to override the base URI of an element explicitly and all descendant elements. The value of this attribute is interpreted as a URI reference as defined in *IETF RFC 2396* (`http://www.ietf.org/rfc/rfc2396.txt`). In namespace-aware XML processors, the `xml` prefix is automatically bound to `http://www.w3.org/XML/1998/namespace`. If the `xml:base` value is itself a relative URI, it's also resolved with respect to the current in-scope base URI (either explicitly set through an ancestor `xml:base` attribute or inherited from the owner entity).

Example

Using XML Base to modify an element's base URI

```
<chapter xml:base='http://www.develop.com/xml/'>
  <title>XSLT</title>
  <sections xml:base='/exmlref/refs/'>
    <xinc:include href='xslt.xml'/>
    <xinc:include
    href='xpath.xml#xpointer(id("section123"))'
        xml:base='http://www.w3.org/TR/'/>
  </sections>
  <xinc:include href='exml.xml#xpointer(//xslt-summary)'/>
</chapter>
```

The three relative URIs used in this document are resolved to

```
http://www.develop.com/exmlref/refs/xslt.xml
http://www.w3.org/TR/xpath.xml#xpointer(id(section123))
http://www.develop.com/xml/exml.xml#xpointer(//xslt-
    summary)
```

4.4   References

XML Pointer Language (XPointer) Version 1.0. *Last-Call Working Draft 8 January 2001.*
Available at *http://www.ietf.org/rfc/rfc2396.txt*
http://www.w3.org/TR/2001/WD-xptr-20010108 and
http://www.w3.org/TR/xptr (current version).

XML Inclusions (XInclude) Version 1.0. *Working draft 26 October 2000.*
Available at *http://www.w3.org/TR/2000/WD-xinclude-20001026* and
http://www.w3.org/TR/xinclude (current version).

XML Base. *Proposed Recommendation 20 December 2000.*
Available at *http://www.w3.org/TR/2000/PR-xmlbase-20001220* and
http://www.w3.org/TR/xmlbase (current version).

For more information of IETF RFC 2396, please visit http://www.ietf.org/rfc/
rfc2396.txt

Chapter 5

XSL Transformations 1.0

XSL Transformations (XSLT) version 1.0 defines an XML-based programming language for transforming XML documents into other text formats. The most common use of XSLT today is for transforming one type of XML document into another type of XML document, which helps alleviate schema incompatibilities (see Figure 5–1).

It's also common to use XSLT for transforming XML documents into HTML or some other presentation-oriented format (for example, see Formatting Objects in XSL). In addition to these scenarios, XSLT can be used to transform XML documents into any other type of text format (for example, comma-separated formats, C++/Java source files, COBOL records, and so on).

```
<v1:emp xmlns:v1='urn:employee:v1'>
  <fname>Bob</fname>
  <lname>Smith</lname>
  <age>45</age>
  <position>Instructor</position>
</v1:emp>
```

```
<v2:employee xmlns:v2='urn:employee:v2'>
  <name>Bob Smith</name>
  <title>Instructor</title>
</v2:employee>
```

Figure 5–1   Transforming between different versions of employee documents.

5.1 Introduction to XSLT programming

XSLT offers three distinct programming models: exemplar-based, procedural, and declarative. The first and simplest programming model is exemplar-based. This model allows you to take an XML document template and fill it in with XSLT programming constructs that produce dynamic content at the appropriate locations. For more information on this programming model, see Section 5.6.

Sample exemplar-based transformation

```
<!-- exemplar document -->
<v2:employee
  xmlns:v1='urn:employee:v1'
  xmlns:v2='urn:employee:v2'
  xmlns:xsl='http://www.w3.org/1999/XSL/Transform'
  xsl:version='1.0'>
  <name><xsl:value-of select="concat(/v1:emp/fname,
    ' ', /v1:emp/lname)"/></name>
  <title><xsl:value-of select='/v1:emp/position'/></title>
</v2:employee>
```

XSLT also makes it possible to separate and generalize transformation logic into reusable templates. Templates in XSLT can be called like functions in procedural programming languages. The action of a template is to output a portion of the result document. See the sections on `template` and `call-template` for more details.

Sample procedural transformation

```
<xsl:transform
  xmlns:v1='urn:employee:v1'
  xmlns:v2='urn:employee:v2'
  xmlns:xsl='http://www.w3.org/1999/XSL/Transform'
  version='1.0'>

  <!-- outputs name element -->
  <xsl:template name="outputName">
    <name><xsl:value-of
      select="concat(v1:emp/fname, ' ', v1:emp/lname)"/></
    name>
  </xsl:template>
```

```
<!-- outputs title element -->
<xsl:template name="outputTitle">
  <title><xsl:value-of select='v1:emp/position'/></
  title>
</xsl:template>

<!-- root template: main entry point -->
<xsl:template match="/">
  <v2:employee>
    <xsl:call-template name="outputName"/>
    <xsl:call-template name="outputTitle"/>
  </v2:employee>
</xsl:template>

</xsl:transform>
```

And finally, XSLT offers a powerful and flexible declarative programming model (similar to that of Prolog, Lisp, and Scheme). The declarative model is based on associating templates with patterns (or rules) relative to the input document.

When the processor begins executing the transformation, it looks for the template with a pattern that matches the root of the input tree (for example, this is how the first template was called in the previous example). Then, inside that template, you indicate which nodes you would like the processor to continue processing through the `apply-templates/apply-imports` elements. After a call to `apply-templates/apply-imports`, the processor identifies and executes the template that best matches each specified node. This continues until the processor reaches a template that doesn't explicitly call `apply-templates/apply-imports`.

XSLT defines several built-in templates that exist as part of every program unless they're explicitly overridden. The built-in templates have a profound effect on the programming model. For the root node and element nodes, the built-in template calls `apply-templates` to continue processing all child nodes. For attribute and text nodes, the built-in template simply outputs the node's value. For all other node types, the built-in template does nothing. See Section 5.5 for more details.

The declarative model allows developers to partition transformation logic into modules that are automatically associated with a portion of the input tree. The developer doesn't have to worry about when or how the template is called. Instead the developer simply declares that a given template should be called for a particular node, and the processor figures out when and how to do it. With this approach, it's possible to build programs that transform extremely complex input documents in a straightforward fashion. For more details on this approach, see the `template`, `apply-templates`, and `apply-imports` sections.

Sample declarative transformation

```
<xsl:transform
  xmlns:v1='urn:employee:v1'
  xmlns:v2='urn:employee:v2'
  xmlns:xsl='http://www.w3.org/1999/XSL/Transform'
  version='1.0'>

  <!-- override built-in template for
       text/attributes -->
  <xsl:template match="text()|@*"/>

  <!-- template for position elements -->
  <xsl:template match="position">
    <title><xsl:value-of select='.'/></title>
  </xsl:template>

  <!-- template for fname elements -->
  <xsl:template match="fname">
    <name><xsl:value-of select="
      concat(., ' ',
        following-sibling::lname)"/></name>
  </xsl:template>

  <!-- template for v1:emp elements -->
  <xsl:template match="v1:emp">
    <v2:employee>
      <xsl:apply-templates select="*"/>
    </v2:employee>
  </xsl:template>
</xsl:transform>
```

Although exemplar-based transformations only allow XML output (or well-formed HTML), the last two approaches make it possible to output XML, HTML, or straight text. See the `output` element for more details on how this works. The last two approaches also make it possible to partition transformations into multiple source files. The `include/import` elements can be used to combine XSLT files into one logical program.

Regardless of which approach you choose, XSLT offers several programming constructs that can be used to write sophisticated transformations. Some of these programming constructs are quite familiar and intuitive (for example, conditionals, loop statements, and so on), whereas others are specific to XSLT (for example, `value-of`, `element`, `attribute`, and so on).

5.2   XSLT types and expressions

XSLT leverages XPath for identifying nodes from the input document (`select` attribute), specifying conditions (`if`/`when` statements), and generating text in the result document (`value-of`). XSLT also defines several new data types and expressions that are used to define the various XSLT constructs throughout the rest of this chapter.

XSLT data types

Type	Description
char	A single UCS character
QName	A qualified name (`prefix:local_name`). The prefix is expanded into a URI using the in-scope namespace declarations.
QNames	A whitespace-separated list of QName values
token	A string that doesn't contain whitespace
tokens	A whitespace-separated list of token values
uri-reference	A valid URI reference
template	A template defines a portion of the result document. It can contain literal output (elements/text) as well as XSLT elements that are instructions for creating dynamic output.

XSLT expressions

Type	Description
expression	A generic XPath expression
node-set-expression	An XPath expression that yields a `node-set`
boolean-expression	An XPath expression with a result that is converted to a boolean (as if by calling the `boolean` function)
number-expression	An XPath expression with a result that is converted to a number (as if by calling the `number` function)

XSLT

Type	Description
`string-expression`	An XPath expression with a result that is converted to a string (as if by calling the `string` function)
`pattern`	A sequence of XPath location paths separated by `|`. Location paths used in patterns may only use the `child` and `attribute` (@) axis identifiers, but they may use the `//` abbreviation for `/descendant-or-self::node()/`. There are no restrictions on what's used in the node test or predicate portion of a location path. The `id` and `key` functions may also be used as a complete pattern. For more details on pattern matching see Section 5.3.

These type/expression names are used when presenting the syntax for each of the XSLT constructs presented in this chapter. For example, the following represents the syntax of the `attribute` element:

```
<xsl:attribute
  name = { qname }
  namespace = { uri-reference }>
  <!-- Content: template -->
</xsl:attribute>
```

The previous tables describe what `QName,` URI reference, and template mean in this context. See Chapter 3 for more details on XPath data types and expressions.

5.3 Patterns

A pattern is a restricted XPath location path (see previous section) that identifies a set of nodes. A pattern identifies an *is-a relationship* rather than a *has-a relationship*. For example, the pattern `child::foo` identifies nodes that *are* child foo elements rather than nodes that *have* child foo elements. Patterns are primarily used to associate templates with nodes in the source document (see **template**). Patterns are also used to define keys (see **key**) and numbering details (see **number**).

A node matches a pattern when the pattern expression evaluated against the node (or any of the node's ancestor nodes) identifies the node itself.

Examples

Pattern example	Description
`*`	Matches any element node.
`v1:*`	Matches any element from the namespace associated with the `v1` prefix.
`@*`	Matches any attribute node.
`text()`	Matches any text node.
`node()`	Matches any node except for the root node (the root node is not a child of another node).
`fname`	Matches any `fname` element that belongs to no namespace.
`child::fname`	Matches any `fname` element that belongs to no namespace.
`fname	lname	@id`	Matches any `fname`/`lname` element or `id` attribute that belong to no namespace.
`fname/text()`	Matches any text node that is a child of an `fname` element (belonging to no namespace).
`emp//text()`	Matches any text node that is a descendant of an `emp` element.
`v1:emp[@id='e101']/fname`	Matches any `fname` element (from no namespace) that is a child of the `emp` element with an `id` attribute equal to `e101`, from the namespace associated with the `v1` prefix.

As you can see from these examples, it's possible for a node to match more than one pattern. XSLT provides a set of conflict resolution rules to define what happens when this occurs (described next).

5.4 Conflict resolution

When a node matches more than one pattern, the following conflict resolution rules are used to determine which template to use:

- All templates with a lower import precedence are eliminated from consideration (see `import` element).

- Of the remaining templates, the one with the highest priority matches. A priority may be explicitly assigned to a template via the `priority` attribute; otherwise, its default priority is automatically calculated (listed next).

- If there are multiple templates remaining of equal priority, the XSLT processor may either signal an error or choose the last one in the document.

Default priorities

Pattern type	Default priority	Examples

Node test by type	-0.50	`*`
		`node()`
		`comment()`
		`text()`
		`processing-instruction()`
		`child::*`
		`child::text()`
		`@*`
		`@node()`
		`attribute::node()`

Namespace wildcard	-0.25	`v1:*`
		`child::v1:*`
		`attribute::v1:*`

QName	0.00	`fname`
		`child::fname`
		`v1:emp`
		`child::v1:emp`
		`@id`
		`attribute::id`
		`@v1:id`

Processing instruction tests by literal	0.00	`processing-instruction(` `'xsl-stylesheet' )`

Everything else	0.50	`v1:emp/fname`
		`v1:emp[@id]`
		`fname[contains(., 'Aaron')]`
		`//fname`
		`//node()`

Multiple patterns (pattern1 | pattern2)	Treated as distinct templates, with priorities that are calculated independently.	`v1:emp	fname` `node()	@*	*`

5.5 Built-in templates

XSLT defines several templates that are built into every transformation. These built-in templates provide default functionality for each node type (as described next). Built-in templates have the lowest possible priority and can be overridden.

Built-in template descriptions for each node type

Node type	Description
Root	Calls `apply-templates` on child nodes.
Element	Calls `apply-templates` on child nodes.
Attribute	Outputs the attribute value using `value-of`.
Text	Outputs the text node using `value-of`.
Processing Instruction	Does nothing.
Comment	Does nothing.
Namespace	Does nothing.

Built-in template syntax

```
<xsl:template match="*|/">
  <xsl:apply-templates/>
</xsl:template>
<xsl:template match="text()|@*">
  <xsl:value-of select="."/>
</xsl:template>
<xsl:template match="processing-instruction()|comment()"/>
```

In addition to these built-in templates, there is also a set of built-in templates for each mode used in the document (see `template` for more details):

```
<xsl:template match="*|/" mode="m">
  <xsl:apply-templates mode="m"/>
</xsl:template>
```

These built-in templates can be explicitly overridden to change this default behavior.

Example

Overriding built-in templates

```
<!-- overrides built-in templates -->
<xsl:template match="*|/"/>
<xsl:template match="text()|@*"/>
```

This example overrides the built-in templates for the root, element, attribute, and text nodes to do nothing by default.

XSLT

5.6 Exemplar-based transformation syntax

An exemplar-based transformation must

- be a well-formed XML document

- specify the XSLT version number on the root element
  (xsl:version='1.0')

An exemplar-based transformation is equivalent to having a single (root) template that contains the entire exemplar document as a literal result element. Because of this, top-level elements may not be used within exemplars. This approach is very similar to the ASP/JSP model, as illustrated by the following example.

Sample exemplar-based transformation

```
<!-- exemplar document -->
<html xmlns:xsl='http://www.w3.org/1999/XSL/Transform'
  xsl:version='1.0' xmlns:v1='urn:employee:v1'>
  <body>
    <h1><xsl:value-of select="concat(/v1:emp/fname,
    ' ', /v1:emp/lname)"/></h1>
    <h2><xsl:value-of select='/v1:emp/position'/></h2>
  </body>
</html>
```

5.7 Attribute value templates

In many situations, it's convenient to assign the value of an attribute dynamically (see attribute). For example, consider the following typical example that uses attribute to generate an id attribute on the new employee element:

```
<xsl:template match="v1:emp">
  <employee>
    <xsl:attribute name="id">
      <xsl:value-of select="lname"/>-<xsl:value-of
    select="@empid"/>
    </xsl:attribute>
  </employee>
</xsl:template>
```

To simplify this process, XSLT provides attribute value templates that make it possible to embed `value-of` expressions within attribute values. To use attribute value templates, enclose the XPath expression that you would have used with `value-of` inside curly braces { } inside the attribute value. Notice how much this simplifies the previous example:

```
<xsl:template match="v1:emp">
  <employee id="{lname}-{@empid}"/>
</xsl:template>
```

Besides using attribute value templates with literal result elements, they also may be used with some of the attributes on certain XSLT elements. The following example illustrates how one could generate an attribute with a name that was determined dynamically by a value in the source document:

```
<xsl:template match="v1:emp">
  <employee>
    <xsl:attribute name="{//id-label}">
      <xsl:value-of select="lname"/>-<xsl:value-of
    select="@empid"/>
    </xsl:attribute>
  </employee>
</xsl:template>
```

Curly braces are not recognized recursively inside expressions. Also, curly braces are not recognized inside attributes of XSLT elements (as shown previously) unless an attribute has been defined to accept attribute value templates. When the syntax is presented for the various XSLT elements throughout this chapter, only those attributes that have curly braces surrounding the type identifier accept attribute value templates.

5.8 Whitespace

In XML, whitespace characters consist of space (#x20), tab (#x9), carriage return (#xD), and new line (#xA). Before an XSLT processor executes a transformation against a given source document, whitespace-only text nodes are stripped from both documents.

A whitespace-only text node only contains whitespace characters. If a text node contains a single non-whitespace character, it's always preserved. It's possible to force the preservation of whitespace-only text nodes. The following rules describe when whitespace-only text nodes are preserved for both the transformation and the source documents:

Preserved in transformation document

- Whitespace within `text` elements (all others are always stripped)

Preserved in source document

- Whitespace-only text nodes with a parent element's name that is in the set of whitespace-preserving element names (see `preserve-space` and `strip-space`)

- Whitespace-only text nodes that have an `xml:space` value of `preserve` (current in-scope value, either declared on the parent element or some ancestor)

5.9 Element library

Namespace

`http://www.w3.org/1999/XSL/Transform`

The following groups the XSLT elements by functional category. The last category lists the elements that may be used as direct children of `transform/stylesheet`, otherwise known as top-level elements. All other elements (that are not top level) must be used within one of the top-level elements. For more information on any individual element, see the corresponding section.

Structural element	Description
`import`	Includes the specified transformation with lower precedence.
`include`	Includes the specified transformation.
`param`	Declares a parameter and binds it to a default value (used with `template` or `transform`).
`template`	Defines a new template rule with the specified pattern and/or name, optional mode, and optional priority.
`transform` (`stylesheet`)	Is the topmost element in an XSLT document.
`variable`	Binds a name to a value (like `param` without a default value).

Flow-control element	Description
`apply-imports`	Facilitates overriding templates by processing the current node using only imported template rules.
`apply-templates`	Instructs the processor to process each node in the identified `node-set`.
`call-template`	Invokes a template by name.
`for-each`	Loops through the identified `node-set`, instantiating the template with each node acting as the current node.
`sort`	Sorts the current node list before processing (used with `for-each` and `apply-templates`).
`with-param`	Passes the specified parameter to the target template (used with `call-template` and `apply-templates`).

Generative element	Description
`attribute`	Generates an attribute in the result document.
`comment`	Generates a comment in the result document.
`copy`	Copies the current node (without attributes or child nodes) to the result document.
`copy-of`	Copies the specified object (and each node's subtree) to the result document.
`element`	Generates an element in the result document.
`processing-instruc-tion`	Generates a processing instruction in the result document.
`text`	Generates the literal text in the result document.
`value-of`	Generates a text node from an expression in the result document.

Conditional element	Description
`choose`	Selects one template from a number of alternatives (defined by `when` and `otherwise`).
`if`	Defines a conditional template.
`otherwise`	Defines the default template for a `choose` instruction.
`when`	Defines a conditional template for a `choose` instruction.

XSLT

Declaration element	Description
attribute-set	Defines a named set of attributes that can be reused across multiple elements.
decimal-format	Declares a decimal format (used by format-number).
namespace-alias	Declares that one namespace URI is an alias for another while processing the transformation.
output	Declares how the author of the stylesheet would like the result document serialized.
preserve-space	Defines the elements in the source document for which whitespace-only text nodes should be preserved.
strip-space	Defines the elements that should be removed from the list of whitespace-preserving elements (defined by preserve-space).

Miscellaneous element	Description
fallback	Defines a fallback template that will be called when the containing XSLT instruction isn't recognized.
key	Declares a new key (used with key function).
message	Outputs a message in a processor-dependent fashion and potentially terminates the program.
number	Inserts a formatted number into the result document.

Top-level element	Description
attribute-set	Defines a named set of attributes that can be reused across multiple elements.
decimal-format	Declares a decimal format (used by format-number).
import	Includes the specified transformation with lower precedence.
include	Includes the specified transformation.
key	Declares a new key (used with key function).
namespace-alias	Declares that one namespace URI is an alias for another while processing the transformation.
output	Declares how the author of the stylesheet would like the result document serialized.
param	Declares a parameter and binds it to a default value (used with template or transform).
preserve-space	Defines the elements in the source document for which whitespace-only text nodes should be preserved.

Top-level element	Description
strip-space	Defines the elements that should be removed from the list of whitespace-preserving elements (defined by preserve-space).
template	Defines a new template rule with the specified pattern and/or name, optional mode, and optional priority.
variable	Binds a name to a value (like param without a default value).

The XSLT programming language is defined in terms of XML elements and attributes. Each of the elements belongs to the XSLT namespace. Attributes are always optional unless stated otherwise.

The syntax for each element/attribute references XSLT-specific type/expression names. For example, the following is the syntax for attribute:

```
<xsl:attribute
  name = { qname }
  namespace = { uri-reference }>
  <!-- Content: template -->
</xsl:attribute>
```

See Section 5.2 for more details on what qname, uri-reference, and template mean in this context. The { } notation identifies that these attributes also accept attribute value templates (see Section 5.7).

5.9.1 apply-imports

```
<xsl:apply-imports />
```

Description

apply-imports facilitates overriding templates. It instructs the processor to process the current node using only imported template rules (see import for details on importing template rules). The node is processed in the same mode as the current template rule (the current template rule is the template that was most recently matched, except for inside of a for-each element where the current template is always null). It is an error if xsl:apply-imports is instantiated when the current template rule is null.

Example

Using apply-imports

```
<!-- employee.xsl -->
...
<xsl:template match="employee">
  Name: <xsl:value-of select="name"/>
</xsl:template>
...

<!-- employeeDetails.xsl -->
...
<xsl:import href="employee.xsl"/>

<xsl:template match="employee">
  <xsl:apply-imports/>
  Title: <xsl:value-of select="title"/>
</xsl:template>
...
```

This example consists of two files: employee.xsl and employeeDetails.xsl. employeeDetails.xsl imports employee.xsl and overrides the employee template. Inside the derived employee template, we first call apply-imports to execute the behavior of the base template in employee.xsl (this is similar to calling a method in a base class from a derived class). In this case, we're extending the behavior of the base template also to output the employee's title.

5.9.2 apply-templates

```
<xsl:apply-templates
  select = node-set-expression
  mode = qname>
  <!-- Content: (xsl:sort | xsl:with-param)* -->
</xsl:apply-templates>
```

Description

Instructs the processor to process each node in the **node-set** identified by the select attribute. For each node in the identified **node-set**, the processor identifies the template rule that best matches the node and instantiates the template with that node as the current node (see Sections 5.3 and 5.4). The identified nodes are traversed in document order unless `apply-templates` contains child `sort` elements to reorder the `node-set` before processing (see `sort`).

If a `mode` attribute is also supplied, only templates that have the same `mode` attribute are candidates to match (see `template` for more details). Modes make it possible to have two templates with the same pattern that produce different results. Remember that there are also built-in templates for each mode specified in the transformation (see Section 5.5 for more details).

Parameters may be passed to templates through child `with-param` elements (see `param` and `with-param` for more details).

Attributes

Name	Default	Description
select	node()	A node-set expression that identifies the node-set to be processed.
mode	""	A qualified name that identifies the particular mode against which to match.

Example

Using apply-templates

```
<xsl:transform
  xmlns:v1='urn:employee:v1'
  xmlns:v2='urn:employee:v2'
  xmlns:xsl='http://www.w3.org/1999/XSL/Transform'
  version='1.0'>

  <!-- override built-in template for text/atts -->
  <xsl:template match="text()|@*"/>

  <!-- template for dependent elements -->
  <xsl:template match="dependent">
    <dep><xsl:value-of select='.'/></dep>
  </xsl:template>

  <!-- template for v1:emp elements -->
  <xsl:template match="v1:emp">
    <name><xsl:value-of
      select="concat(fname, ' ', lname)"/></name>
```

XSLT

```
    <xsl:apply-templates select="dependents"/>
  </xsl:template>

  <!-- root template, main entry point -->
  <xsl:template match="/">
    <v2:employee>
      <xsl:apply-templates/>
    </v2:employee>
  </xsl:template>

</xsl:transform>
```

In this example, the first call to `apply-templates` occurs in the root template (`match='/'`). Because the `select` attribute was omitted, it defaults to processing all the child nodes of the current context node—in this case, the root node. Assuming that `v1:emp` is the root element, the `v1:emp` template will be the next one to match. Inside the `v1:emp` template, the call to `apply-templates` selects the child **dependents** elements. Because there isn't a template that matches **dependents**, the built-in template for elements kicks in, which simply calls `apply-templates` again selecting all of **dependents** child nodes (see Section 5.5 for more details).

Assuming that the **dependents** element has child **dependent** elements, each of those will then be processed by the **dependent** template. If there were any additional elements under **dependents**, they would be recursively processed by the built-in template for elements until reaching the child text nodes. This example overrides the built-in template for text nodes to do nothing (this ensures that the text won't be output for any unhandled elements).

5.9.3 attribute

```
<xsl:attribute
  name = { qname }
  namespace = { uri-reference }>
  <!-- Content: template -->
</xsl:attribute>
```

Description

`attribute` generates an attribute in the result document with the specified name and namespace identifier. The new attribute is associated with the element containing the `attribute` instruction, whether that was generated through a literal resulting element or the `element` instruction. The content of the `attribute` becomes the value of the new attribute.

Instead of using `attribute`, one could also use attribute value templates to accomplish the same goal, unless of course you needed to specify the name of the attribute dynamically. To provide for that, notice that both the `name` and `namespace` attributes accept attribute value templates (see Section 5.7).

Attributes

Name	Default	Description
name	(required)	The qualified name of the new attribute
namespace	""	The namespace identifier of the new attribute

Examples

Generating attributes

```
...
<xsl:template match="/">
  <employee>
    <xsl:attribute name="i:id"
      namespace="urn:ids-r-us:format-x">
  <xsl:value-of select="concat(*/lname, '-', */fname)"/>
    </xsl:attribute>
    <name>
      <xsl:attribute name="first">
        <xsl:value-of select="*/fname"/>
      </xsl:attribute>
      <xsl:attribute name="last">
        <xsl:value-of select="*/lname"/>
      </xsl:attribute>
    </name>
  </employee>
</xsl:template>
...
```

This template generates the following element:

```
<employee i:id='Bob-Billy'
  xmlns:i='urn:ids-r-us:format-x'>
```

```
   <name first='Billy' last='Bob'/>
</employee>
```

Generating attributes with attribute value templates

```
...
<xsl:template match="/">
  <employee i:id="{concat(*/lname,'-',*/fname)}"
    xmlns:i="urn:ids-r-us:format-x">
    <name first="{*/fname}" last="{*/lname}"/>
  </employee>
</xsl:template>
...
```

This example generates the same document as the previous example.

Dynamically specifying attribute names

```
...
<xsl:template match="/">
  <employee>
    <name>
      <xsl:attribute name="{labels/fnameLabel}"
        <xsl:value-of select="*/fname"/>
      </xsl:attribute>
      ...
    </name>
  </employee>
</xsl:template>
```

This example generates an attribute with a dynamic name, the value of the fnameLabel element in the source document.

5.9.4 attribute-set

```
<xsl:attribute-set
  name = qname
  use-attribute-sets = qnames>
  <!-- Content: xsl:attribute* -->
</xsl:attribute-set>
```

Description

`attribute-set` defines a named set of attributes that can be reused across multiple elements. The content of `attribute-set` consists of zero or more `attribute` elements that specify the attributes in the set. The contained attribute templates are instantiated each time the `attribute-set` is used on an element, using the same current node that was used to instantiate the element itself. `attribute-set`s are used by `element` through the `use-attribute-sets` attribute (see `element` for more details). They may also be used on literal resulting elements through the `xsl:use-attribute-sets` global attribute.

Attributes

Name	Default	Description
name	(required)	The name of the `attribute-set`
use-attribute-sets	""	A whitespace-separated list of other `attribute-set` names that are to be added to the beginning of this new set

Example

Using `attribute-set`

```
...
<xsl:attribute-set name="nameAtts">
  <xsl:attribute name="first">
    <xsl:value-of select="fname"/>
  </xsl:attribute>
  <xsl:attribute name="last">
    <xsl:value-of select="lname"/>
  </xsl:attribute>
</xsl:attribute-set>

<xsl:template match="/">
  <employees>
    <xsl:for-each select="//emp">
      <xsl:element name="employee"
        use-attribute-sets="nameAtts">
        <xsl:attribute="mi">
          <xsl:value-of select="middle"/>
        </xsl:attribute>
      </xsl:element>
```

XSLT

```
    </xsl:for-each>
  </employees>
</xsl:template>
...
```

This example defines an `attribute-set` named `nameAtts`, which is then used on the `employee` elements generated below. The `employee` element also defines the `mi` attribute inline. (Note: Inline attribute definitions can override attributes in `attribute-sets`.)

5.9.5 call-template

```
<xsl:call-template
  name = qname>
  <!-- Content: xsl:with-param* -->
</xsl:call-template>
```

Description

`call-template` invokes a template by name. The `name` attribute specifies the QName of the template to call. The template with the same expanded name is invoked by the processor (see `template` for more details on naming templates). `call-template` may contain `with-param` elements for passing the expected parameters into the template. Invoking templates by name doesn't affect the context in any way (for example, the current node and node list are the same within the called template).

Attribute

Name	Default	Description
name	(required)	The qualified name of the template to invoke

Example

Using call-template

```
...
<!-- outputs employee info -->
<xsl:template name="outputEmpInfo">
  <xsl:param name="empNode"/>
  <xsl:param name="getTitle" select="false()"/>
```

```
  <name><xsl:value-of select="concat($empNode/fname, ' ',
    $empNode/lname)"/></name>
  <xsl:if test="$getTitle">
    <title><xsl:value-of select='$empNode/title'/></title>
  </xsl:if>
</xsl:template>

<!-- root template: main entry point -->
<xsl:template match="/">
  <employee>
    <xsl:call-template name="outputEmpInfo">
      <xsl:with-param name="empNode"
        select="//emp[@id='e102']"/>
      <xsl:with-param name="getTitle" select="true()"/>
    </xsl:call-template>
  </employee>
</xsl:template>
...
```

XSLT

This example invokes the `outputEmpInfo` element by name and passes in two parameters, `empNode` (the employee node to output) and `getTitle` (a boolean value indicating whether to output the employee's title).

5.9.6 choose

```
<xsl:choose>
  <!-- Content: (xsl:when+, xsl:otherwise?) -->
</xsl:choose>
```

Description

`choose` selects exactly one template from a number of alternatives (similar to a switch statement in C++/Java or a Select statement in Visual Basic). The content of `choose` consists of a sequence of `when` elements followed by an optional `otherwise` element (default case). Each `when` element has a single `test` attribute, which specifies an XPath expression. Each of the `when` elements is tested in turn, by evaluating the expression and converting the resulting object to a boolean. The content of the first `when` element with a test that is `true` is instantiated. If no `when` is `true`, the content of the `otherwise` element is instantiated.

Example

Using choose

```
...
<xsl:template match="/">
  <employees>
    <xsl:for-each select="//emp">
      <xsl:choose>
        <xsl:when test="@dept = 'sales'">
          <salesRep><xsl:apply-templates/></salesRep>
        </xsl:when>
        <xsl:when test="@dept = 'dev'">
          <programmer><xsl:apply-templates/></programmer>
        </xsl:when>
        <xsl:otherwise>
          <employee><xsl:apply-templates/></employee>
        </xsl:otherwise>
      </xsl:choose>
    </xsl:for-each>
  </employees>
</xsl:template>
...
```

This example illustrates how to use a `choose` element to select from a number of different conditions.

5.9.7 comment

```
<xsl:comment>
  <!-- Content: template -->
</xsl:comment>
```

Description

Generates a comment in the result document. The content of the `comment` instruction becomes the content of the new comment in the result document.

Example

Using comment

```
...
<xsl:template match="/">
  <xsl:comment>
    new employee file: <xsl:value-of select="*/fname"/>
  </xsl:comment>
  ...
</xsl:template>
...
```

This example produces a comment that would look something like this in the result document:

```
<!--new employee file: Bob-->
```

5.9.8 copy

```
<xsl:copy
  use-attribute-sets = qnames>
  <!-- Content: template -->
</xsl:copy>
```

Description

copy copies the current node to the result document along with all associated namespace nodes, but without attributes or other child nodes. The content of the copy instruction is a template for the attributes and children of the newly created node (in the result document). The use-attribute-sets attribute may also be used to add a set of attributes automatically to newly created element nodes (see attribute-set).

Attributes

Name	Default	Description
use-attribute-sets	""	A whitespace-separated list of attribute-set names

Example

Using copy to write an identity transformation

```
...
<xsl:template match="lname">
  <lastName><xsl:apply-templates/></lastName>
</xsl:template>

<!-- the identity transformation -->
<xsl:template match="node()|@*">
  <xsl:copy>
    <xsl:apply-templates select="node()|@*"/>
  </xsl:copy>
</xsl:template>
...
```

This example illustrates how to use copy to write the identity transformation. The identity template copies each node it encounters from the source document into the result document without changes. This would be useful if you wanted to leave the entire document unchanged, except for a few specific elements that needed alterations. Using this template in conjunction with more specific templates makes this possible. This example has a template for lname elements, which simply changes the element name to lastName. Besides this change, everything else is copied as is to the result document.

5.9.9 copy-of

```
<xsl:copy-of
  select = expression />
```

Description

Copies the result of the specified expression to the result document. If the expression yields a result tree fragment (see variable), the entire result tree fragment is copied directly to the result document. If the expression yields a node-set, each node is copied to the result document in document order (along with all namespace, attribute, and child nodes). If the expression yields an object of any other type, the object is converted to a string, which is then copied to the result document.

Attribute

Name	Default	Description
select	(required)	A generic XPath expression

Example

Using copy-of to copy a set of nodes

```
...
<xsl:template match="/">
  <employeesOfTheMonth>
    <xsl:copy-of select="//employee[@eom]"/>
  </employeesOfTheMonth>
</xsl:template>
...
```

This example copies all the employee elements from the source document that have an eom attribute into the result document.

XSLT

5.9.10 decimal-format

```
<xsl:decimal-format
  name = qname
  decimal-separator = char
  grouping-separator = char
  infinity = string
  minus-sign = char
  NaN = string
  percent = char
  per-mille = char
  zero-digit = char
  digit = char
  pattern-separator = char />
```

Description

decimal-format declares a decimal format that controls the interpretation of a format string used by the format-number function. If there is a name attribute, then the element declares a named decimal format; otherwise, it declares the default decimal format for the transformation.

A decimal format controls how the XSLT processor converts a decimal number to a string. It specifies what characters in the format string and the resulting output string represent the decimal sign (.), grouping separator (,), percent sign (%), and per-mille sign (‰). It also specifies what strings represent NaN and infinity in the output string. In addition, the format string controls where a number must appear (zero digit) and where a number may appear (digit). The following summarizes the meaning of each format string construct.

Attributes

Name	Default	Description
name	" "	The qualified name of the decimal format; if no name, it becomes the default decimal format
decimal-separator	.	The character used for the decimal sign
grouping-separator	,	The character used as the grouping separator
infinity	Infinity	The string used to represent infinity
minus-sign	–	The character used as the minus sign
NaN	NaN	The string used to represent the NaN value
percent	%	The character used as the percent sign
per-mille	‰	The character used as a per-mille sign
zero-digit	0	The character used as the digit zero
digit	#	The character used for a digit in the format string
pattern-separator	;	The character used to separate positive and negative subpatterns in a pattern

Example

Using decimal-format

```
...
<xsl:decimal-format
  decimal-separator = ","
  grouping-separator = "."
  NaN = "Invalid number"
  infinity = "Out of Bounds"/>

<xsl:template match="/">
  <!-- root template -->
```

```
  <numbers>
    <number><xsl:value-of
    select="format-number('29895.9','#.##0,00')"/></number>
    <number><xsl:value-of
    select="format-number('10000000','#.##0,##')"/></
    number>
    <number><xsl:value-of
    select="format-number('foo','#.##0,00')"/></number>
    <number><xsl:value-of
    select="format-number(1 div 0,'#.##0,00')"/></number>
  </numbers>
</xsl:template>
...
```

This example illustrates how to declare a default decimal format that modifies the decimal and grouping separators as well as the string representations for NaN and infinity. The following shows the result of this transformation:

```
<numbers>
  <number>29.895,90</number>
  <number>10.000.000</number>
  <number>Invalid number</number>
  <number>Out of Bounds</number>
</numbers>
```

5.9.11 element

```
<xsl:element
  name = { qname }
  namespace = { uri-reference }
  use-attribute-sets = qnames>
  <!-- Content: template -->
</xsl:element>
```

Description

Generates an element in the result document with the specified name, namespace identifier, and set of `attribute-sets`. Both the `name` and `namespace` attributes accept attribute value templates, making it possible to assign element names dynamic values. The content of the `element` instruction becomes the content of the new element.

Attributes

Name	Default	Description
name	(required)	The qualified name of the new element
namespace	""	The namespace identifier of the new element
use-attribute-sets	""	A whitespace-separated list of attribute-set names that are to be added to this element (see attribute-set for more details)

Example

Using element to generate elements dynamically

```
...
<xsl:template match="/">
  <xsl:element name="v2:employees"
    namespace="urn:employee:v2">
    <xsl:for-each select="//emp">
      <xsl:element name="employee">
        <xsl:value-of select="concat(fname, ' ', lname)"/>
      </xsl:element>
    </xsl:for-each>
  </xsl:element>
</xsl:template>
...
```

This example dynamically generates the v2:employees element. Then it iterates through all the source document's emp elements, generating a new element called employee for each one that contains the concatenation of emp's child fname and lname elements.

5.9.12 fallback

```
<xsl:fallback>
  <!-- Content: template -->
</xsl:fallback>
```

Description

Defines a fallback template that will be called when the containing XSLT instruction isn't recognized by the XSLT processor.

Example

Using `fallback`

```
...
<xsl:template match="/">
  <xsl:document href="managers.xml">
    <managers>
      <xsl:apply-templates select="//emp[@manage]"/>
    </managers>
    <xsl:fallback>
      <xsl:call-template name="copyManagersInternally"/>
    </xsl:fallback>
  </xsl:document>
  <xsl:apply-templates/>
</xsl:template>
...
```

This example attempts to use an XSLT 1.1 working draft (WD) instruction, **docu-ment**, which creates multiple output files. If this stylesheet is used with an XSLT 1.0 processor, the **document** element would fail and the contained `fallback` would be instantiated, which in this case calls an alternate template.

5.9.13 for-each

```
<xsl:for-each
  select = node-set-expression>
  <!-- Content: (xsl:sort*, template) -->
</xsl:for-each>
```

Description

`for-each` loops through the specified **node-set**, instantiating the contained template with each node as the current node. The nodes are traversed in docu-ment order by default, unless `for-each` contains child `sort` elements that reor-der the **node-set** (see `sort`).

Attribute

Name	Default	Description
select	(required)	An XPath expression that must yield a node-set

Example

Looping through a node-set

```
...
<xsl:template match="/">
  <xsl:for-each select="//emp">
    <xsl:sort select="lname"/>
    <employee>
      <xsl:value-of select="concat(fname,' ',lname)"/>
    </employee>
  </xsl:for-each>
</xsl:template>
...
```

This example loops through all emp elements in the document, sorted by the lname child element in alphabetical order. For each one, it outputs an employee element, which contains the concatenation of the fname and lname string values (separated by a space character).

5.9.14 if

```
<xsl:if
  test = boolean-expression>
  <!-- Content: template -->
</xsl:if>
```

Description

Defines a conditional template that's instantiated when the test expression evaluates to true. Use choose for if/else semantics.

Attribute

Name	Default	Description
test	(required)	An XPath expression with a result that is coerced to a boolean (as if by calling the boolean function)

Example

Using if to test conditions

```
...
<xsl:if test="@dept = 'sales'">
  <salesRep><xsl:apply-templates/></salesRep>
<xsl:if>
...
```

This fragment uses the if element to test whether the context node's dept attribute has a value of sales. If it does, it outputs the salesRep element.

5.9.15 import

```
<xsl:import
  href = uri-reference />
```

Description

import includes the transformation identified by the href attribute in the current transformation and gives the imported templates lower precedence in terms of conflict resolution (see Section 5.4). import elements must precede all other children of the stylesheet/transform element including include elements. It's also possible to override imported templates through the apply-imports element (see apply-imports). Use include to include templates without affecting their precedence (see include).

Attribute

Name	Default	Description
href	(required)	The URI reference of the transformation to import

Example

Using import to override templates

```
<!-- employee.xsl -->
...
<xsl:template match="employee">
  Name: <xsl:value-of select="name"/>
</xsl:template>
...
```

```
<!-- employeeDetails.xsl -->
..
<xsl:import href="employee.xsl"/>

<xsl:template match="employee">
  <xsl:apply-imports/>
  Title: <xsl:value-of select="title"/>
</xsl:template>
...
```

This example consists of two files: `employee.xsl` and `employeeDetails.xsl`. `employeeDetails.xsl` imports `employee.xsl` and overrides the `employee` template. Inside of the derived employee template, we first call `apply-imports` to execute the behavior of the base template in `employee.xsl` (this is similar to calling a method in a base class from a derived class). In this case, we're extending the behavior of the base template to output the employee's title as well.

5.9.16 include

```
<xsl:include
  href = uri-reference />
```

Description

`include` includes the transformation identified by the `href` attribute in the current transformation. `include` is different than `import` in that it has no effect on the precedence of the included templates (see `import`). `include` must be a top-level element.

Attribute

Name	Default	Description
href	(required)	The URI reference of the transformation to import

Example

Using `include`

```
<!-- employee.xsl -->
...
<xsl:template match="employee">
```

```
  Name: <xsl:value-of select="name"/>
</xsl:template>
...

<!-- employeeDetails.xsl -->
...
<xsl:include href="employee.xsl"/>

<!-- employee template available here -->
<xsl:template match="/">
  <xsl:apply-templates select="//employee"/>
</xsl:template>
...
```

This example consists of two distinct files. `employeeDetails.xsl` includes `employee.xsl`. All of the templates within the former are now also available in the latter. `include` has no effect on the conflict resolution rules.

XSLT

5.9.17 key

```
<xsl:key
  name = qname
  match = pattern
  use = expression />
```

Description

`key` declares a new key with the specified name for the nodes that match the specified pattern. An XSLT key is analogous to an attribute of type ID except it doesn't require a DTD. A key is given a name so it can be referred to later by the `key` function. The `match` attribute identifies the nodes to which the key applies. The `use` attribute contains an XPath expression that is evaluated relative to the nodes identified by the `match` pattern to produce the key value. See the `key` function for more details.

Attributes

Name	Default	Description
name	(required)	The qualified name of the key
match	(required)	A pattern that identifies the nodes to which the key applies

Name	Default	Description
use	(required)	An XPath expression that is evaluated relative to the nodes identified by the match attribute to produce the key value

Example

Using key to process cross-references

```
...
<xsl:key name="employeeId" match="employees/employee"
    use="@id"/>

<xsl:template match="courses/course">
  <h2><xsl:value-of select="name"/></h2>
  <h3>Instructors</h3>
  <ul>
<xsl:for-each select="key('employeeId', ./instructors/*)">
      <li><xsl:value-of select="."/></li>
</xsl:for-each>
  </ul>
</xsl:template>

<xsl:template match="text()|@*"/>
...
```

The following example illustrates how to use keys to take advantage of cross-references in the source document that aren't of type ID/IDREF. If this transformation were used against the following example document:

```
<courses>
  <course>
    <name>Essential XML</name>
    <instructors>
      <instructor>e103</instructor>
    </instructors>
  </course>
  <course>
    <name>Guerrilla XML</name>
    <instructors>
      <instructor>e101</instructor>
```

```
      <instructor>e102</instructor>
      <instructor>e103</instructor>
    </instructors>
  </course>
  <employees>
    <employee id='e101'>
      <name>Martin Gudgin</name>
    </employee>
    <employee id='e102'>
      <name>Don Box</name>
    </employee>
    <employee id='e103'>
      <name>Aaron Skonnard</name>
    </employee>
  </employees>
</courses>
```

it would produce the following output:

```
<h2>Essential XML</h2>
<h3>Instructors</h3>
<ul>
   <li>Aaron Skonnard </li>
</ul>
<h2>Guerrilla XML</h2>
<h3>Instructors</h3>
<ul>
   <li>Martin Gudgin </li>
   <li>Don Box </li>
   <li>Aaron Skonnard </li>
</ul>
```

5.9.18 message

```
<xsl:message
  terminate = "yes" | "no">
  <!-- Content: template -->
</xsl:message>
```

Description

Outputs a message in a processor-dependent fashion and potentially terminates the program.

Attribute

Name	Default	Description
terminate	"no"	Specifies whether the processor should terminate processing after sending the message.

Example

Using message

```
...
<xsl:template match="/">
  <xsl:document href="managers.xml">
    <managers>
      <xsl:apply-templates select="//emp[@manage]"/>
    </managers>
    <xsl:fallback>
      <xsl:message terminate="yes">XSLT 1.1 document
          element not supported </xsl:message>
    </xsl:fallback>
  </xsl:document>
  <xsl:apply-templates/>
</xsl:template>
...
```

This example attempts to use an XSLT 1.1 (WD) element, which fails with all XSLT 1.0 processors. When this stylesheet is used with an XSLT 1.0 processor, the fallback template is instantiated, which outputs a message and instructs the processor to terminate processing.

5.9.19 namespace-alias

```
<xsl:namespace-alias
  stylesheet-prefix = prefix | "#default"
  result-prefix = prefix | "#default" />
```

Description

`namespace-alias` declares that one namespace URI is an alias for another while processing the transformation. In the result document, the namespace URI associated with the `alias` prefix is replaced with the namespace URI associated with the `result` prefix. Use `#default` to refer to the default namespace as opposed to an explicit prefix. `namespace-alias` greatly facilitates writing transformations that output elements from the XSLT namespace.

Attributes

Name	Default	Description
`stylesheet-prefix`	`""`	The prefix of the alias namespace
`result-prefix`	`""`	The prefix of the original namespace (the one being aliased)

Example

Using namespace-alias

```
<xsl:transform
  xmlns:xsl='http://www.w3.org/1999/XSL/Transform'
  xmlns:a='urn:this-is-an-alias'
  version='1.0'>

  <xsl:namespace-alias stylesheet-prefix="a"
    result-prefix="xsl"/>
  <xsl:template match="/">
    <!-- output XSLT elements using namespace alias -->
    <a:transform version='1.0'>
      <a:template match="/">
        ...
      <a:template>
    </a:transform>
  </xsl:template>
</xsl:transform>
```

This example outputs XSLT 1.0 elements. To avoid confusing the XSLT processor, the `namespace-alias` element is used to define a namespace alias while processing the document. The namespace alias is swapped with the real namespace in the result document as shown here:

```
<a:transform
  xmlns:a='http://www.w3.org/1999/XSL/Transform'
  version='1.0'>
  <a:template match="/">

     ...

  <a:template>
</a:transform>
```

5.9.20 number

```
<xsl:number
  level = "single" | "multiple" | "any"
  count = pattern
  from = pattern
  value = number-expression
  format = { string }
  lang = { nmtoken }
  letter-value = { "alphabetic" | "traditional" }
  grouping-separator = { char }
  grouping-size = { number } />
```

Description

number inserts a formatted number into the result document. The value attribute contains an XPath expression with a result that is coerced to a number (as if by calling the number function) and is inserted into the result document.

If the value attribute isn't specified, the current position is inserted into the result document. The level, count, and from attributes determine how the current node's position is evaluated. The count attribute determines what nodes are to be counted. The from attribute determines from where to start counting (how far to go back in the tree) whereas the level attribute determines how many levels in the tree should be considered.

The remaining attributes (format, lang, letter-value, grouping-separator, and grouping-size) determine how the resulting number is converted into a string. See the following for more details.

Attributes

Name	Default	Description
`level`	`"single"`	Specifies what levels of the source tree should be considered during the counting process (see below for more details).
`count`	the pattern that matches the current node's type and name (if any)	A pattern that specifies what nodes should be counted at the specified levels (see `level` attribute below).
`from`	`/`	A pattern that specifies where counting starts.
`value`	position (based on other attributes)	An XPath expression with a result that is coerced to a number. If not specified, the value is evaluated as the current node's position with respect to the `level`, `count`, and `from` attributes.
`format`	1	Specifies the format to use for numbering (see below for more details).
`lang`	determined from system environment	Specifies which language's alphabet to use when numbering with an alphabetical sequence (same value space as `xml:lang`).
`letter-value`	(none)	Disambiguates between different numbering schemes for a given language. In English, the a format token identifies an alphabetical sequence (for example, `a`, `b`, `c`, `...`, `aa`, `ab`, `ac`, `...`) whereas the i format token identifies a numerical-alphabetical sequence (for example, `i`, `ii`, `iii`, `iv`, `...`). In some languages both numbering schemes start with the same letter. In these cases, a `letter-value` of `alphabetic` identifies the alphabetical sequence whereas a `letter-value` of `traditional` identifies the other form.
`grouping-separator`	(none)	Specifies the separator used as a grouping separator in decimal numbering sequences (for example, `1,000,000`).
`grouping-size`	(none)	Specifies the size of the grouping (for example, 3 in the `grouping-separator` example).

level

Specifies what levels of the source tree should be considered during the counting process

Value	Description
single	Counts the siblings that precede the target node (same as XPath preceding-sibling axis). If the current node matches the count pattern or count is not specified, it is the target node. Otherwise, the target node is the first ancestor to match the count pattern. The first ancestor node (of the current node) that matches the from pattern identifies the start node, where counting begins. Only those nodes that come after the start node up to the current node are considered in the count.
any	Counts the nodes, identified by the count pattern, that come before the current node in document order (same as the union of XPath's preceding and ancestor-or-self axes). The first node (which comes before the current node) that matches the from pattern identifies the start node, where counting begins. Only those nodes that come after the start node up to the current node are considered in the count.
multiple	Produces a sequence of numbers, each of which is produced in the same way as a single level count (for example, 1.1.1, 1.1.2, 1.2.1, and so on). The count of the outermost ancestor that matches the count pattern becomes the first number in the sequence. The count of the next outermost ancestor that matches the count pattern becomes the second number in the sequence, and so on. The count of the innermost ancestor that matches the count pattern becomes the last number in the sequence. The count of each ancestor is determined like a single level count.

format

The format attribute is split into a sequence of tokens in which each token is either a format token (alphanumerical) or a separator token (nonalphanumerical). Format tokens specify the format to be used for each number in the list. Separator tokens are used to join numbers in the list (for example, 1.1.1). The nth format token will be used to format the nth number in the list. If there are more numbers than format tokens, then the last format token will be used to format the remaining numbers. 1 is the default format token whereas . is the default separator token.

If the first and last characters in the format string are nonalphanumerical, they are included in the final output string as is, surrounding the generated number (for example, [1.1.1]). The following illustrates the types of sequences generated by the different format tokens.

Token	Sequence
1	1, 2, 3, 4, ..., 10, 11, 12, ..., 20, 21, ...
01	01, 02, 03, 04, ..., 10, 11, 12, ..., 100, 101, ...
A	A, B, C, D, ..., Z, AA, AB, AC, ...
a	a, b, c, d, ..., z, aa, ab, ac, ...
I	I, II, III, IV, V, VI, ..., X, XI, ...
i	i, ii, iii, iv, v, vi, ..., x, xi, ...

Example

Using number

```
...
<xsl:template match="instructor">
  <xsl:number level="multiple"
    count="course|instructor" format="1-a)"/>
  <xsl:text> </xsl:text><xsl:value-of select="."/>
</xsl:template>

<xsl:template match="course">
  <xsl:number level="single" format="1)"/>
  <xsl:text> </xsl:text><xsl:value-of select="name"/>
  <xsl:apply-templates select="instructors"/>
</xsl:template>
...
```

Assuming a source document that contains a list of course elements, each of which contains a list of instructor elements (see **key** for an example), this example would produce the following output:

```
1) Essential XML
     1-a) Aaron Skonnard
     1-b) Martin Gudgin

2) Guerrilla XML
     2-a) Aaron Skonnard
     2-b) Martin Gudgin
     2-c) Don Box

  ...
```

5.9.21 otherwise

```
<xsl:otherwise>
  <!-- Content: template -->
</xsl:otherwise>
```

Description

Defines the default template within a choose instruction. See choose for more details and an example.

5.9.22 output

```
<xsl:output
  method = "xml" | "html" | "text" | qname
  version = nmtoken
  encoding = string
  omit-xml-declaration = "yes" | "no"
  standalone = "yes" | "no"
  doctype-public = string
  doctype-system = string
  cdata-section-elements = qnames
  indent = "yes" | "no"
  media-type = string />
```

Description

Declares how the author of the stylesheet would like the result document serialized, although processors are not required to follow these instructions.

Attributes

Name	Default	Description
method	html if root element of result document is 'html' (case insensitive), otherwise xml	Indicates the output method for the result document. XML, HTML, and text are the only widely supported output methods, although others may be specified through a qualified name. The XML output method always outputs well-formed XML. The HTML output method makes several adjustments to produce friendlier HTML documents (for example, empty elements don't have end tags, script/style tags are not escaped, and so on). And the text output method simply outputs all of the result document's text nodes without modification.
version	XML:1.0, HTML:4.0	Specifies the version of the output method.
encoding	XML:UTF-8/UTF-16, text: system dep.	Specifies the preferred character encoding that the XSLT processor should use to encode sequences of characters as sequences of bytes.
omit-xml-declaration	XML:no	Specifies whether the XSLT processor should output an XML declaration.
standalone	(none)	Specifies whether the XSLT processor should output a stand-alone DTD.
doctype-public	(none)	Specifies the public identifier to be used in the DTD.
doctype-system	(none)	Specifies the system identifier to be used in the DTD.
cdata-section-elements	(none)	Specifies a list of the names of elements with text node children that should be output using CDATA sections.
indent	XML:no, HTML:yes	Specifies whether the XSLT processor may add additional whitespace when outputting the result tree.
media-type	XML:text/xml, HTML:text/html, text:text/plain	Specifies the media type (MIME content-type) of the result tree.

XSLT

Example

Using output to control serialization details

```
<xsl:transform
  xmlns:xsl='http://www.w3.org/1999/XSL/Transform'
  version='1.0'>

  <xsl:output method="xml"
    version="1.0"
    omit-xml-declaration="yes"
    indents="yes"
    encoding="iso-8859-1"
    cdata-section-elements="codefrag syntax"/>

  ...
</xsl:transform>
```

This example specifies that the output document should be serialized using XML 1.0 syntax without an XML declaration using the ISO-8859-1 character encoding. In addition, it specifies that pretty printing/indenting should be used and that all codefrag/syntax elements should be enclosed in CDATA sections.

5.9.23 param

```
<xsl:param
  name = qname
  select = expression>
  <!-- Content: template -->
</xsl:param>
```

Description

param declares a parameter with the specified qualified name and default value. The syntax for referring to parameters is $name. Parameters behave just like variables (see variable for more details) except for the fact that parameters may also have default values. Parameters may be declared globally for the entire transformation or locally within a template. Parameters are passed to templates via the with-param element. Parameters are passed to transformations in a processor-specific fashion.

As with variables, a parameter's default value can be set either through the select attribute or through the param element's content; otherwise, the parameter's default value is the empty string. When a parameter's default value is specified through the `select` attribute, the value is the result of the XPath expression (either a `node-set, boolean, number, or string`) and the content of the element must be empty. When the parameter's default value is specified through the element's content, the value is a result tree fragment (see `variable` for more details).

Attributes

Name	Default	Description
name	(required)	The name of the parameter
select	""	An XPath expression

Example

Parameterizing templates and transformation documents

```
...
<!-- global parameter -->
<xsl:param name="dept" select="string('manager')"/>

<!-- outputs employee info -->
<xsl:template name="outputEmpInfo">
  <!-- local parameters -->
  <xsl:param name="empNode"/>
  <xsl:param name="getTitle" select="false()"/>
  <name><xsl:value-of
    select="concat($empNode/fname, ' ', $empNode/lname)"/>
    </name>
  <xsl:if test="$getTitle">
    <title><xsl:value-of select='$empNode/title'/></title>
  </xsl:if>
</xsl:template>

<!-- root template: main entry point -->
<xsl:template match="/">
  <employee>
    <xsl:call-template name="outputEmpInfo">
      <xsl:with-param name="empNode"
        select="//emp[@dept = $dept]"/>
      <xsl:with-param name="getTitle" select="true()"/>
  </xsl:call-template>
```

```
    </employee>
  </xsl:template>
  ...
```

This example declares a global parameter, dept, and two parameters local to the outputEmpInfo template.

5.9.24 preserve-space

```
<xsl:preserve-space
  elements = tokens />
```

Description

Defines the elements in the source document, for which whitespace-only text nodes should be preserved (see Section 5.8 for more details). The elements attribute contains a whitespace-separated list of name tests (for example, QNames, *, and so on) that identify the set of whitespace-preserving elements for the source document. The strip-space element can be used in conjunction with this element to preserve all whitespace for all elements except for a few specified by name (see strip-space).

Attribute

Name	Default	Description
elements	""	A whitespace-separated list of name tests (QNames, *, and so on)

Example

Using preserve-space

```
<xsl:transform version='1.0'
  xmlns:xsl='http://www.w3.org/1999/XSL/Transform'>

  <xsl:preserve-space elements="code"/>
  ...
</xsl:transform>
```

This example preserves space within all code elements in the source document.

5.9.25 `processing-instruction`

```
<xsl:processing-instruction
  name = { ncname }>
  <!-- Content: template -->
</xsl:processing-instruction>
```

Description

Generates a processing instruction with the specified name (target) in the result document. The content of the `processing-instruction` instruction becomes the content of the new processing instruction (everything after the target) in the result document.

Attribute

Name	Default	Description
name	(required)	The target of the processing instruction

Example

Generating processing instructions in the result document

```
...
<xsl:param name="stylesheet" select="'employee.xsl'"/>
<xsl:template match="/">
  <xsl:processing-instruction name="xsl-stylesheet">
    type='text/xsl'
    href='<xsl:value-of select="$stylesheet"/>'
  </xsl:processing-instruction>
  ...
</xsl:template>
...
```

This example generates a processing instruction that would look something like this in the result document: `<?xsl-stylesheet type='text/xsl' href= 'employee.xsl'?>`, depending on the value of the `stylesheet` parameter.

5.9.26 `sort`

```
<xsl:sort
  select = string-expression
  lang = { nmtoken }
```

```
data-type = { "text" | "number" | qname }
order = { "ascending" | "descending" }
case-order = { "upper-first" | "lower-first" } />
```

Description

sort is used as a child of for-each and apply-templates to sort the current node list before processing. The first sort child specifies the primary sort key; the second sort child specifies the secondary sort key, and so on. The select attribute takes an XPath expression that is evaluated against each node in the current node list. The results are coerced to strings, as if by calling the string function, and the resulting strings become the sort keys.

Attributes

Name	Default	Description
select	"."	An XPath expression that identifies the sort key
lang	(system default)	Specifies the language of the sort key (same value space as xml:lang attribute).
data-type	"text"	Specifies the data type of the sort key. "text" indicates that the sort key should be sorted in a manner that makes sense for the specified language. "number" indicates that the sort key values should be coerced to numbers and then sorted according to numerical value. If the value is a qualified name, the qualified name identifies an application-specific data type for the sort key.
order	"ascending"	Specifies whether the sort key should be sorted in ascending or descending order.
case-order	(language dependent)	Specifies that uppercase letters should be sorted before lowercase, or vice versa.

Example

Using sort to sort node-sets

```
...
<xsl:template match="/">
  <xsl:for-each select="//emp">
    <xsl:sort select="age" lang="en" data-type="number"
      order="descending"/>
    <xsl:sort select="lname" lang="en" data-type="text"
      order="ascending" case-order="upper-first"/>
```

```
    <employee>
      <xsl:value-of select="concat(fname,' ',lname)"/>
    </employee>
  </xsl:for-each>
</xsl:template>
...
```

This example sorts the `for-each` node list (all `emp` elements) first by `age` (descending) and then by `lname` (ascending).

5.9.27 strip-space

```
<xsl:strip-space
  elements = tokens />
```

Description

Defines the elements in the source document that should be removed from the list of whitespace-preserving elements (defined by `preserve-space`). The `elements` attribute contains a whitespace-separated list of name tests (for example, QNames, *, and so on).

Attribute

Name	Default	Description
elements	""	A whitespace-separated list of name tests (QNames, *, and so on)

Example

Using strip-space

```
<xsl:transform version='1.0'
  xmlns:xsl='http://www.w3.org/1999/XSL/Transform'>

  <xsl:preserve-space elements="*"/>
  <xsl:strip-space elements="name title"/>
  ...
</xsl:transform>
```

This example preserves space within all elements except for `name` and `title` elements.

5.9.28 stylesheet

Description

stylesheet is a (less appropriate) alias for the transform element. The transform and stylesheet elements may be used interchangeably in XSLT documents. See transform for details.

5.9.29 template

```
<xsl:template
  match = pattern
  name = qname
  priority = number
  mode = qname>
  <!-- Content: (xsl:param*, template) -->
</xsl:template>
```

Description

template defines a new template rule with the specified pattern and/or name. Patterns facilitate a declarative programming model whereas named templates facilitate a procedural programming model (see Section 5.1). The match attribute specifies the template's pattern (see Section 5.3) and the name attribute specifies the template's name.

When the name attribute is used, you can explicitly call the template from another template, in a procedural fashion (see call-template for more details). When the match attribute is used, the supplied pattern identifies the source nodes to which the template rule applies. When the processor begins executing the transformation, it looks for the template with a pattern that matches the root of the input tree. Then, inside that template, you indicate which nodes you would like the processor to continue processing through the apply-templates/apply-imports elements. After a call to apply-templates/apply-imports, the processor identifies and executes the template that best matches each specified node, according to their associated patterns. This continues until the processor reaches a template that doesn't explicitly call apply-templates/apply-imports. For more details on this approach, see Sections 5.1, 5.3, and 5.5.

If a particular mode matches more than one template rule, the processor follows the well-defined conflict resolution rules to choose the best match (see Section

5.4). In general, the template with the highest priority is considered the best match. The `priority` attribute may be used to set the template's priority value explicitly. Otherwise, it's automatically calculated by the XSLT processor (see Section 5.4 for more details).

The content of `template` defines a portion of the result document. It can contain literal output (elements, text, and so on) as well as other XSLT elements that are instructions for dynamically generating portions of the result document.

Templates may accept parameters as defined by the child `param` elements. This makes it possible to generalize the functionality of a given template to facilitate reusability. The `with-param` element can be used with either `call-template` or `apply-templates` to pass parameters into a template. Templates may also be assigned a mode. Modes make it possible to have multiple template rule definitions for a single pattern. To execute a template of a particular mode, you specify the mode you wish to use in the call to `apply-templates`.

XSLT

Attributes

Name	Default	Description
match	(none)	Specifies a pattern that identifies the nodes to which this template applies.
name	(none)	Specifies the qualified name of the template.
priority	See rules in Section 5.4	Specifies a numerical value specifying the template's priority (for conflict resolution).
mode	(none)	Specifies the template's mode.

Examples

Sample procedural transformation

```
<xsl:transform
  xmlns:v1='urn:employee:v1'
  xmlns:v2='urn:employee:v2'
  xmlns:xsl='http://www.w3.org/1999/XSL/Transform'
  version='1.0'>

  <!-- outputs name element -->
  <xsl:template name="outputName">
    <name><xsl:value-of
      select="concat(v1:emp/fname, ' ', v1:emp/lname)"/>
        </name>
```

```
  </xsl:template>

  <!-- outputs title element -->
  <xsl:template name="outputTitle">
    <title><xsl:value-of select='v1:emp/position'/></
    title>
  </xsl:template>

  <!-- root template: main entry point -->
  <xsl:template match="/">
    <v2:employee>
      <xsl:call-template name="outputName"/>
      <xsl:call-template name="outputTitle"/>
    </v2:employee>
  </xsl:template>

</xsl:transform>
```

This example illustrates how to define three templates. As you can see, this example uses the procedural approach by naming the templates and explicitly calling them through `call-template`.

Sample declarative transformation

```
<xsl:transform
  xmlns:v1='urn:employee:v1'
  xmlns:v2='urn:employee:v2'
  xmlns:xsl='http://www.w3.org/1999/XSL/Transform'
  version='1.0'>

  <!-- override built-in template for
       text/attributes -->
  <xsl:template match="text()|@*"/>

  <!-- template for position elements -->
  <xsl:template match="position">
    <title><xsl:value-of select='.'/></title>
  </xsl:template>

  <!-- template for fname elements -->
  <xsl:template match="fname">
```

```
    <name><xsl:value-of select="
      concat(., ' ',
        following-sibling::lname)"/></name>
  </xsl:template>

  <!-- template for v1:emp elements -->
  <xsl:template match="v1:emp">
    <v2:employee>
      <xsl:apply-templates select="*"/>
    </v2:employee>
  </xsl:template>
</xsl:transform>
```

This example illustrates how to define three template rules for different types of nodes in the source document. As you can see, this template leverages the declarative approach by assigning each template a match attribute and using apply-templates.

Sample using modes/priority

```
...
<xsl:param name="outputFormat" select="'xml'"/>

<!-- other templates omitted -->

<!-- toHTML mode templates -->
<xsl:template match="v1:emp" mode="toHTML">
  <html>
    <body>
      <h1><xsl:value-of
        select="concat(fname, ' ', lname)"/></h1>
  <xsl:apply-templates select="position" mode="toHTML"/>
    </body>
  </html>
</xsl:template>

<xsl:template match="position" mode="toHTML">
  <h2><xsl:value-of select="."/></h2>
</xsl:template>
```

```
<xsl:template match="text()|@*" mode="toHTML"/>

<!-- root template, main entry point -->
<xsl:template match="/">
  <xsl:choose>
    <xsl:when test="$outputFormat = 'html'">
      <xsl:apply-templates select="v1:emp" mode="toHTML">
    </xsl:when>
    <xsl:otherwise>
      <xsl:apply-templates select="v1:emp">
    </xsl:otherwise>
  </xsl:choose>
</xsl:template>
...
```

This transformation is capable of processing `v1:emp` elements in different modes. The default mode (no mode) outputs the employee information in a different XML format (as illustrated in the previous example). The toHTML mode outputs employee information as an HTML document. Note that to use the toHTML mode, it has to be specified when calling `apply-templates`.

5.9.30 text

```
<xsl:text
  disable-output-escaping = "yes" | "no">
  <!-- Content: #PCDATA -->
</xsl:text>
```

Description

text generates the contained literal text in the result document including whitespace. The `disable-output-escaping` attribute controls whether unsafe XML characters are escaped in the result document.

Attribute

Name	Default	Description
disable-output-escaping	"no"	Enables/disables the escaping of unsafe XML characters in the result document.

Example

Using text to output whitespace

```
...
<xsl:template match="/">
  <xsl:text disable-output-escaping="yes">
  if (age &lt; maxAge)
    processEmployee();
</xsl:text>
</xsl:template>
...
```

This transformation uses text to preserve whitespace and to output unsafe XML characters. It produces the following result document:

```
    if (age < maxAge)
      processEmployee();
```

5.9.31 transform (stylesheet)

```
<xsl:transform
  id = id
  extension-element-prefixes = tokens
  exclude-result-prefixes = tokens
  version = number>
  <!-- Content: (xsl:import*, top-level-elements) -->
</xsl:transform>

<xsl:stylesheet
  id = id
  extension-element-prefixes = tokens
  exclude-result-prefixes = tokens
  version = number>
  <!-- Content: (xsl:import*, top-level-elements) -->
</xsl:stylesheet>
```

Description

transform is the root of every XSLT document unless the transformation uses the exemplar-based syntax (see Exemplar-based transformations). stylesheet is a synonym for `transform`. `transform` must have a `version` attribute that specifies the version of XSLT required by the transformation. For this version of XSLT, the value should be 1.0. The `id` attribute makes it possible to give the transformation a unique ID to facilitate embedding XSLT transformations within other types of XML documents. All other XSLT elements are nested within `transform`.

Attributes

Name	Default	Description
id	" "	Specifies a unique identifier for the transformation element.
extension-element-prefixes	" "	Specifies a whitespace-separated list of name-space prefixes used for extension (non-XSLT) elements. The namespace bound to each of the prefixes is designated as an extension namespace and therefore will not be treated as literal output. It is an error if there is no namespace bound to the prefix on the element bearing the element. The default namespace may be designated as an extension namespace by including #default in the list of namespace prefixes.
exclude-result-prefixes	" "	Specifies a whitespace-separated list of namespace prefixes that indicate which namespaces should be excluded from the result document. It is an error if there is no namespace bound to the prefix on the element bearing the exclude-result-prefixes or xsl:exclude-result-prefixes attribute. The default namespace may be designated as an excluded namespace by including #default in the list of namespace prefixes.
version	(required)	Specifies the version of XSLT required by this transformation.

Example

Writing a transformation

```
<xsl:transform version='1.0'
  xmlns:xsl='http://www.w3.org/1999/XSL/Transform'>

  <!-- XSLT instructions go here -->

<xsl:transform>
```

This example illustrates how to begin writing an XSLT transformation.

5.9.32 value-of

```
<xsl:value-of
  select = string-expression
  disable-output-escaping = "yes" | "no" />
```

Description

value-of generates a text node in the result document from the select expression. The result of the XPath expression is coerced to a string, as if by calling the string function. The disable-output-escaping attribute can be used to control how unsafe XML characters are handled in the result document (see text for more details).

Attributes

Name	Default	Description
select	(required)	Specifies an XPath expression with a result that is coerced to a string.
disable-output-escaping	"no"	Enables/disables the escaping of unsafe XML characters in the result document.

Example

Using value-of

```
...
<xsl:template match="/">
  <employee>
    <first><xsl:value-of select="*/fname"/></first>
    <last><xsl:value-of select="*/lname"/></last>
    <fullname><xsl:value-of
      select="concat(*/fname, ' ', */lname)"/></fullname>
  </employee>
</xsl:template>
...
```

This example uses value-of to generate three text nodes in the output, one in the first, last, and fullname elements respectively.

5.9.33 variable

```
<xsl:variable
  name = qname
  select = expression>
  <!-- Content: template -->
</xsl:variable>
```

Description

variable binds a qualified name to a value. The syntax for referring to variables is $name. The value to which a variable is bound can be an object of any of the types that can be returned by XPath expressions (node-set, boolean, number, string). This is accomplished through the select attribute:

```
<!-- emps variable bound to a node-set -->
<xsl:variable name="emps" select="//employee"/>
```

Instead of using the select attribute, variables can also be initialized from the element's content. This approach introduces an additional data type known as a result tree fragment, to which variables may also be bound:

```
<!-- emps variable bound to a result tree fragment -->
<xsl:variable name="emps">
  <employee>Aaron</employee>
  <employee>Martin</employee>
  <employee>Don</employee>
</xsl:variable>
```

A result tree fragment represents a portion of the result tree and is treated equivalently to a node-set that contains just a single root node, which contains each of the elements that make up the document fragment. The operations permitted on a result tree fragment are a subset of those permitted on a node-set. Only operations that are permitted on XPath strings are also allowed on result tree fragments. The /, //, and [ ] operators are not allowed on result tree fragments. When result tree fragments are operated on, they are treated just like the equivalent node-set. Expressions can only return result tree fragments when referencing variables (or parameters) of type result tree fragment.

Result tree fragments are often the source of confusion. The following conditional appears to return false, when it really returns true:

```
<xsl:variable name="index">0</xsl:variable>
<xsl:if test="$index">...</xsl:if>
```

The reason for this is that when $index is evaluated, it's coerced to a bool-ean, which in this case returns true because the result tree fragment isn't empty (the coercion works the same as for node-sets). To avoid this, you would use one of the following alternatives:

```
<xsl:variable name="index">0</xsl:variable>
<xsl:if test="number($index)">...</xsl:if>
```

or

```
<xsl:variable name="index" select="0"/>
<xsl:if test="$index">...</xsl:if>
```

If a variable's value is not specified through either the select attribute or the ele-ment's content, the value is automatically assigned to the empty string. XSLT parameters are just like variables, as described here; plus they provide the notion of default values (see param).

Variables are primarily used to cache the results of expressions for later use. Vari-ables are also the only way to return values from templates (see the following examples).

Attributes

Name	Default	Description
name	(required)	Specifies the variable's qualified name.
select	""	Specifies an XPath expression with a result that becomes the value of the variable.

Examples

Using variables to cache expression results

```
...
<xsl:template match="/">
  <xsl:variable name="emps" select="//emp"/>
  <xsl:variable name="aaron" select="$emps[@id='e102']"/>
  <xsl:variable name="fullname"
    select="concat($aaron/fname,' ',$aaron/lname)"/>
```

```
  <employee>
    <fullname><xsl:value-of select="$fullname"/></
    fullname>
    <title><xsl:value-of select="$aaron/title"/></title>
  </employee>

</xsl:template>
. . .
```

This example stores the results of several expressions in variables for later use.

Returning values from templates

```
. . .
<xsl:template name="add">
  <xsl:param name="x"/>
  <xsl:param name="y"/>
  <xsl:value-of select="$x+$y"/>
</xsl:template>

<xsl:template match="/">
  <xsl:variable name="sum">
    <xsl:call-template name="add">
      <xsl:with-param name="x" select="30"/>
      <xsl:with-param name="y" select="70"/>
    </xsl:call-template>
  </xsl:variable>
  <sum><xsl:value-of select="$sum"/></sum>
</xsl:template>
. . .
```

This example illustrates how to use a variable to return a value from a template. Notice that the call-template instruction is contained within a variable element. Because of this, anything that is output within the add template is added to the result tree fragment for the sum variable.

Using variables with recursive templates

```
. . .
<xsl:template name="totalSalaries">
  <xsl:param name="empList"/>
  <xsl:choose>
```

```
   <xsl:when test="$empList">
     <xsl:variable name="first" select="$empList[1]"/>
     <xsl:variable name="total">
       <xsl:call-template name="totalSalaries">
         <xsl:with-param name="empList"
           select="$empList[postion()!=1]"/>
       </xsl:call-template>
     </xsl:variable>
     <xsl:value-of select="$first/salary + $total"/>
   </xsl:when>
   <xsl:otherwise>0</xsl:otherwise>
 </xsl:choose>
</xsl:template>

<xsl:template match="/">
 <xsl:variable name="salaries">
   <xsl:call-template name="totalSalaries">
     <xsl:with-param name="empList" select="//emp"/>
   </xsl:call-template>
 </xsl:variable>
 Total Salaries: <xsl:value-of select="$salaries"/>
</xsl:template>
...
```

This example illustrates how to call a template recursively to total a list of employee salaries.

5.9.34 when

```
<xsl:when
  test = boolean-expression>
  <!-- Content: template -->
</xsl:when>
```

Description

Defines a conditional template that is used within the choose element. See choose for more details and an example.

Attribute

Name	Default	Description
test	(required)	Specifies an XPath expression that is evaluated as a boolean.

5.9.35 `with-param`

```
<xsl:with-param
  name = qname
  select = expression>
  <!-- Content: template -->
</xsl:with-param>
```

Description

Passes the specified parameter to the target template (used with `call-template` and `apply-templates`). The value of the parameter is set in the same way as parameters and variables (see `variable/param`). The value can be set through the `select` attribute (any XPath object) or the content of the `with-param` element (result tree fragment). Otherwise, the default value is the empty string. See `call-template` for an example.

Attributes

Name	Default	Description
name	(required)	Specifies the qualified name of the parameter.
select	""	Specifies a generic XPath expression that yields an object of any type.

5.10 XSLT function library

XSLT supports the entire XPath function library as well as several XSLT-specific functions that all implementations are required to support. If a function expects an argument of a specific type and an object of a different type is used, it's implicitly coerced as if by calling the appropriate coercion function (`string()`, `number()`, or `boolean()`).

All of the XSLT function names belong to no namespace, which means their names don't require a namespace prefix. XSLT implementations may augment this core library with implementation-specific extension functions. When this is the case, the extension function names must be qualified with a namespace prefix. Each function is described next.

XSLT functions

Name	Description
`current`	Returns the current node.
`document`	Facilitates processing multiple input documents.
`element-available`	Returns `true` if the processor supports the specified element.
`format-number`	Converts the argument number to a string according to the specified decimal format.
`function-available`	Returns `true` if the processor supports the specified function.
`generate-id`	Returns a `string` that uniquely identifies the first node in the argument `node-set`.
`key`	Returns the nodes that have the specified key value.
`system-property`	Returns the value of the specified system property.
`unparsed-entity-uri`	Returns the URI of the unparsed entity with the specified name.

5.10.1 current

```
node-set current()
```

Description

`current` returns a `node-set` that has the current node as its only member. XSLT defines the notion of a current node to facilitate working with `for-each` and `apply-templates`. When using either of these, the current node is defined as the node currently being processed. For expressions that don't occur within other expressions, this is always the same as the context node (see Chapter 3 for more details on context node). For example, the following two `value-of` expressions return the same value:

```
<xsl:for-each select="fname">
   <xsl:value-of select="current()"/>
</xsl:for-each>
```

```
<xsl:for-each select="fname">
   <xsl:value-of select="."/>
</xsl:for-each>
```

When expressions appear within other expressions (for example, predicates), the current node is typically different than the context node. In the following example, the `employeeOfTheMonth` element is the current node whereas the `employee` element is the context node within the predicate expression:

```
<xsl:for-each select="employeeOfTheMonth">
  <xsl:value-of select="//employee[@id = current()/@eid]"/>
</xsl:for-each>
```

Had it used `.` instead of `current()` in the predicate, `eid` would have been treated as an attribute of `employee` instead of `employeeOfTheMonth`. Without the `current` function, one would have to bind the current node to a variable before evaluating the XPath expression as follows:

```
<xsl:for-each select="employeeOfTheMonth">
   <xsl:variable name="eom" select="."/>
   <xsl:value-of select="//employee[@id = $eom/@eid]"/>
</xsl:for-each>
```

5.10.2 document

```
node-set document(object, node-set?)
```

Description

`document` makes it possible to process multiple input documents. The `object` argument is treated as a URI reference (or a set of URI references) relative to the base URI of the first node in the optional `node-set` argument. When the `object` argument identifies a single document, the resulting `node-set` contains that document's root node. When the `object` argument identifies multiple documents, the resulting `node-set` contains the union of the root nodes, one from each document.

Fragment identifiers may also be used in the supplied URI references to identify subsets of the specified documents (other than the root node). See Chapter 4 for more details on this approach. The following describes exactly how this function behaves for each type of `object` argument.

Type	Description
node-set	Returns the union of the `node-set`s that result from calling the document function again with each node in the argument `node-set`.
other	The argument is coerced to a string and the string is treated as a URI reference. The document identified by the URI reference is retrieved and the root node of the document is returned in the resulting `node-set`.

Examples

document example	Description
document('aaron.xml')	Returns the root node of `aaron.xml`.
document(concat(employee/ fname, '.xml'))	Returns the root node of the file identified by the result of the `concat` function.
document(./fileName, /*)	Returns the union of the `node-set`s returned by calling the document function with the value of each `fileName` child element. If any of the URI references are relative, they're resolved against the base URI of the input document's root element node.
document('aaron.xml#xpointer(//dependent)')	Returns a `node-set` that contains all of the `dependent` elements within `aaron.xml`.

Using with `apply-templates`

```
...
<xsl:template match="employeeRecords">
  <xsl:apply-templates
    select="document('aaron.xml')"/>
</xsl:template>
...
```

This example instructs the processor to `apply-templates` to the root node of the `aaron.xml` document.

Using with `for-each`

```
...
<xsl:template match="employeeRecords">
```

XSLT

```
  <xsl:for-each

    select="document(./fileName)">
      <!-- process each root node here -->
  </xsl:for-each>
</xsl:template>
...
```

This example iterates through the root node of each document identified by the child `fileName` elements.

Using with `variable`

```
...
<xsl:template match="employeeRecords">
  <xsl:variable name='aaronsDoc'
    select="document('aaron.xml')"/>
  <xsl:for-each select="$aaronsDoc//dependents">
    <!-- process dependent elements here -->
  </xsl:for-each>
</xsl:template>
...
```

This example selects the root node from `aaron.xml` into the `aaronsDoc` variable. Then it iterates through each of the descendant `dependent` elements from that same document.

5.10.3 `element-available`

`boolean element-available(string)`

Description

`element-available` returns `true` if and only if the specified name is the name of an element that the processor supports. The argument string is evaluated as a QName. If the QName's expanded name has a namespace URI equal to the XSLT namespace URI, then it refers to an element defined by XSLT. Otherwise, it refers to a processor-specific extension element. If the expanded name has a null namespace URI, the `element-available` function returns `false`.

Examples

Testing for an XSLT element

```
...
<xsl:if test="element-available('xsl:message')">
<xsl:message>Error transforming employee/name</xsl:message>
</xsl:if>
...
```

This example tests to see if the XSLT processor supports the `xsl:message` element before using it.

Testing for a processor-specific element

```
<xsl:transform version='1.0'
  xmlns:xsl='http://www.w3.org/1999/XSL/Transform'
  xmlns:saxon='http://icl.com/saxon'
  extension-element-prefixes="saxon">

  <xsl:template match="/">
    <xsl:if test="element-available('saxon:output')">
      <xsl:for-each select="//employee">
        <saxon:output file="{./fname}.xml">
          <xsl:copy-of select="."/>
        </saxon:output>
      </xsl:for-each>
    </xsl:if>
  </xsl:template>
<xsl:transform>
```

This example tests to see if the processor supports the Saxon-specific `output` element before attempting to use it.

5.10.4 format-number

```
string format-number(number, string, string?)
```

Description

Converts the **number** argument to a string according to the format string specified by the second argument and the decimal format named by the third argument (or the default decimal format if there is no third argument). Decimal formats are defined by the decimal-format element (see decimal-format for details). The syntax of the format string is defined by the JDK 1.1 DecimalFormat class (see the JDK 1.1 documentation for more details). See the decimal-format element for an example.

5.10.5 function-available

```
boolean function-available(string)
```

Description

function-available returns true if and only if the specified name is the name of a function that the processor supports. The argument string is evaluated as a QName. If the QName's expanded name has a null namespace URI, it refers to a function defined by XPath or XSLT. Otherwise, it refers to a processor-specific extension function.

Examples

Testing for an XSLT function

```
...
<xsl:if test="function-available('document')">
  <xsl:apply-templates select="document('aaron.xml')"/>
</xsl:if>
...
```

This example tests to see if the XSLT processor supports the document function before using it.

Testing for a processor-specific function

```
<xsl:transform version='1.0'
  xmlns:xsl='http://www.w3.org/1999/XSL/Transform'
  xmlns:saxon='http://icl.com/saxon'>
  <xsl:param name="expr"/>

  <xsl:template match="/">
    <xsl:if test="function-available('saxon:evaluate')">
      <xsl:apply-templates select="saxon:evaluate($expr)"/>
    </xsl:if>
```

```
  </xsl:template>
<xsl:transform>
```

This example tests to see if the processor supports the Saxon-specific `evaluate` function before attempting to use it.

5.10.6 generate-id

`string generate-id(node-set?)`

Description

`generate-id` returns a string that uniquely identifies the first node in the argument `node-set`. Implementations are always required to generate the same identifier for the same node. If the argument `node-set` is empty, the empty string is returned. If the argument is omitted, it defaults to the context node.

Examples

generate-id example	Description
`generate-id()`	Generates a unique ID for the context node.
`generate-id(employee)`	Generates a unique ID for the first child `employee` element.
`generate-id(document('aaron.xml'))`	Generates a unique ID for the root node of `aaron.xml`.
`generate-id(document('aaron.xml')) = generate-id(document('aaron.xml'))`	Returns `true`.

5.10.7 key

`node-set key(string, object)`

Description

Returns a `node-set` containing the nodes that have the specified key value. The first argument is the qualified name of the key (see `key` element) whereas the second argument is the key value. If the second argument is a `node-set`, the result is the union of `node-set`s that results from applying the `key` function to each node in the argument `node-set` using the node's string-value as the second parameter. If the second argument is not a **node-set**, the argument is coerced to a string (as if by calling the **string** function), which is treated as the key value. The following describes how the second argument is treated based on object type. See the **key** element for an example.

Type	Description
node-set	The result is the union of the **node-set**s that results from applying the key function to each node in the argument **node-set** using the node's string-value as the second parameter.
other	Coerced to a string (as if by calling the **string** function).

5.10.8 system-property

```
object system-property(string)
```

Description

system-property returns the value of the argument system property. The argument string is evaluated as a QName, which is used to identify the system property by namespace-qualified name. If the system property doesn't exist, an empty string is returned. Implementations must provide the following system properties, which are all in the XSLT namespace:

System property	Description
version	Specifies a number that identifies the version of XSLT implemented by the processor (1.0).
vendor	Specifies a string identifying the vendor of the XSLT processor.
vendor-url	Specifies a string containing the vendor's URL.

Examples

system-property example	Description
system-property('xsl:version')	1.0
system-property('xsl:vendor')	Microsoft, Apache Software Foundation, and so on
system-property('xsl:vendor-url')	*http://www.microsoft.com, http://xml.apache.org/xalan,* and so on

5.10.9 `unparsed-entity-uri`

```
string unparsed-entity-uri(string)
```

Description

`unparsed-entity-uri` returns the URI of the unparsed entity with the specified name in the same document as the context node, or an empty string if it doesn't exist.

Example

`unparsed-entity-uri` example	Description
`unparsed-entity-uri('aaronsImage')`	Returns the URI of the unparsed enity named `aaronsImage`.

5.11 References

XSL Transformations 1.0 Recommendation.

Available at *http://www.w3.org/TR/1999/REC-xslt-19991116*. James Clark, editor, 1999.

XML Path Language.

Available at *http://www.w3.org/TR/1999/REC-xpath-19991116*. James Clark, Steve DeRoy, editors, 1999.

JDK 1.1 Documentation.

Available at *http://www.java.sun.com/products/jdk/1.1/docs*

Chapter 6
SAX 2.0

The Simple API for XML (SAX) 2.0 is a set of abstract programmatic interfaces that project an XML document onto a stream of well-known method calls. SAX provides a streaming model that can be used to both process XML documents as well as produce (or write) XML documents. Because SAX offers a streaming model, it's often preferred over the DOM when performance is an issue.

One implements the SAX interfaces to process XML documents. And one calls into the SAX interfaces to produce XML documents. Because most developers need to both process and produce XML documents in a given application, they often find themselves on both sides of the SAX interfaces (for example, implementing versus calling).

SAX was designed for the Java programming language by a group of developers on the XML-DEV mailing list and has since become widely supported throughout the industry. Today there are numerous SAX 2.0 implementations available for a wide range of programming languages and platforms. As an example, Microsoft introduced support for SAX 2.0 in MSXML 3.0, which can be used from both C++ and VB.

This SAX reference presents the SAX 2.0 core interface definitions for both Java and Visual Basic (VB). The interfaces are presented in alphabetical order. When describing interface members, both the Java and VB names will be given, in that order, when not identical. For all sample code, assume that the appropriate Java `import` statement or VB type library reference has been provided.

6.1 SAX UML quick reference

The UML diagram in Figure 6–1 provides a quick reference for the core and auxiliary interfaces/classes as well as their relationships to one another.

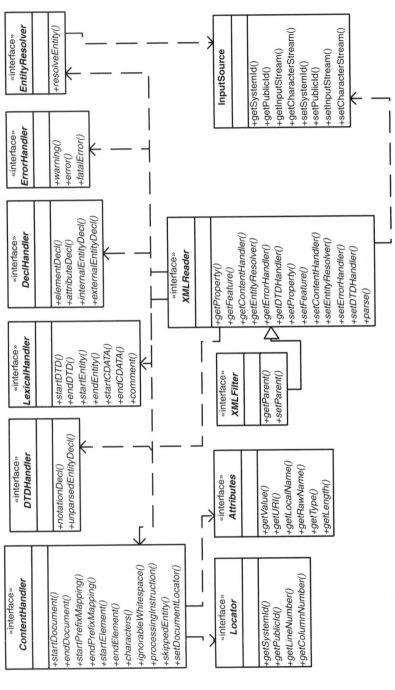

Figure 6-1 SAX 2.0 UML.

6.2   SAX interfaces and classes

The SAX API is divided into the following four areas: core interfaces, core classes, extended interfaces, and helper classes. The core interfaces and classes facilitate working with the core information contained in an XML document. The extended interfaces model aspects of a document with which most developers aren't concerned (for example, lexical details, DTD declarations, comments, and so on). And finally, the helper classes consist of several convenience classes as well as default implementations of certain core interfaces.

Most SAX developers find themselves working with the core interfaces 95 percent of the time. Because the extended interfaces are rarely used and the core/helper classes differ between SAX implementations, this chapter focuses strictly on the SAX 2.0 core interfaces. The following provides a quick description of each interface/class defined by SAX 2.0. For more details on the core interfaces, see the following sections. Otherwise refer to the SAX documentation (see Section 6.4).

Core interface	Description
`Attributes`	Models the attributes of an element.
`ContentHandler`	Models the core information in an XML document as an ordered sequence of method calls (primary SAX interface).
`DTDHandler`	Models notations and unparsed entities.
`EntityResolver`	Allows implementations to provide custom resolution of external entities.
`ErrorHandler`	Models well-formed errors, validation errors, and warnings.
`Locator`	Models the current location in the underlying document (for example, line number, column number, and so on).
`XMLFilter`	Provides pipeline-style processing by allowing multiple `ContentHandler` implementations to be chained together.
`XMLReader`	Models the XML parser (or other type of XML producer) by providing methods for registering handlers (for example, a `ContentHandler` implementation), parser configuration methods (properties/features), and parse methods.

SAX

Core class	Description
InputSource	Models a native input/output stream.
SAXException	Models a generic SAX exception.
SAXNotRecognizedException	Models an exception that occurs when a given feature/property isn't recognized.
SAXNotSupportedException	Models an exception that occurs when a given feature/property is recognized but isn't supported.
SAXParseException	Models a parser exception.

Extended interface	Description
DeclHandler	Models DTD declarations.
LexicalHandler	Models lexical information such as comments and CDATA section boundaries.

Helper class	Description
AttributesImpl	Convenience implementation of the Attributes interface.
DefaultHandler	Default implementation of the core interfaces (just stubbed): `ContentHandler`, `ErrorHandler`, `EntityResolver`, and `DTDHandler`.
LocatorImpl	Is the convenience implementation of the `Locator` interface.
NamespaceSupport	Helper class for managing in-scope namespaces, for dealing with QNames in attribute/element content.
XMLFilterImpl	Is the convenience implementation of the `XMLFilter` interface.
XMLReaderFactory	Is the class factory for implementations of `XMLReader`.

6.2.1 `Attributes`

The `Attributes` interface models the attributes of an element (passed as a parameter to `ContentHandler::startElement`). Attributes are exposed as an unordered property bag that can be traversed by name or position.

Java definition

```
package org.xml.sax;

public interface Attributes {
    int getLength();
    String getURI(int index);
    String getLocalName(int index);
    String getQName(int index);
    int getIndex(String qName);
    int getIndex(String uri, String localPart);
    String getValue (String uri, String localName);
    String getValue (int index);
    String getValue (String qName);
    String getType(String uri, String localName);
    String getType(int index);
    String getType(String qName);
}
```

VB definition

```
' IVBSAXAttributes Members
Property length As Long
Function getURI(nIndex As Long) As String
Function getLocalName(nIndex As Long) As String
Function getQName(nIndex As Long) As String
Function getIndexFromQName(strQName As String) As Long
Function getIndexFromName(strURI As String, strLocalName _
    As String) As Long
Function getValueFromName(strURI As String, strLocalName _
    As String) As String
Function getValue(nIndex As Long) As String
Function getValueFromQName(strQName As String) As String
Function getTypeFromName(strURI As String, strLocalName _
    As String) As String
Function getType(nIndex As Long) As String
Function getTypeFromQName(strQName As String) As String
```

Member	Description
getLength length	Returns the number of attributes in the list.
getURI	Retrieves an attribute's namespace URI by index.
getLocalName	Retrieves an attribute's local name by index.

SAX

Member	Description
getQName	Retrieves an attribute's QName by index.
getIndex getIndexFromQName	Retrieves an attribute's index by QName.
getIndex getIndexFromName	Retrieves an attribute's index by namespace name.
getValue getValueFromName	Retrieves an attribute's value by namespace name.
getValue	Retrieves an attribute's value by index.
getValue getValueFromQName	Retrieves an attribute's value by QName.
getType getTypeFromName	Retrieves an attribute's type by namespace name.
getType	Retrieves an attribute's type by index.
getType getTypeFromQName	Retrieves an attribute's type by QName.

Examples

Accessing attributes by name and index

These examples access the value of the id attribute by namespace name and QName; then they access the index of the id attribute by QName. Then they walk through the collection of attributes by index, accessing the local name, QName, value, and type of each one individually. Note: The order in which the attributes appear is insignificant and processor specific.

Java

```
public void startElement(String namespaceURI, String
   localName, String QName, Attributes atts)
{
   // accessing an attribute by namespace name
   String value;
   value = atts.getValue("urn:dm:employees", "id");
   if (!value.equals(""))
   {
   ... // process employee id attribute
   }

   // accessing an attribute by QName
   value = atts.getValue("d:id");
```

```
    // get attribute index by QName
    int index;
    index = atts.getIndex("d:id");

    // traverse attributes by index
    int i;
    String local, QName, type;
    for (i = 0; i<atts.getLength(); i++)
    {
        local = atts.getLocalName(i);
        qName = atts.getQName(i);
        value = atts.getValue(i);
        type = atts.getType(i);
        ... // process attribute here
    }
}
```

VB

```
Private Sub IVBSAXContentHandler_startElement( _
    strNamespaceURI As String, strLocalName As String, _
    strQName As String, ByVal oAttributes As _
    IVBSAXAttributes)

    ' accessing an attribute by namespace name
    Dim strAttValue As String
    strAttValue = oAttributes.getValueFromName( _
        "urn:dm:employees", "id")
    If (strAttValue <> "") Then
        ... ' process employee id attribute
    End If

    ' accessing an attribute by QName
    strAttValue = oAttributes.getValueFromQName("d:id")

    ' get attribute index by QName
    Dim index As Integer
    index = oAttributes.getIndexFromName("d:id")

    ' traverse attributes by index
    Dim i As Integer
```

SAX

```
    Dim strLocal As String, strQName As String
    Dim strType As String
    For i = 0 To oAttributes.length - 1
        strLocal = oAttributes.getLocalName(i)
        strQName = oAttributes.getQName(i)
        strAttValue = oAttributes.getValue(i)
        strType = oAttributes.getType(i)
        ... ' process attribute here
    Next
End Sub
```

6.2.2 ContentHandler

ContentHandler is the primary SAX interface. ContentHandler models the core information of an XML document as an ordered sequence of method calls. The remaining document information is modeled by the DTDHandler, DeclHandler, and LexicalHandler interfaces.

You implement ContentHandler to process XML documents. And you call into ContentHandler to produce XML documents. Because most developers need to both process and produce XML documents in a given application, they often find themselves on both sides of ContentHandler (for example, implementing versus calling).

Java definition

```
package org.xml.sax;

public interface ContentHandler {
    void startDocument() throws SAXException;
    void endDocument() throws SAXException;
    void startElement(String namespaceURI, String localName,
        String qName, Attributes atts) throws SAXException;
    void endElement(String namespaceURI, String localName,
        String qName) throws SAXException;
    void startPrefixMapping(String prefix, String uri)
        throws SAXException;
    void endPrefixMapping(String prefix) throws SAXException;
    void characters(char ch[], int start, int length)
        throws SAXException;
    void ignorableWhitespace(char ch[], int start, int length)
```

```
      throws SAXException;
   void processingInstruction(String target, String data)
      throws SAXException;
   void skippedEntity(String name) throws SAXException;
   void setDocumentLocator(Locator locator)
      throws SAXException;
}
```

VB definition

```
' IVBSAXContentHandler Members

Sub startDocument()
Sub endDocument()
Sub startElement(strNamespaceURI As String, strLocalName As _
   String, strQName As String, oAttributes As _
   IVBSAXAttributes)
Sub endElement(strNamespaceURI As String, _
   strLocalName As String, strQName As String)
Sub startPrefixMapping(strPrefix As String, strURI As String)
Sub endPrefixMapping(strPrefix As String)
Sub characters(strChars As String)
Sub ignorableWhitespace(strChars As String)
Sub processingInstruction(strTarget As String, strData As _
   String)
Sub skippedEntity(strName As String)
Property documentLocator As IVBSAXLocator
```

Member	Description
startDocument	Models the beginning of a document. Every method call that comes after startDocument and before endDocument models a part of the document's content (for example, a child or descendant).
endDocument	Models the end of a document. Signals that there is no more document content left to process (for example, no more children or descendants).
startElement	Models the beginning of an element. Every method call that comes after startElement and before endElement models a part of the element's content. Each element has a namespace identifier, a local name, a qualified name (QName: the raw name from the source document including the prefix if any), and a collection of attributes.

Member	Description
endElement	Models the end of the element's content. Signals that there is no more element content left to process.
startPrefixMapping	Models a namespace declaration entering scope. A namespace declaration consists of a prefix and the associated namespace identifier. The prefix of '' represents a default namespace declaration. This prefix is considered in scope within any subsequent method call until endPrefixMapping.
endPrefixMapping	Models a namespace declaration leaving scope. The specified prefix is no longer considered in scope within subsequent method calls.
characters	Models character data in element content. In Java/C++, a character array is used (for buffering purposes) along with a start position and the number to read. In VB, the characters are sent in a normal VB String.
ignorableWhitespace	Models ignorable whitespace in element content. In Java/C++, a character array is used (for buffering purposes) along with a start position and the number to read. In VB, the whitespace is sent in a normal VB String. Only called for whitespace in element-only content models when DTD/Schema is present.
processingInstruction	Models a processing instruction. A processing instruction consists of a target and the target-specific data. The target is the string that comes after <? until the first whitespace character. The data is everything after that first whitespace character.
skippedEntity	Models an entity that was skipped by the XML parser. This can occur with nonvalidating processors that don't expand external entities.
setDocumentLocator documentLocator	Supplies context information about the caller. A ContentHandler implementation can cache the locator object reference for future use (for example, determine the line and column number of the caller).

Examples

Using ContentHandler to generate a document

The following examples generate a simple XML document using ContentHandler. The generated document could be serialized as follows:

```xml
<?xsl-stylesheet type='text/xsl' href='inv.xsl'?>
<d:employee xmlns:d='urn:schemas-develop-com:staff'
  id='ss-102-22-3323'>
  <name>Keith Brown</name>
  <title>Dark Prince</title>
</d:employee>
```

Java

```java
void genEmployeeDocument(ContentHandler handler)
  throws SAXException {
  handler.startDocument();
  handler.processingInstruction("xsl-stylesheet",
    "type='text/xsl' href='inv.xsl'");
  handler.startPrefixMapping("d",
    "urn:schemas-develop-com:staff");
  Attributes a =
    new AttributesImpl();
  a.addAttribute("", "id", "id", "ID", "ss-102-22-3323");
  handler.startElement("urn:schemas-develop-com:staff",
    "employee", "d:employee", a);
  a.clear();
  handler.startElement("", "name", "name", a);
  String ch = "Keith Brown";
  handler.characters(ch.toCharArray(), 0, ch.length()-1);
  handler.endElement("", "name", "name");
  handler.startElement("", "title", "title", a);
  ch = "Dark Prince";
  handler.characters(ch.toCharArray(), 0, ch.length()-1);
  handler.endElement("", "title", "title");
  handler.endElement("urn:schemas-develop-com:staff",
    "employee", "d:employee");
  handler.endPrefixMapping("d",
    "urn:schemas-develop-com:staff");
  handler.endDocument();
}
```

SAX

VB

```
Public Sub genEmployeeDocument(handler as
   IVBSAXContentHandler)
   Dim a As New SAXAttributes
   handler.startDocument
   handler.processingInstruction "xsl-stylesheet", _
      "type='text/xsl' href='inv.xsl'"
   handler.startPrefixMapping "d", _
      "urn:schemas-develop-com:staff"
   a.addAttribute "", "id", "id", "ID", "ss-102-22-3323"
   handler.startElement "urn:schemas-develop-com:staff",_
      "employee", "d:employee", a
   a.clear
   handler.startElement "", "name", "name", a
   Dim ch as String
   ch  = "Keith Brown"
   handler.characters ch
   handler.endElement "", "name", "name"
   handler.startElement "", "title", "title"
   ch = "Dark Prince"
   handler.characters ch
   handler.endElement "", "title", "title"
   handler.endElement "urn:schemas-develop-com:staff", _
      "employee", "d:employee"
   handler.endPrefixMapping "d", _
      "urn:schemas-develop-com:staff"
   handler.endDocument
End Sub
```

Implementing ContentHandler to process a document

The following examples process an XML document, similar to the one shown in the previous example, by loading its information into an application-specific class (Employee). This requires implementing a finite state machine that keeps track of the document position.

Java

```
public class EmployeeHandler implements ContentHandler
{
   Stack m_elementContext;
```

```
Employee m_emp;
String m_data;

// state machine constants
private final int STATE_EMPLOYEE = 1;
private final int STATE_NAME = 2;
private final int STATE_TITLE = 3;

public void startDocument()
{
   m_elementContext = new Stack();
   m_emp = null;
   m_data = "";
}

public void startElement(String uri, String localName,
   String qName, Attributes atts)
{
  if (uri.equals("urn:schemas-develop-com:staff") &&
      localName.equals("employee"))
  {
    m_emp = new Employee();
    m_elementContext.push(new Integer(STATE_EMPLOYEE));
  }
  else if (localName.equals("name"))
  {
    m_elementContext.push(new Integer(STATE_NAME));
  }
  else if (localName.equals("title"))
  {
    m_elementContext.push(new Integer(STATE_TITLE));
  }
}

public void endElement(String uri, String localName,
   String qName)
{
  if (uri.equals("urn:schemas-develop-com:staff") &&
      localName.equals("employee")) ;
  else if (localName.equals("name"))
    if (m_emp) m_emp.name = m_data;
```

```
      else if (localName.equals("title"))
         if (m_emp) m_emp.title = m_data;
      else return;
      m_elementContext.pop();
      m_data = "";
   }

   public void characters(char[] ch, int start, int len)
   {
      if (m_emp != null &&
          !m_elementContext.isEmpty())
      {
         Integer context = (Integer)m_elementContext.peek();

         switch (context.intValue())
         {
         case STATE_NAME:
         case STATE_TITLE:
            m_data += new String(ch, start, len);
            break;
         case STATE_EMPLOYEE:
         default:
            break;
         }
      }
   }

   public void endDocument()
   {
      if (m_emp != null)
         ... // process Employee instance here
   }

   ... // other methods omitted for clarity
}
```

VB

```vb
Implements IVBSAXContentHandler

Dim m_elementContext as Stack
Dim m_emp as Employee
Dim m_data as String

Private Enum EmployeeStates
   STATE_EMPLOYEE = 1
   STATE_NAME
   STATE_TITLE
End Enum

Private Sub IVBSAXContentHandler_startDocument()
   Set m_elementContext = New Stack
   Set m_emp = Nothing
   m_data = ""
End Sub

Private Sub IVBSAXContentHandler_startElement( _
   strNamespaceURI As String, strLocalName As String, _
   strQName As String, ByVal oAttributes As _
   IVBSAXAttributes)

   Select Case strLocalName
     Case "employee"
        If strNamespaceURI = _
           "urn:schemas-develop-com:staff" Then
           set m_emp = New Employee
           m_elementContent.push STATE_EMPLOYEE
        End If
     Case "name"
           m_elementContent.push STATE_NAME
     Case "title"
           m_elementContent.push STATE_TITLE
   End Select
End Sub

Private Sub IVBSAXContentHandler_endElement( _
   strNamespaceURI As String, strLocalName As String, _
   strQName As String)
```

SAX

```vb
   Select Case strLocalName
      Case "employee"
         If strNamespaceURI <> _
            "urn:schemas-develop-com:staff" Then
            Exit Sub
         End If
      Case "name"
         m_emp.name = m_data
      Case "title"
         m_emp.title = m_data
      Case Else
         Exit Sub
   End Select
   m_elementContext.pop
   m_data = ""
End Sub

Private Sub IVBSAXContentHandler_characters( _
   strChars As String)
   If Not m_emp Is Nothing And Not _
      m_elementContext.IsEmpty Then
      Dim state as EmployeeStates
      state = m_elementContext.peek
      Select Case state
         Case STATE_NAME, STATE_TITLE
            m_data = m_data & strChars
      End Select
   End If
End Sub

Private Sub IVBSAXContentHandler_endDocument()
   If Not m_emp Is Nothing Then
      ... ' process Employee instance here
   End If
End Sub

... ' other methods omitted for clarity
```

6.2.3 DTDHandler

DTDHandler models the notations and unparsed entities in an XML document.

Java definition

```
package org.xml.sax;

public interface DTDHandler {
  notationDecl(String name, String publicId, String systemId);
  void unparsedEntityDecl(String name, String publicId,
  String systemId, String notationName) throws SAXException;
}
```

VB definition

```
' IVBSAXDTDHandler Members
Sub notationDecl(strName As String, strPublicId As String, _
  strSystemId As String)
Sub unparsedEntityDecl(strName As String, strPublicId As _
  String, strSystemId As String, strNotationName As String)
```

Member	Description
notationDecl	Models a notation declaration. The notation name is used in unparsed entity declarations to declare the resource type. The type identifier is the corresponding public/system identifier.
unparsedEntityDecl	Models an unparsed entity declaration. The name is used to refer to the unparsed entity within the XML document. The public/system identifiers specify the location of the resource whereas the notation name identifies the resource type.

Examples

Processing an unparsed entity

This example processes unparsed entities based on the media type, which is identified through the associated notation.

Java

```
public Class EmployeeHandler implements DTDHandler,
  ContentHandler
{
```

```
   // ContentHandler methods omitted for clarity

   public void notationDecl(String name, String publicId,
      String systemId)
   {
      CacheNotationInfoForLater(name, publicId, systemId);
   }

   public void unparsedEntityDecl(String name, String
    publicId,
      String systemId, String notationName)
   {
      String nId = GetNotationId(notationName);
      if (nId.equals("urn:mime:img/gif"))
         LaunchImageAppAndProcess(publicId, systemId);
      else if (nId.equals("urn:dm:video-presentation"))
         LaunchMediaPlayer(publicId, systemId);
      else
         ThrowUnknownMediaTypeError();
   }
}
```

VB

```
Implements DTDHandler
Implements ContentHandler

' ContentHandler methods omitted for clarity

Private Sub IVBSAXDTDHandler_notationDecl(strName As _
   String, strPublicId As String, strSystemId As String)
   CacheNotationInfoForLater strName, strPublicId, _
      strSystemId
End Sub

Private Sub IVBSAXDTDHandler_unparsedEntityDecl(strName _
   As String, strPublicId As String, strSystemId As _
   String, strNotationName As String)
   String nId = GetNotationId(notationName)
   Select Case nId
      Case "urn:mime:img/gif"
```

```
          LaunchImageAppAndProcess publicId, systemId
       Case "urn:dm:video-presentation"
          LaunchMediaPlayer publicId, systemId
       Case Else
          ThrowUnknownMediaTypeError
   End Select
End Sub
```

6.2.4 EntityResolver

EntityResolver is an interface that allows implementations to provide custom resolution of external entities. When an implementation supports EntityResolver, the SAX parser will call its resolveEntity method before resolving the public/ system identifier. This gives the implementation a chance to provide its own InputSource that represents the given resource.

Java definition

```
package org.xml.sax;

public interface EntityResolver {
   InputSource resolveEntity(String publicId, String systemId)
   throws SAXException, java.io.IOException;
}
```

VB definition

```
' IVBSAXEntityResolver Members
Function resolveEntity(strPublicId As String, strSystemId _
   As String)
```

Member	Description
resolveEntity	Returns an InputSource object representing the entity or null to indicate systemId should be used as the URI.

Examples

Custom resolution of external entities

This example attempts to retrieve the specified external entity from an in-memory cache of frequently accessed entities. If it's found in the cache, the cached resource is simply wrapped in an `InputSource` instance and returned to the processor. Otherwise, the method returns `null`, signaling the processor to use the `systemId` for resolution.

Java

```
public class EmployeeHandler implements EntityResolver,
   ContentHandler
{
   // ContentHandler methods omitted for clarity

   public InputSource resolveEntity(String pId, String
    sysId)
   {
      InputSource res =
        RetrieveResourceFromInMemoryCache(res, pId, sysId))
      return res;
   }
}
```

VB

```
Implements EntityResolver
Implements ContentHandler

' ContentHandler methods omitted for clarity

' NOTE: at the time of publication, resolveEntity was not
  called by the MSXML 3.0 parser

Private Function IVBSAXEntityResolver_resolveEntity( _
   strPublicId As String, strSystemId As String) As Variant

   Set IVBSAXEntityResolver_resolveEntity = _
      RetrieveResourceFromInMemoryCache(pId, sysId))

End Function
```

6.2.5 ErrorHandler

ErrorHandler models well-formed errors, validation errors, and warnings. The consumer of a ContentHandler implementation uses this interface to abort the stream of method invocations resulting from a caller-side error. Typically the SAX parser uses this to notify the ContentHandler implementation that something is wrong with the document's byte stream.

Java definition

```
package org.xml.sax;

public interface ErrorHandler {
    void warning(SAXParseException exception)
        throws SAXException;
    void error(SAXParseException exception)
        throws SAXException;
    void fatalError(SAXParseException exception)
        throws SAXException;
}
```

VB definition

```
' IVBSAXErrorHandler Members
Sub ignorableWarning(oLocator As IVBSAXLocator, _
    strErrorMessage As String, nErrorCode As Long)
Sub error(oLocator As IVBSAXLocator, strErrorMessage _
    As String, nErrorCode As Long)
Sub fatalError(oLocator As IVBSAXLocator, strErrorMessage _
    As String, nErrorCode As Long)
```

Member	Description
warning ignorableWarning	Models exceptional conditions that are less serious than errors or fatal errors.
error	Models an XML 1.0 nonfatal error. According to the XML 1.0 Recommendation, nonfatal errors are typically violations of validity constraints imposed by element and attribute list declarations (3.2.1) and XML version mismatches (2.8).
fatalError	Models an XML 1.0 fatal error. According to the XML 1.0 Recommendation, fatal errors are either violations of XML's well-formed rules (1.2), encountering an unrecognized character encoding (4.3.3), or certain illegal uses of entity or character references (4.4.4).

Examples

Handling errors

This example illustrates how to handle errors in the document byte stream sent to the ContentHandler implementation.

Java

```java
public class EmployeeHandler implements ErrorHandler,
    ContentHandler
{
    // ContentHandler methods omitted for clarity

    public void error(SAXParseException e)
      throws SAXException
    {
        logErrorAndBail(e);
    }

    public void fatalError(SAXParseException p1)
      throws SAXException
    {
        logErrorAndBail(e);
    }

    public void warning(SAXParseException p1)
      throws SAXException
    {
        logWarningAndContinue(e);
    }
}
```

VB

```vb
Implements IVBSAXErrorHandler
Implements IVBSAXContentHandler

' ContentHandler methods omitted for clarity

Private Sub IVBSAXErrorHandler_error(ByVal oLocator As _
    IVBSAXLocator, strErrorMessage As String, _
    ByVal nErrorCode As Long)
```

```
   LogErrorAndBail oLocator, strErrorMessage, nErrorCode
End Sub

Private Sub IVBSAXErrorHandler_fatalError(ByVal oLocator _
     As IVBSAXLocator, strErrorMessage As String, _
     ByVal nErrorCode As Long)
   LogErrorAndBail oLocator, strErrorMessage, nErrorCode
End Sub

Private Sub IVBSAXErrorHandler_ignorableWarning(ByVal _
     oLocator As IVBSAXLocator, strErrorMessage As _
     String, ByVal nErrorCode As Long)
   LogWarningAndContinue oLocator, strErrorMessage, _
     nErrorCode
End Sub
```

6.2.6 Locator

Because SAX is commonly used to interface with XML parsers, it is occasionally
useful for a ContentHandler implementation to discover to which part of the
underlying document the current method corresponds. To support this function-
ally, SAX defines the Locator interface, which is typically implemented by SAX-
aware parsers to allow implementations of ContentHandler to discover
exactly where the current method corresponds in the underlying document.

A reference to a Locator object is sent to the ContentHandler implementation through the setDocumentLocator method before processing begins.

Java definition

```
package org.xml.sax;

public interface Locator {
    String getPublicId( );
    String getSystemId( );
    int getLineNumber( );
    int getColumnNumber( );
}
```

VB definition

```
' IVBSAXLocator Members
Property publicId As String
Property systemId As String
Property lineNumber As Long
Property columnNumber As Long
```

Member	Description
getPublicId publicId	Returns the public identifier of the entity (document or external parsed) that is currently being processed.
getSystemId systemId	Returns the system identifier of the entity (document or external parsed) that is currently being processed.
getLineNumber lineNumber	Returns the 1-based line number where the serialization of the information item being processed ends.
getColumnNumber columnNumber	Returns the 1-based column number where the serialization of the information item being processed ends.

Examples

Using the Locator interface

Java

```java
public class EmployeeHandler implements ContentHandler
{
    Locator m_loc;

    public void setDocumentLocator(Locator loc)
    {
        m_loc = loc;
    }

    public void startElement(String uri, String localName,
        String qName, Attributes atts)
    {
        Console.out.println(m_loc.getLineNumber())
        Console.out.println(m_loc.getColumnNumber());
        Console.out.println(m_loc.getSystemId());
        Console.out.println(m_loc.getPublicId());
    }
    ... // other methods omitted for clarity
}
```

VB

```
Implements ContentHandler

Dim m_loc as IVBSAXLocator

Private Property Set
   IVBSAXContentHandler_documentLocator(_
       ByVal loc As IVBSAXLocator)
   set m_loc = loc
End Property

Private Sub IVBSAXContentHandler_startElement( _
       strNamespaceURI As String, strLocalName As String, _
    strQName As String, ByVal oAttributes As _
    IVBSAXAttributes)
   Debug.Print m_loc.lineNumber
   Debug.Print m_loc.columnNumber
   Debug.Print m_systemId
   Debug.Print m_publicId
End Sub

... ' other methods omitted for clarity
```

SAX

6.2.7 XMLFilter

Most SAX interfaces are amenable to pipeline-style processing, where an implementation of, say, ContentHandler can intercept certain information items it recognizes but pass along unrecognized information items to a downstream processor that also implements ContentHandler. SAX makes this model concrete via its XMLFilter interface. XMLFilter extends the XMLReader interface by adding two methods—one to discover the upstream XMLReader implementation and one to set it.

Java definition

```
package org.xml.sax;

public interface XMLFilter extends XMLReader {
   XMLReader getParent();
   void setParent(XMLReader parent);
}
```

VB definition

```
' IVBSAXXMLFilter Members
Property parent As SAXXMLReader
```

Member	Description
getParent parent	Returns the upstream XMLReader implementation.
setParent parent	Sets the upstream XMLReader implementation.

Examples

Using an SAX filter for XInclude processing

This example uses an XMLReader to parse an XML document from disk as well as a ContentHandler implementation that serializes the stream of method calls back out to an XML 1.0 byte stream. It also uses a filter, which sits between the reader and the serializer, for processing XInclude-based inclusions within the document. The filter adds XInclude functionality without affecting either of the existing components.

Java

```
public void ProcessFileForXInclude(String file)
{
    // implements XMLFilter, ContentHandler, etc.
    ' and provides XInclude functionality
    MyXIncludeFilter f = new MyXIncludeFilter();
    XMLFilter xf = f;
    XMLReader rf = f;

    ' XMLReader implementation - parses XML 1.0 document
    XMLReader r = new
    org.apache.xerces.parsers.SAXParser();

    ' implementation of ContentHandler that serializes a
    ' file back out to XML 1.0
    Serializer ser = new Serializer();
    ser.setOutputStream("c:\temp\out.xml");

    xf.setParent(r);
    rf.setContentHandler(ser);
    rf.parse(file);
}
```

VB

```vb
Public Sub ProcessFileForXInclude(file as String)

    ' implements IVBSAXXMLFilter, IVBSAXContentHandler, etc.
    ' and provides XInclude functionality
    Dim f As New MyXIncludeFilter
    Dim xf As IVBSAXXMLFilter
    Dim rf as IVBSAXXMLReader

    ' XMLReader implementation - parses XML 1.0 document
    Dim r As New SAXXMLReader30

    ' implementation of ContentHandler that serializes a
    ' file back out to XML 1.0
    Dim ser As New Serializer
    ser.setOutputStream "c:\temp\out.xml"

    Set xf = f
    Set xf.parent = r
    Set rf = f
    Set rf.contentHandler = ser
    rf.parseURL file
End Sub
```

SAX

6.2.8 XMLReader

SAX defines the XMLReader interface to tie together many of the other SAX interfaces. This interface is implemented by SAX parsers but could also be implemented by other applications that produce XML document streams. The XMLReader interface has three groups of methods: handler registration methods, configuration methods (properties/features), and parse methods.

Java definition

```java
package org.xml.sax;

public interface XMLReader {
    void setContentHandler(ContentHandler handler);
    ContentHandler getContentHandler();
    void setDTDHandler(DTDHandler handler);
```

```
    DTDHandler getDTDHandler();
    void setEntityResolver(EntityResolver handler);
    EntityResolver getEntityResolver();
    void setErrorHandler(ErrorHandler handler);
    ErrorHandler getErrorHandler();
    void setProperty(String name, Object value)
        throws SAXNotRecognizedException,
        SAXNotSupportedException;
    Object getProperty(String name) throws
        SAXNotRecognizedException, SAXNotSupportedException;
    void setFeature(String name, boolean value) throws
        SAXNotRecognizedException, SAXNotSupportedException;
    boolean getFeature(String name) throws
        SAXNotRecognizedException, SAXNotSupportedException;
    void parse(String systemId) throws SAXException,
        java.io.IOException;
    void parse(InputSource source) throws SAXException,
        java.io.IOException;
}
```

VB definition

```
' IVBSAXXMLReader Members
Property contentHandler As IVBSAXContentHandler
Property dtdHandler As IVBSAXDTDHandler
Property entityResolver As IVBSAXEntityResolver
Property errorHandler As IVBSAXErrorHandler
Sub putProperty(strName As String, varValue)
Function getProperty(strName As String)
Sub putFeature(strName As String, fValue As Boolean)
Function getFeature(strName As String) As Boolean
Sub parseURL(strURL As String)
Sub parse(varInput)
Property baseURL As String
Property secureBaseURL As String
```

Member	Description
setContentHandler contentHandler	Registers a `ContentHandler` implementation with the reader.
getContentHandler contentHandler	Returns the current `ContentHandler` implementation or null if one hasn't yet been registered.

Member	Description
setDTDHandler dtdHandler	Registers a DTDHandler implementation with the reader.
getDTDHandler dtdHandler	Returns the current DTDHandler implementation or null if one hasn't yet been registered.
setEntityResolver entityResolver	Registers an EntityResolver implementation with the reader.
getEntityResolver entityResolver	Returns the current EntityResolver implementation or null if one hasn't yet been registered.
setErrorHandler errorHandler	Registers an ErrorHandler implementation with the reader.
getErrorHandler errorHandler	Returns the current ErrorHandler implementation or null if one hasn't yet been registered.
setProperty putProperty	Sets the value of a property (object).
getProperty	Returns the specified property's value (object).
setFeature putFeature	Sets the state of a feature (true/false).
getFeature	Returns the specified feature's state (true/false).
parse parseURL	Instructs an XMLReader implementation to parse the XML document specified by the system identifier.
parse	Instructs an XMLReader implementation to parse the XML document specified by the InputSource.

SAX

Examples

Using XMLReader to parse a document

This example instantiates a SAX parser that implements XMLReader as well as a receiver object that implements ContentHandler, ErrorHandler, DTDHandler, EntityResolver, and LexicalHandler. The individual handlers are registered with the reader through the appropriate "set" (for example, setContentHandler) method calls. Notice, however, that the LexicalHandler implementation must be registered through a call to setProperty because it's not considered part of core SAX but rather an extension interface. This example also enables the namespace-prefixes property, which allows namespace declarations to appear as attributes in the document stream. Finally, once the XMLReader has been completely configured, parse is used to begin parsing the specified file.

Java

```java
public void processEmployeeDocument()
{
    // instantiate Xerces-J SAX parser
    XMLReader reader =
        new org.apache.xerces.parsers.SAXParser();

    // EmployeeHandler implements ContentHandler,
    // ErrorHandler, DTDHandler, and EntityResolver
    ContentHandler handler = new EmployeeHandler();

    // register handlers with XMLReader
    reader.setContentHandler(handler);
    reader.setErrorHandler(handler);
    reader.setDTDHandler(handler);
    reader.setEntityResolver(handler);

    try
    {
        // register LexicalHandler implementation
        reader.setProperty(
            "http://xml.org/sax/properties/lexical-handler",
            handler);

        reader.setFeature(
            "http://xml.org/sax/features/namespaces",
            true);
        reader.setFeature(
            "http://xml.org/sax/features/namespace-
            prefixes", true);

        // start parsing
        reader.parse("file://c:\temp\employee.xml");
    }
    catch(Exception e)
    {
        ... // handle errors here
    }
}
```

VB

```
Public Sub processEmployeeDocument()

    On Error Goto HandleError

    ' instantiate MSXML 3.0 SAX parser
    Dim reader as New SAXXMLReader

    ' EmployeeHandler implements ContentHandler,
    ' ErrorHandler, DTDHandler, & EntityResolver
    Dim handler as New EmployeeHandler

    ' register handlers with XMLReader
    set reader.contentHandler = handler
    set reader.errorHandler = handler
    set reader.dtdHandler = handler
    set reader.entityResolver = handler

    ' register LexicalHandler implementation
    reader.putProperty _
        "http://xml.org/sax/properties/lexical-handler",_
        handler

    reader.putFeature _
        "http://xml.org/sax/features/namespaces",_
        true
    reader.putFeature _
        "http://xml.org/sax/features/namespace-prefixes",_
        true

    reader.parseURL "file://c:\temp\employee.xml"

    Exit Sub
HandleError:
    ... ' handle errors here
End Sub
```

SAX

6.3 Features and properties

XMLReader has four configuration methods: two that deal with properties and two that deal with features. Properties are uniquely named values that can be associated with an XMLReader instance. Features can be viewed as configuration-specific boolean properties that are used to turn specific processing features on or off.

SAX predefines a set of well-known properties and features. These properties and features are as follows. SAX implementations may add custom features and properties that have implementation-specific URI-based names.

Features

The full feature name should be prefixed with http://xml.org/sax/features/ (for example, http://xml.org/sax/features/namespaces).

Name	Description
namespaces	Performs namespace processing.
namespace-prefixes	Reports the original prefixed names and attributes used for namespace declarations.
string-interning	Internalizes all element names, prefixes, attribute names, namespace identifiers, and local names using java.lang.String.intern.
external-general-entities	Includes external general (text) entities.
external-parameter-entities	Includes external parameter entities and the external DTD subset.
validation	Reports all validation errors (implies external-general-entities and external-parameter-entities).

Properties

The full property name should be prefixed with http://xml.org/sax/properties/ (for example, http://xml.org/sax/properties/dom-node).

Name	Description
dom-node	Returns the DOM node currently being visited, if SAX is being used as a DOM iterator. If the parser recognizes and supports this property but is not currently visiting a DOM node, returns null. [Read Only]

Name	Description
`xml-string`	Returns the string of characters associated with the current event. If the parser recognizes and supports this property but is not currently parsing text, it should return `null`. [Read Only]
`lexical-handler`	An optional extension handler for lexical events (for example, comments).
`decl-handler`	An optional extension handler for DTD-related events other than notations and unparsed entities.

6.4 References

For more information about Simple API for XML,

please go to http://www.megginson.com/SAX/index.html.

Chapter 7

DOM Level 2

The Document Object Model is a set of abstract programmatic interfaces that project the Infoset of an XML document onto a tree of nodes. The DOM is defined as a set of Object Management Group (OMG) Interface Definition Language (IDL) interface definitions along with a set of Java language bindings and a set of ECMAScript (JavaScript, JScript) language bindings. Various other language bindings have been inferred from the IDL; however, this reference covers the Java and VB language bindings.

Level 1 of the DOM was standardized prior to namespaces or the Infoset and requires proprietary extensions to be useful for modern XML applications. For that reason, this chapter ignores DOM Level 1 and uses the term DOM as a synonym for DOM Level 2.

7.1 DOM UML

Figure 7–1 is a quick-reference UML diagram representing the core DOM level 2 interfaces.

7.2 DOM interfaces

The DOM interfaces are listed in alphabetical order with a brief description, Java and VB interface definitions, and a table of members. The members table gives the name of the method or property and a short description. In cases when two names appear in the name column, the first is the Java name and the second is the VB name. In many cases, examples are also provided.

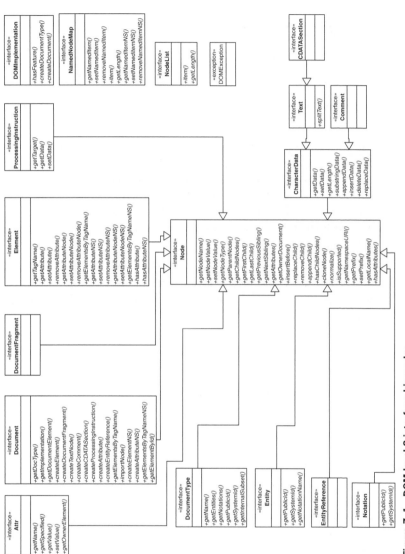

Figure 7–1 DOM level 2 interface hierarchy.

7.2.1 `Attr`

The `Attr` interface models an attribute in an XML document providing access to the various properties of the attribute. Despite extending the `Node` interface, attribute nodes are not considered part of the DOM tree.

Java definition

```
package org.w3c.dom;

public interface Attr extends Node {
    public String getName();
    public boolean getSpecified();
    public String getValue();
    public void setValue(String value) throws DOMException;
    public Element getOwnerElement();
}
```

VB definition

```
'IXMLDOMAttribute
Property name As String 'readonly
Property value As Variant
```

Member	Description
`getName` `name`	Returns the QName of the attribute.
`getSpecified`	Returns `true` if the attribute was specified in the original document. Returns `false` if the attribute is present because of a default value in a DTD.
`getValue` `value`	Retrieves an attribute's value.
`setValue` `value`	Sets the value of an attribute.
`getOwnerElement`	Returns a reference to the Element node that owns the attribute or null if the attribute is currently unowned. An example of an unowned attribute node would be one that had just been created but not yet attached to a particular element.

DOM

Examples

Accessing the name and value of an attribute

These examples check the name of an attribute, retrieve the value, and finally return the owner element. In addition, the Java example checks whether the attribute was specified or defaulted in by the DTD.

Java

```
Element ProcessAttributeAndReturnOwnerElement ( Attr att )
{
  if ( att.getName().equals ( "id" ))
  {
    // Retrieve attribute value
    String value = att.getValue();
    // Process employee id
    // ...
  }

  if ( att.getSpecified() == true )
  {
    // attribute was specified in instance document
    // rather than being defaulted in from a DTD
  }

  return att.getOwnerElement();
}
```

VB

```
Sub ProcessAttribute ( att As IXMLDOMAttribute )
  If att.name = "id" Then
    ' Retrieve attribute value
    Dim value As String
    value = att.value
    ' Process employee id
    ' ...
  End If
End Sub
```

7.2.2 CDATASection

The CDATASection interface is a signature interface (it adds no further methods to org.w3c.dom.Text). It is used to denote a text node in the tree that was either read from a CDATA section or should be written as a CDATA section, or both.

7.2.3 CharacterData

There are no CharacterData nodes in a DOM tree. Rather, the CharacterData interface provides a base interface for the org.w3c.dom.Text and org.w3c.dom.Comment node types. It provides methods for retrieving and manipulating the character data in these nodes.

Java definition

```
package org.w3c.dom;

public interface CharacterData extends Node {
    public String getData() throws DOMException;
    public void setData(String data) throws DOMException;
    public int getLength();
    public String substringData(int offset, int count)
        throws DOMException;
    public void appendData(String arg) throws DOMException;
    public void insertData(int offset, String arg)
        throws DOMException;
    public void deleteData(int offset, int count)
        throws DOMException;
    public void replaceData(int offset, int count,
        String arg) throws DOMException;
}
```

VB definition

```
' IXMLDOMCharacterData
Property data As String
Property length As Long ' read-only
Function substringData ( offset As Long, count As Long ) _
    As String
Sub appendData ( data As String )
Sub insertData ( offset As Long, data As String )
Sub deleteData ( offset As Long, count As Long )
```

```
Sub replaceData ( offset As Long, count As Long, data _
    As String )
```

Member	Description
getData data	Returns the character data associated with the node.
setData data	Replaces any existing character data with the string provided.
getLength length	Returns the number of characters in the character data.
substringData	Returns a range of data from the available character data.
appendData	Appends the provided string to the end of the current character data.
insertData	Inserts the provided string at the specified offset.
deleteData	Deletes a range of character data.
replaceData	Replaces a range of characters with the provided string. replaceData can be thought of as a call to deleteData followed by a call to insertData.

Examples

Using the CharacterData interface

These examples show setting, appending, inserting, deleting, and replacing text in a CharacterData node. The text that the CharacterData node contains after each operation is shown in the following comment. In addition a call to the substringData method is shown along with the returned text.

Java

```
String PopulateCharacterDataNode ( CharacterData cd ) {
    cd.setData ( "A man" );          // 'A man'
    cd.appendData ( " a plan" );     // 'A man a plan'
    cd.appendData ( " panama" );     // 'A man a plan panama'
    cd.insertData ( 12, " a canal" );
        // 'A man a plan a canal panama'
    cd.deleteData ( 12, 4 );         // 'A man a plananal panama'
    cd.replaceData ( 12, 4, " a canal" );
        // 'A man a plan a canal panama'

    String sub = cd.substringData ( 6, 6 ); // 'a plan'
```

```
    return cd.getData();
}
```

VB

```
Function PopulateCharacterDataNode ( ByRef cd  As
    IXMLDOMCharacterData ) As String
    cd.data = "A man"                    ' "A man" '
    cd.appendData " a plan"              ' "A man a plan" '
    cd.appendData " panama"              ' "A man a plan panama" '
    cd.insertData 12, " a canal" _
      ' "A man a plan a canal panama" '
    cd.deleteData 12, 4 _
      ' "A man a plananal panama" '
    cd.replaceData 12, 4, " a canal" _
      ' "A man a plan a canal panama" '

    Dim sub As String
    sub = cd.substringData ( 6, 6, )  ' "a plan" '

    PopulateCharacterDataNode = cd.data
End Function
```

7.2.4 Comment

The Comment interface is a signature interface (it adds no further methods to org.w3c.dom.CharacterData). It is used to denote a comment node in the tree.

7.2.5 Document

The Document interface represents the root of a DOM tree. It also acts as a factory for other node types. When working with XML that includes namespace information, the methods with names that end with NS should be used instead of the methods without that suffix.

Java definition

```
package org.w3c.dom;

public interface Document extends Node {
    public DocumentType getDoctype();
    public DOMImplementation getImplementation();
    public Element getDocumentElement();
    public Element createElement(String tagName)
        throws DOMException;
    public DocumentFragment createDocumentFragment();
    public Text createTextNode(String data);
    public Comment createComment(String data);
    public CDATASection createCDATASection(String data)
        throws DOMException;
    public ProcessingInstruction
        createProcessingInstruction(String target, String data)
        throws DOMException;
    public Attr createAttribute(String name)
        throws DOMException;
    public EntityReference createEntityReference
        (String name) throws DOMException;
    public NodeList getElementsByTagName(String tagname);
    public Node importNode(Node importedNode, boolean deep)
        throws DOMException;
    public Element createElementNS(String namespaceURI,
        String qualifiedName) throws DOMException;
    public Attr createAttributeNS(String namespaceURI,
        String qualifiedName) throws DOMException;
    public NodeList getElementsByTagNameNS(String
        namespaceURI, String localName);
    public Element getElementById(String elementId);
}
```

VB definition

```
' IXMLDOMDocument
Property docType As IXMLDOMDocumentType ' read-only
Property implementation As IXMLDOMImplementation ' read-only
Property documentElement As IXMLDOMElement
Function createElement ( tagName As String ) _
    As IXMLDOMElement
Function createDocumentFragment() As IXMLDOMDocumentFragment
Function createTextNode ( data As String ) As IXMLDOMText
```

```
Function createComment ( data As String ) As IXMLDOMComment
Function createCDATASection ( data As String ) _
    As IXMLDOMCDATASection
Function createProcessingInstruction ( target As String, _
    data As String ) As IXMLDOMProcessingInstruction
Function createAttribute ( name As String ) _
    As IXMLDOMAttribute
Function createEntityReference ( name As String ) _
    As IXMLDOMEntityReference
Function getElementsByTagName ( tagName As String ) _
    As IXMLDOMNodeList
Function createNode ( Type As Variant, name As String, _
    namespaceURI As String ) As IXMLDOMNode
Function nodeFromID ( idString As String ) As IXMLDOMNode
Function load ( xmlSource As Variant ) As Boolean
Property readyState As Long ' read-only
Property parseError As IXMLDOMParseError ' read-only
Property url As String ' read-only
Property async As Boolean
Sub abort()
Function loadXML ( bstrXML As String ) As Boolean
Sub save ( destination As Variant )
Property validateOnParse As Boolean
Property resolveExternals As Boolean
Property preserveWhiteSpace As Boolean
Property onreadystatechange As Variant ' write-only
Property ondataavailable As Variant ' write-only
Property ontransformnode As Variant ' write-only
```

DOM

Member	Description
getDocType docType	Returns the DTD for this document or null if no Document Type Declaration is available.
getImplementation implementation	Returns the DOMImplementation that deals with this document.
getDocumentElement documentElement	Returns the element child of the Document node.
createElement	Creates and returns an element node with the provided name. The localName, prefix, and namespaceURI properties of the element node will be null.
createDocumentFragment	Creates an empty DocumentFragment node.

Member	Description
createTextNode	Creates a Text node containing the provided string.
createComment	Creates a Comment node containing the provided string.
createCDATASection	Creates a CDATASection node containing the provided string.
createProcessingInstruction	Creates a ProcessingInstruction node with the provided target and data.
createAttribute	Creates an Attribute node with the provided name. The localName, prefix, and namespaceURI properties of the Attribute node will be null.
createEntityReference	Creates an EntityReference node with the provided name. If the name corresponds to a known Entity in the DTD, then the descendants of the createEntityReference node correspond to those specified by the entity declaration, otherwise the created node has no descendants.
getElementsByTagName	Returns a list of all Elements in the document with a nodeName property that matches the provided name. The string value "*" matches all Elements. The Elements are returned in document order. Use of this method should be avoided when working with XML containing namespace information because the results are implementation dependent.
importNode	Creates a copy of a node created in another document such that the copy can be used in the importing document. For Attribute nodes, any Text node children are also copied. For DocumentFragment nodes, if deep was set to true, then all descendant nodes are also copied. Otherwise, an empty DocumentFragment node is created. For Element nodes, any specified Attribute nodes are copied. Defaulted Attribute nodes are not copied. If deep is set to true then all descendant nodes are also copied. For EntityReference nodes only the entity reference is copied. If the importing document provides a definition for an entity with the same name as the imported entity, then the value of that entity

Member	Description
	definition is assigned to the new node. For `ProcessingInstruction` nodes a straight copy is created. For Text, `CDATASection`, and `Comment` nodes a straight copy is created. `importNode` is undefined or not useful for `Notation`, `Entity`, `DocumentType`, and `Document` nodes.
`createElementNS`	Creates a namespace-qualified `Element` node with the specified QName. At serialization time, the relevant namespace declaration will be written out. This method supersedes `createElement`.
`createAttributeNS`	Creates a namespace-qualified `Attribute` node with the specified QName. At serialization time, the relevant namespace declaration will be written out. This method supersedes `createAttribute`.
`getElementsByTagNameNS`	Returns a list of all `Elements` in the document with `namespaceURI` and `localName` properties that match the provided parameters. The string value "*" matches all `Elements`. The `Elements` are returned in document order.
`getElementById` `nodeFromID`	Returns the `Element` whose ID attribute matches the supplied string. Note that the ID attribute is the one whose type is ID, not the one (if any) whose name is ID. The DOM implementation needs a DTD or schema to determine the type of an attribute. If no `Element` with the specified ID can be found, or the implementation does not know which attributes are of type ID, then the method returns null.

Examples

Creating elements, attributes, and text nodes

These examples show creating a namespace qualified element, a namespace qualified attribute, and associated text node and retrieving a list of nodes. The element is appended to the document element. The Visual Basic example uses `createNode` rather than `createElementNS`/`createAttributeNS` and `getElementsByTagName` rather than `getElementsByTagNameNS` as MSXML does not support the "NS" methods of the `Document` interface.

Java

```
NodeList addElementAndGetList ( Document doc ) {
  Element docelt = doc.getDocumentElement();
  Element e = doc.createElementNS
    ( "urn:develop-com:employees", "employee" );
  docelt.appendChild ( e );
  Attr a = doc.createAttributeNS ( null, "id" );
  Text t = doc.createTextNode ( "5" );
  a.appendChild ( t );
  e.setAttributeNodeNS ( a );

  return doc.getElementsByTagNameNS
    ( "urn:develop-com:employees", "employee" );
}
```

VB

```
Function addElementAndGetList ( doc As IXMLDOMDocument ) _
    As IXMLDOMNodeList
  Dim docelt As IXMLDOMElement
  Set docelt = doc.documentElement
  Dim e As IXMLDOMElement
  Set e = doc.createNode(NODE_ELEMENT, "employee", _
    "urn:develop-com:employees")
  docelt.appendChild e
  Dim a As IXMLDOMAttribute
  Set a = doc.createNode(NODE_ATTRIBUTE, "id", "")
  Dim t As IXMLDOMText
  Set t = doc.createTextNode("5")
  a.appendChild t
  e.setAttributeNode a

  set addELementAndGetList = _
    doc.getElementsByTagName ( "employee" )
End Function
```

7.2.6 DocumentFragment

The DocumentFragment interface is a signature interface (it adds no further methods to org.w3c.dom.Node). It is used to denote a DocumentFragment node. The descendants of a DocumentFragment node need not conform to the structure rules laid down in the XML Infoset. For example, a DocumentFragment may have multiple element children. When a DocumentFragment is inserted into a DOM tree, the children are inserted rather than the DocumentFragment node.

7.2.7 DocumentType

The DocumentType interface provides access to the Entity and Notation collections of the document along with certain aspects of the internal and external subsets of the DTD. Both the Entity and Notation collections are read-only.

Java definition

```
package org.w3c.dom;

public interface DocumentType extends Node {
    public String getName();
    public NamedNodeMap getEntities();
    public NamedNodeMap getNotations();
    public String getPublicId();
    public String getSystemId();
    public String getInternalSubset();
}
```

VB definition

```
' IXMLDOMDocumentType
Property name As String ' read-only
Property entities As IXMLDOMNamedNodeMap ' read-only
Property notations As IXMLDOMNamedNodeMap ' read-only
```

Member	Description
getName name	Returns the name of the DTD. This is the name that immediately follows the DOCTYPE keyword and corresponds to the name of the document element.

Member	Description
getEntities entities	Returns a read-only collection containing general entities declared in the internal or external subset of the DTD. All nodes in the returned map implement the Entity interface.
getNotations notations	Returns read-only collection notations declared in the internal or external subset of the DTD. All nodes in the returned map implement the Notation interface.
getPublicId	Returns the public identifier of the external subset of the DTD.
getPublicId	Returns the system identifier of the external subset of the DTD.
getInternalSubset	Returns the internal subset of the DTD as a string.

7.2.8 DOMImplementation

A bootstrapping interface typically used for creating the initial **Document** node of a DOM tree. DOMImplementation also allows a given DOM implementation to be interrogated with regard to supported features.

Java definition

```
package org.w3c.dom;

public interface DOMImplementation {
    public boolean hasFeature(String feature, String
    version);
    public DocumentType createDocumentType(String
    qualifiedName, String publicId, String systemId) throws
    DOMException;
    public Document createDocument(String namespaceURI,
    String qualifiedName, DocumentType doctype) throws
    DOMException;
}
```

VB definition

```
' IXMLDOMImplementation
Function hasFeature ( feature As String, version As String )
    As Boolean
```

Member	Description
hasFeature	Returns **true** if the DOM implementation supports the specified version of the specified feature; **false** otherwise. Defined features include Core, XML, HTML, Views, StyleSheets, CSS, CSS2, Events, UIEvents, MouseEvents, MutationEvents, HTMLEvents, Range, and Traversal. Other specifications may define new features. Feature names are case sensitive. For DOM level 2, the version string for all features is "2.0."
createDocumentType	Creates an empty **DocumentType** node with the specified name and public and system IDs. Because the notation and entity collections are read-only, the resulting **DocumentType** node is not very useful.
createDocument	Creates a **Document** node of the specified **DocumentType** along with the document Element.

Examples

Creating the document element

This example shows creating a DocumentType node, the **Document** node, and the document element. The resulting XML document could be serialized as follows:

```
<!DOCTYPE e:employees SYSTEM "employees.dtd" >
<e:employees xmlns:e='urn:develop-com:employees' />
```

Java

```
Document CreateDocument ( DOMImplementation dom ) {
  DocumentType dt = dom.createDocumentType ( "e:employees",
    null, "employees.dtd" );
  Document doc = dom.createDocument ( "urn:develop-
    com:employees", "e:employees", dt );
  return doc;
}
```

DOM

7.2.9 **Element**

The **Element** interface provides methods for access to and modification of the attributes of an element along with methods for retrieving some of the properties of the element. When working with XML that includes namespace information, the

methods with names that end with NS should be used instead of the methods
without that suffix.

Java definition

```
package org.w3c.dom;

public interface Element extends Node {
    public String getTagName();
    public String getAttribute(String name);
    public void setAttribute(String name, String value)
      throws DOMException;
    public void removeAttribute(String name) throws
      DOMException;
    public Attr getAttributeNode(String name);
    public Attr setAttributeNode(Attr newAttr) throws
      DOMException;
    public Attr removeAttributeNode(Attr oldAttr) throws
      DOMException;
    public NodeList getElementsByTagName(String name);
    public String getAttributeNS(String namespaceURI,
      String localName);
    public void setAttributeNS(String namespaceURI, String
      qualifiedName, String value) throws DOMException;
    public void removeAttributeNS(String namespaceURI,
      String localName) throws DOMException;
    public Attr getAttributeNodeNS(String namespaceURI,
      String localName);
    public Attr setAttributeNodeNS(Attr newAttr) throws
      DOMException;
    public NodeList getElementsByTagNameNS(String
      namespaceURI, String localName);
    public boolean hasAttribute(String name);
    public boolean hasAttributeNS(String namespaceURI,
      String localName);
}
```

VB definition

```
' IXMLDOMElement
Property tagName As String ' read-only
Function getAttribute ( ByRef name As String ) As Variant
Sub setAttribute ( ByRef name As String, ByRef value As _
    Variant )
```

```
Sub removeAttribute ( ByRef name As String )
Function getAttributeNode ( ByRef name As String ) As _
    IXMLDOMAttribute
Function setAttributeNode ( ByRef DOMAttribute As _
    IXMLDOMAttribute ) As IXMLDOMAttribute
Function removeAttributeNode ( ByRef DOMAttribute As _
    IXMLDOMAttribute ) As IXMLDOMAttribute
Function getElementsByTagName ( ByRef tagName As String ) _
    As IXMLDOMNodeList
Sub normalize()
```

Member	Description
getTagName	Returns the nodeName property of the element. The value of this property is the same as that of the nodeName property of the org.w3c.dom.Node interface. Use of this method should be avoided when working with XML containing namespace information because the results are implementation dependent.
getAttribute	Returns the value of the attribute with a name that matches the supplied parameter. When two attributes share the same nodeName (but have different namespace URIs), the value returned is undefined. This method has been superseded by getAttributeNS.
setAttribute	Creates a new Attribute node with the specified name and value or overwrites an existing attribute with the specified name. This method has been superseded by setAttributeNS.
removeAttribute	Removes the attribute with the specified name. This method has been superseded by removeAttributeNS.
getAttributeNode	Returns the Attribute node with a name that matches the supplied parameter. When two attributes share the same nodeName (but have different namespace URIs) the value returned is undefined. This method has been superseded by getAttributeNodeNS.
setAttributeNode	Attaches the provided attribute to the element. If an attribute already exists on the element that has the same name as the attribute being added, then the old attribute is returned. Otherwise, the return value is null. This method has been superseded by setAttributeNodeNS.

DOM

Member	Description
removeAttributeNode	Removes the specified attribute node. The removed attribute is returned to the caller.
getElementsByTagName	Returns a list of all descendant Elements of this Element node with a nodeName property that matches the provided name. The string value "*" matches all Elements. The Elements are returned in document order.
getAttributeNS	Returns the value of the attribute with the local name and namespace URI that match the supplied parameters.
setAttributeNS	Creates a new Attribute node with the specified namespace URI, QName, and value or overwrites an existing attribute with the specified namespace URI and QName.
removeAttributeNS	Removes the attribute with the specified namespace URI and local name.
getAttributeNodeNS	Returns the Attribute node with the namespace URI and local name that matche the supplied parameters.
getElementsByTagNameNS	Returns a list of all descendant Elements of this Element node with a namespaceURI and localName properties that match the provided parameters. The string value "*" matches all Elements. The Elements are returned in document order.
hasAttribute	Returns true if an attribute with the specified name exists. When two attributes share the same node-Name (but have different namespace URIs), the value returned is undefined. This method has been superseded by hasAttributeNS.
hasAttributeNS	Returns true if an attribute with the specified namespace URI and local name exists; otherwise, returns false.

Examples

Add an attribute to an element

These examples check for the existence of a named attribute and, if the attribute does not exist, add such an attribute. The VB example uses a QName rather than a namespace name/local name pair because of the lack of support for NS methods in MSXML. Similarly, `createNode` is used rather than `setAttributeNS`.

Java

```java
void AttachAttributes ( Element e ) {
  if ( !e.hasAttributeNS ( "urn:example-
        org:weightsandmeasures", "units" ))
    e.setAttributeNS ( "urn:example-
        org:weightsandmeasures", "p:units", "inches" );
}
```

VB

```vb
Sub AttachAttributes ( ByRef e As IXMLDOMElement )
  If e.getAttributeNode ( "p:units" ) Is Nothing Then
    Dim doc As IXMLDOMDocument
    Set doc = e.ownerDocument
    Dim a As IXMLDOMAttribute
    Set a = doc.createNode ( NODE_ATTRIBUTE, "p:units", _
      "urn:example-org:weightsandmeasures" )
    a.value = "inches"
    e.setAttributeNode a
  End If
End Sub
```

7.2.10 Entity

The Entity interface represents an internal or external entity in an XML document.

DOM

Java definition

```java
package org.w3c.dom;

public interface Entity extends Node {
    public String getPublicId();
    public String getSystemId();
    public String getNotationName();
}
```

VB definition

```vb
' IXMLDOMEntity
Property publicId As Variant ' read-only
Property systemId As Variant ' read-only
```

```
Property notationName As String ' read-only
```

Member	Description
getPublicId publicId	Returns the public identifier of the entity, if any; otherwise, returns null.
getSystemId systemId	Returns the system identifier of the entity, if any; otherwise, returns null.
getNotationName notationName	Returns the notation name associated with an unparsed entity. If the entity is not an unparsed entity, then this method returns null.

7.2.11 EntityReference

The EntityReference interface is a signature interface (it adds no further methods to org.w3c.dom.Node). It is used to denote a node in the tree that is a reference to a general entity. The nodeName property contains the name of the entity to which this node is a reference.

7.2.12 NamedNodeMap

The NamedNodeMap interface models a set of named but unordered nodes in the DOM tree. Such nodes include Attribute nodes and Entity nodes.

Java definition

```
package org.w3c.dom;

public interface NamedNodeMap {
    public Node getNamedItem(String name);
    public Node setNamedItem(Node arg) throws DOMException;
    public Node removeNamedItem(String name) throws
        DOMException;
```

```
      public Node item(int index);
      public int getLength();
      public Node getNamedItemNS(String namespaceURI,
         String localName);
      public Node setNamedItemNS(Node arg) throws
         DOMException;
      public Node removeNamedItemNS(String namespaceURI,
      String localName) throws DOMException;
}
```

VB definition

```
' IXMLDOMNamedNodeMap
Function getNamedItem ( ByVal name As String ) As IXMLDOMNode
Function setNamedItem ( ByRef newItem As IXMLDOMNode ) As _
   IXMLDOMNode
Function removeNamedItem ( ByVal name As String ) As _
   IXMLDOMNode
Property item ( ByVal index As Long ) As IXMLDOMNode
   ' read-only
Property length As Long ' read-only
Function getQualifiedItem ( ByVal baseName As String, _
   ByVal namespaceURI As String ) As IXMLDOMNode
Function removeQualifiedItem ( ByVal baseName As String, _
   ByVal namespaceURI As String ) As IXMLDOMNode
Function nextNode() As IXMLDOMNode
Function reset()
Property _newEnum As IUnknown ' read-only
```

DOM

Member	Description
getNamedItem	Retrieves the node with the nodeName property that matches the specified name.
setNamedItem	Adds the specified node to the map. If a node with the same nodeName property as the added node exists in the map, the existing item is replaced. In this case the replaced node is returned; otherwise, null is returned.
removeNamedItem	Removes from the map the node with the nodeName property that matches the specified name. The removed node is returned.

Member	Description
item	Returns the node at the specified index. Returns null if the index specified equals or exceeds the number of nodes in the map.
getLength length	Returns the number of nodes in the map.
getNamedItemNS getQualifiedItem	Returns the node in the map with the specified namespaceURI and localName properties.
setNamedItemNS	Adds the specified node to the map. If a node with the same namespaceURI and localName properties as the added node exists in the map, the existing node is replaced. In this case, the replaced node is returned; otherwise, null is returned.
removeNamedItemNS removeQualifiedItem	Removes from the map the node with namespaceURI and localName properties that match the specified namespaceURI and Localname.

Examples

Adding an attribute to a NamedNodeMap

These examples show adding an Attribute node to the attributes collection of an element. Note that the Java example also creates a namespace declaration as an attribute in the http://www.w3.org/2000/xmlns/ namespace. MSXML automatically puts in namespace declarations as needed.

Java

```
void AddAttribute ( Element e ) {
   NamedNodeMap map = e.getAttributes();

   // Create units attribute in urn:example-org namespace
   and add to map
   Attr a = doc.createAttributeNS ( "urn:example-org",
      "pre:units" );
   a.setValue ( "inches" );
   map.setNamedItemNS ( a );

   // Create namespace declaration for urn:example-
   org:measurements and add to map
   a = doc.createAttributeNS (
      "http://www.w3.org/2000/xmlns/", "xmlns:pre" );
   a.setValue ( "urn:example-org" );
```

```
      map.setNamedItemNS ( a );
}
```

VB

```
Sub AddAttribute ( e As IXMLDOMElement )
  Dim map As IXMLDOMNamedNodeMap
  Set map = e.Attributes

  ' Create units attribute in urn:example-org:measurements
    namespace and add to map
  Dim a As IXMLDOMAttribute
  Set a = doc.createNode(NODE_ATTRIBUTE, "pre:units", _
    "urn:example-org")
  a.value = "inches"
  map.setNamedItem a

End Sub
```

7.2.13 Node

The Node interface is the base interface for all other interfaces in the DOM and provides access to generic node properties, traversal methods, and tree modification methods.

Java definition

```
package org.w3c.dom;

public interface Node {
    // NodeType
    public static final short ELEMENT_NODE              = 1;
    public static final short ATTRIBUTE_NODE            = 2;
    public static final short TEXT_NODE                 = 3;
    public static final short CDATA_SECTION_NODE        = 4;
    public static final short ENTITY_REFERENCE_NODE     = 5;
    public static final short ENTITY_NODE               = 6;
    public static final short PROCESSING_INSTRUCTION_
       NODE                                             = 7;
    public static final short COMMENT_NODE              = 8;
```

```
public static final short DOCUMENT_NODE              = 9;
public static final short DOCUMENT_TYPE_NODE          = 10;
public static final short DOCUMENT_FRAGMENT_NODE      = 11;
public static final short NOTATION_NODE               = 12;
public String getNodeName();
public String getNodeValue() throws DOMException;
public void setNodeValue(String nodeValue)
   throws DOMException;
public short getNodeType();
public Node getParentNode();
public NodeList getChildNodes();
public Node getFirstChild();
public Node getLastChild();
public Node getPreviousSibling();
public Node getNextSibling();
public NamedNodeMap getAttributes();
public Document getOwnerDocument();
public Node insertBefore(Node newChild, Node refChild)
   throws DOMException;
public Node replaceChild(Node newChild, Node oldChild)
   throws DOMException;
public Node removeChild(Node oldChild)
   throws DOMException;
public Node appendChild(Node newChild)
   throws DOMException;
public boolean hasChildNodes();
public Node cloneNode(boolean deep);
public void normalize();
public boolean isSupported(String feature, String
   version);
public String getNamespaceURI();
public String getPrefix();
public void setPrefix(String prefix)
   throws DOMException;
public String getLocalName();
public boolean hasAttributes();
}
```

VB definition

```
' IXMLDOMNode
Property nodeName As String ' read-only
Property nodeValue As String
Property nodeType As DOMNodeType ' read-only
Property parentNode As IXMLDOMNode ' read-only
Property childList As IXMLDOMNodeList ' read-only
Property firstChild As IXMLDOMNode ' read-only
Property lastChild As IXMLDOMNode ' read-only
Property previousSibling As IXMLDOMNode ' read-only
Property nextSibling As IXMLDOMNode ' read-only
Property attributes As IXMLDOMNamedNodeMap ' read-only
Function insertBefore ( ByRef newChild As IXMLDOMNode, _
    ByRef refChild As Variant ) As IXMLDOMNode
Function replaceChild ( ByRef newChild As IXMLDOMNode, _
    ByRef oldChild As IXMLDOMNode ) As IXMLDOMNode
Function removeChild ( ByRef childNode As IXMLDOMNode ) _
    As IXMLDOMNode
Function appendChild ( ByRef newChild As IXMLDOMNode ) _
    As IXMLDOMNode
Function hasChildNodes() As Boolean
Property ownerDocument As IXMLDOMDocument
Function cloneNode ( ByVal deep As Boolean ) As IXMLDOMNode
Property nodeTypeString As String ' read-only
Property text As String
Property specified As Boolean ' read-only
Property definition As IXMLDOMNode ' read-only
Property nodeTypeValue As Variant
Property dataType As String
Property xml As String ' read-only
Function transformNode ( ByRef stylesheet As IXMLDOMNode ) _
    As String
Function selectNodes ( ByVal queryString As String ) As _
    IXMLDOMNodeList
Function selectSingleNode ( ByVal queryString As String ) _
    As IXMLDOMNode
Property parsed As Boolean ' read-only
Property namespaceURI As String ' read-only
Property prefix As String ' read-only
Property baseName As String ' read-only
Function transformNodeToObject ( ByRef stylesheet As _
    IXMLDOMNode ) As Variant
```

Member	Description
getNodeName nodeName	Retrieves the name of the node. For Element and Attribute nodes, the name is the QName. For ProcessingInstruction nodes, the name is the target portion of the processing instruction. For Entity and EntityReference nodes, the name is the entity name. For Notation nodes, the name is the notation name. For Document nodes, the name is "#document". For Comment nodes, the name is "#comment". For Text nodes, the name is "#text". For CDATASection nodes, the name is "#cdata". For DocumentFragment nodes the name is #document-fragment. For DocumentType nodes the name is the tagname of the document element.
getNodeValue nodeValue	Retrieves the value of the node. For Attribute, CDATA, Comment, and Text nodes the value is the text of the node. For ProcessingInstruction nodes, the value is the data portion of the processing instruction. For all other node types the value is null.
setNodeValue nodeValue	Sets the value of the node. Only Attribute, Comment, CDATASection, ProcessingInstruction, and Text nodes can have their node value set.
getNodeType nodeType	Retrieves the type of the node.
getParentNode parentNode	Retrieves the parent node. For Attribute, Document and DocumentFragment nodes this property is null.
getChildNodes childList	Retrieves an ordered collection containing the children of the node. Only Attribute, Document, DocumentFragment, Element, and Entity nodes can have children.
getFirstChild firstChild	Retrieves the first child of the node.
getLastChild lastChild	Retrieves the last child of the node.
getPreviousSibling previousSibling	Retrieves the previous node in the tree whose parent is the same as that of the current node.
getNextSibling nextSibling	Retrieves the next node in the tree whose parent is the same as that of the current node.
getAttributes attributes	Retrieves an unordered collection containing the attributes of the node. Only element nodes can have attributes.
getOwnerDocument ownerDocument	Retrieves the owning document node.

Member	Description
insertBefore	Inserts a node into the children collection of the current node, immediately before the provided reference node. Returns the new node.
replaceChild	Replaces a node in the children collection of the current node. Returns the replaced node.
removeChild	Removes a node from the children collection of the current node. Returns the removed node.
appendChild	Appends a node to the children collection of the current node. Returns the appended node.
hasChildNodes	Returns true if the node has children; otherwise, returns false.
cloneNode	Creates and returns a copy of the current node. If the deep parameter is set to true, descendants are also copied.
normalize	Converts adjacent text node children into single text nodes.
isSupported	Returns true if the specified feature and version are supported; otherwise, returns false. Defined features include Core, XML, HTML, Views, StyleSheets, CSS, CSS2, Events, UIEvents, MouseEvents, MutationEvents, HTMLEvents, Range, and Traversal. Other specifications may define new features. Feature names are case sensitive. For DOM level 2, the version string for all features is "2.0."
getNamespaceURI	Returns the namespace URI of the node. Only element and attribute nodes have namespace URIs.
getPrefix	Returns the namespace prefix of the node. Only element and attribute nodes have namespace prefixes.
setPrefix	Sets the namespace prefix of the node. Only element and attribute nodes have namespace prefixes.
getLocalName	Returns the localname of the node. Only element and attribute nodes have local names.
hasAttributes	Returns true if the node has attributes; otherwise, returns false.

DOM

Examples

Traversing the tree

These examples show traversing a DOM tree depth first using the firstChild and nextSibling properties of the Node interface.

Java

```java
void TraverseTree ( Node n ) {
    // Process node ...

    // Recursively process first child...
    Node p = n.getFirstChild();

    if ( p != null )
        TraverseTree ( p );

    // ... and siblings
    p = n.getNextSibling();

    if ( p != null )
        TraverseTree ( p );
}
```

VB

```vb
Sub TraverseTree ( n As IXMLDOMNode )
  ' Process node ...

  ' Recursively process first child...
  Dim p As IXMLDOMNode
  Set p = n.firstChild

  If Not p Is Nothing Then
    TraverseTree p
  End If

  ' ... and siblings
  Set p = n.nextSibling

  If Not p Is Nothing Then
    TraverseTree p
  End If
End Sub
```

Adding nodes to the tree

These examples show removing, creating, and adding several nodes to a DOM tree using a combination of **removeChild**, **appendChild**, and **insertBefore**. Note that the Java example has to add explicitly an attribute representing the namespace declaration whereas MSXML automatically inserts it. The resulting tree could be serialized as follows:

```
<e:employees xmlns:e='urn:develop-com:employees'>
  <e:employee>Aaron</e:employee>
  <e:employee>Don</e:employee>
</e:employees>
```

Java

```
void CreateNodes ( Document doc ) {
  Element emps, emp1, emp2;
  Text t;

  // Remove current document element
  doc.removeChild ( doc.getDocumentElement());

  // Create document element
  emps = doc.createElementNS ( "urn:develop-com:employees",
    "e:employees" );
  doc.appendChild ( emps );

  // Create namespace declaration for urn:develop-
    com:employees and add to document element
  emps.setAttributeNS ( "http://www.w3.org/2000/xmlns/",
    "xmlns:e", "urn:develop-com:employees" );

  // Create first child element and append
  emp1 = doc.createElementNS ( "urn:develop-com:employees",
    "e:employee" );
  t = doc.createTextNode ( "Don" );
  emp1.appendChild ( t );
  emps.appendChild ( emp1 );

  // Create second child element and insert before first
```

DOM

```
  emp2 = doc.createElementNS ( "urn:develop-com:employees",
    "e:employee" );
  t = doc.createTextNode ( "Aaron" );
  emp2.appendChild ( t );
  emps.insertBefore ( emp2, emp1 );
}
```

VB

```
Sub CreateNodes ( doc As IXMLDOMDocument )
  Dim emps As IXMLDOMElement
  Dim emp1 As IXMLDOMElement
  Dim emp2 As IXMLDOMElement
  Dim t As IXMLDOMText

  ' Remove current document element
  doc.removeChild doc.documentElement

  ' Create document element
  Set emps = doc.createNode ( NODE_ELEMENT, _
    "e:employees", "urn:develop-com:employees" )
  doc.appendChild emps

  ' Create first child element and append
  Set emp1 = doc.createNode ( NODE_ELEMENT, _
    "e:employee", "urn:develop-com:employees" )
  Set t = doc.createTextNode ( "Don" )
  emp1.appendChild t
  emps.appendChild emp1

  ' Create second child element and insert before first
  Set emp2 = doc.createNode ( NODE_ELEMENT, _
    "e:employee", "urn:develop-com:employees" )
  Set t = doc.createTextNode ( "Aaron" )
  emp2.appendChild t
  emps.insertBefore emp2, emp1
End Sub
```

7.2.14 NodeList

The NodeList interface is used to model an ordered collection of nodes.

Java definition

```
package org.w3c.dom;

public interface NodeList {
  public Node item(int index);
  public int getLength();
}
```

VB definition

```
' IXMLDOMNodeList
Property item As IXMLDOMNode ' read-only
Property length As Long ' read-only
Function nextNode() As IXMLDOMNode
Sub reset()
Property _newEnum As IUnknown ' read-only
```

Member	Description
item	Returns the node at the specified index. Indices are zero based.
getLength	Returns the number of nodes in the collection.

Examples

Traversing the tree

These examples show a method, TraverseTree, traversing a DOM tree depth first using the NodeList interface retrieved from the childNodes collection.

Java

```
void TraverseTree ( Node n ) {
  // Process node ...

  // Recursively process children
  NodeList nl = n.getChildNodes();

  for(int i=0;i<nl.getLength();i++)
    TraverseTree ( nl.item ( i ));
}
```

DOM

VB

```vb
Sub TraverseTree ( n As IXMLDOMNode )
  ' Process node ...

  ' Recursively process children
  Dim nl As IXMLDOMNodeList
  Set nl = n.childNodes
  Dim i As Integer
  For i = 0 To nl.length - 1
    TraverseTree nl.Item ( i )
  Next i
End Sub

Sub TraverseTreeForEach ( n As IXMLDOMNode )
  ' Process node ...

  ' Recursively process children
  Dim nl As IXMLDOMNodeList
  Set nl = n.childNodes
  Dim x As IXMLDOMNode

  If nl.length > 0 Then
    For Each x In nl
      TraverseTreeForEach x
    Next x
  End If
End Sub

Sub TraverseTreeNextNode ( n As IXMLDOMNode )
  ' Process node ...

  ' Recursively process children
  Dim nl As IXMLDOMNodeList
  Set nl = n.childNodes
  Dim x As IXMLDOMNode
  Set x = nl.nextNode

  While Not x Is Nothing
    TraverseTreeNextNode x
    Set x = nl.nextNode
  Wend
End Sub
```

7.2.15 Notation

The Notation interface models a notation declaration in a DTD.

Java definition

```
package org.w3c.dom;

public interface Notation extends Node {
    public String getPublicId();
    public String getSystemId();
}
```

VB definition

```
' IXMLDOMNotation
Property publicId As Varint ' read-only
Property systemId As Variant ' read-only
```

Member	Description
getPublicId	Returns the public identifier of the notation.
getSystemId	Returns the system identifier of the notation.

7.2.16 ProcessingInstruction

The ProcessingInstruction interface models processing instructions.

Java definition

```
package org.w3c.dom;

public interface ProcessingInstruction extends Node {
    public String getTarget();
    public String getData();
    public void setData(String data) throws DOMException;
}
```

VB definition

```
' IXMLDOMProcessingInstruction
Property target As String ' read-only
Property data As String
```

Member	Description
getTarget	Returns the target of the processing instruction.
getData	Returns the data of the processing instruction.
setData	Sets the data of the processing instruction to the specified string.

7.2.17 Text

The Text interface models text nodes.

Java definition

```
package org.w3c.dom;

public interface Text extends CharacterData {
    public Text splitText(int offset) throws DOMException;
}
```

VB definition

```
' IXMLDOMText
Function splitText ( ByVal offset As Long ) As IXMLDOMText
```

Member	Description
splitText	Splits the text node into two adjacent text nodes.

7.3 References

LeHors, Arnaud, et al., editors. *Document Object Model (DOM) Level 2 Core Specification*.
Available at *http://www.w3.org/TR/DOM-Level-2-Core/*.   1999

Chapter 8
XML Schema Datatypes

XML Schema provides a set of built-in datatypes. Some of these types are primitives, described in the specification, whereas others are derived types described in a schema. Both primitive and derived types are available to schema authors to use as is or to derive new types from.

This chapter provides a reference for the parts of the schema language related to defining simple types. For reasons of brevity, not all examples are full schemas. In all examples, the xs namespace prefix is mapped to the namespace name of the XML Schema language, http://www.w3.org/2001/XMLSchema, even if no such namespace declaration appears in the example. Similarly, the tns namespace prefix is mapped to the same namespace name as the targetNamespace attribute of the schema element even if that element is not shown.

8.1 Datatype grouping

The following group the built-in datatypes according to various criteria.

Numeric types

Type	Description
decimal	An arbitrary-precision decimal number
integer	An arbitrary-length integer
negativeInteger	An arbitrary-length negative integer
nonNegativeInteger	An arbitrary-length integer with a value of zero or more
positiveInteger	An arbitrary-length positive integer
nonPositiveInteger	An arbitrary-length integer with a value of zero or less
long	A 64-bit signed integer
int	A 32-bit signed integer
short	A 16-bit signed integer
byte	An 8-bit signed integer

Schema I

Type	Description
unsignedLong	A 64-bit unsigned integer
unsignedShort	A 16-bit unsigned integer
unsignedInt	A 32-bit unsigned integer
unsignedByte	An 8-bit unsigned number
float	A single-precision floating point number
double	A double-precision floating point number

Date and time types

Type	Description
date	A Gregorian calendar date
dateTime	An instant in time
duration	A duration in time
gDay	A Gregorian day-long monthly recurring period
gMonth	A Gregorian month
gMonthDay	A Gregorian day-long annually recurring period
gYear	A Gregorian calendar year
gYearMonth	A Gregorian month-long annually recurring period
time	An instant in time

XML 1.0 types

Type	Description
ID	An XML 1.0 ID
IDREF	An XML 1.0 IDREF
IDREFS	A list of XML 1.0 IDREF instances
ENTITY	An XML 1.0 ENTITY
ENTITIES	A list of XML 1.0 ENTITY instances
NMTOKEN	An XML 1.0 NMTOKEN
NMTOKENS	A list of XML 1.0 NMTOKEN instances
NOTATION	An XML 1.0 NOTATION

Name and string types

Type	Description
string	A general string type
normalizedString	A string with normalized whitespace
token	A string with normalized whitespace and with preceding and trailing whitespace removed
QName	An XML Name
Name	An XML Name
NCName	An XML noncolonized name

8.2 Datatypes

Datatypes in the XML Schema specification are defined in terms of a value space, the set of values the type can hold, and a lexical space; in other words, how those values are represented as characters in XML. Some datatypes have multiple lexical representations whereas others only have one. Types that have multiple lexical representations also have a canonical representation of the lexical space for use in situations in which canonicalization is important, such as digital signature scenarios.

In this section the built-in datatypes are listed in alphabetical order, each with a description, a base type (if the type is a derived type), whether the type is atomic or list based, notes about the value and lexical spaces of the type, canonical representation, list of facets that are applicable to the type, built-in types that are derived from the type, and examples.

Figure 8–1 shows the type hierarchy for the built-in types derived from decimal while Figure 8–2 shows the built-in types derived from string. Built-in types not shown in either figure do not serve as the base type for any other built-in type and are derived from anySimpleType—an abstract type that serves as the root of the simple type hierarchy.

8.2.1 anyURI

The anyURI datatype represents a URI reference according to RFC 2396 and RFC 2732. (See References at the end of the chapter.)

Value space: Any absolute or relative URI reference including those with a fragment identifier.

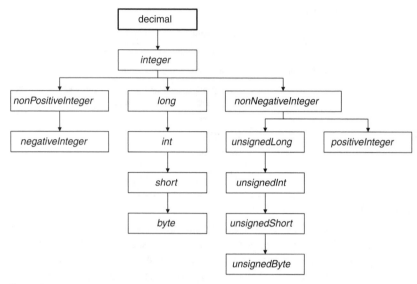

Figure 8-1   Type hierarchy for numerical types.

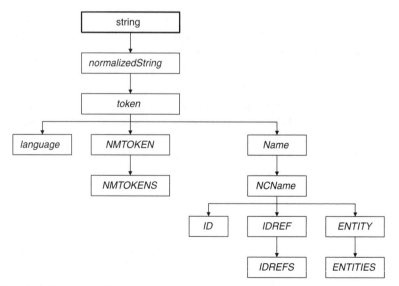

Figure 8-2   Type hierarchy for string types.

Lexical space: The set of strings matching the URI reference production of RFC 2396, as amended by RFC 2732.

Applicable facets: `enumeration`, `length`, `maxLength`, `minLength`, `pattern`, and `whiteSpace`.

Examples

Absolute URI references

```
<a href='http://example.org/People' />
<uri>http://example.org/People/people.xml#xpointer(//
    Person[@name='Martin'])</uri>
<uri>uuid:f6cbe76a-cf75-4ce2-af2b-214e64acca75</uri>
```

Various absolute URI references as element and attribute content

Relative URI references

```
<a href='xml/xmlfiles/myfile.xml' />
<uri>urn:com-develop-demos</uri>
<music src='/music/Bowie/fashion.mp3' />
<uri>People/people.xml#xpointer(//
    Person[@name='Martin'])</uri>
```

Various relative URI references as element and attribute content

---

8.2.2 base64Binary

The `base64Binary` datatype represents base64-encoded binary data.

Value space: Any finite sequence of binary octets.

Lexical space: Any finite sequence of binary octets encoded according to the Base64 Content-Transfer-Encoding per RFC 2045.

Applicable facets: `enumeration`, `length`, `maxLength`, `minLength`, `pattern` and `whiteSpace`.

Example

base64 encoded data

```
<data>AQIDBQcJCw0REwAA</data>
```

A prime number sequence for the numbers 1, 2, 3, 5, 7, 9, 11, 13, 17, and 19 encoded in base64.

8.2.3 boolean

The `boolean` datatype represents two-value logic.

Value space: true, false.

Lexical space: true, false, 1, 0 (where 1 and 0 correspond to true and false respectively).

Canonical representation: true, false.

Applicable facets: `pattern` and `whiteSpace`.

Examples

An attribute

```
<row inserted='true' />
```

A `boolean` attribute set to `true`.

An element

```
<checked>0</checked>
```

A `boolean` element set to `false`.

8.2.4 byte

The `byte` datatype represents the range of integer values that can be stored in an 8-bit signed field.

Base type: short.

Value space: +127 to –128.

Lexical space: A finite sequence of decimal digits with an optional leading sign character (+ or –). The default sign is positive. Leading zeros may appear.

Canonical representation: Leading zeros are prohibited, as is the preceding + sign.

Applicable facets: enumeration, fractionDigits, maxExclusive, maxInclusive, minExclusive, minInclusive, pattern, totalDigits, and whiteSpace.

Examples

byte values

```
<num>+12</num>
<num>-127</num>
<num>0000056</num>
<num>0</num>
```

Various byte values as element content.

Canonical byte values

```
<num>12</num>
<num>-127</num>
<num>56</num>
<num>0</num>
```

Canonical representation of the byte values in the preceding example.

8.2.5 date

The date datatype represents a Gregorian calendar date.

Value space: Any date.

Lexical space: CCYY-MM-DD where CC, YY, MM, and DD correspond to the century, year, month, and day respectively. Additional digits may appear to the left of CC to indicate years greater than 9999. An optional following Z indicates that the date is specified in Coordinated Universal Time. Alternatively, a time zone may be indicated by providing a following + or – sign followed by the offset from UTC as hh:mm where hh and mm correspond to hours and minutes respectively. The mm and the preceding colon may be omitted if the minutes are zero.

Applicable facets: enumeration, maxExclusive, maxInclusive, minExclusive, minInclusive, pattern, and whiteSpace.

Examples

A date

```
<date>2001-02-13</date>
```

February 13th 2001

A date with negative time zone modifier

```
<date>2001-02-13-05:00</date>
```

February 13th 2001, Eastern Standard Time

A date with positive time zone modifier

```
<date>2001-02-13+01:00</date>
```

February 13th 2001, Central European Time

8.2.6 dateTime

The dateTime datatype represents an instant in time as a combination of Gregorian date and time-of-day values.

Value space: Any instant in time as a combination of Gregorian date and time-of-day values.

Lexical space: CCYY-MM-DDThh:mm:ss.sss where T is the date/time separator and CC, YY, MM, DD, hh, mm, and ss.sss correspond to the century, year, month, day, hour, minute, and second (with fractions) respectively. Additional digits may appear to the left of CC to indicate years greater than 9999. A preceding – sign is allowed. An optional following Z indicates the dateTime is specified in Coordinated Universal Time. Alternatively, a time zone may be indicated by providing a following + or – sign followed by the offset from UTC as hh:mm where hh and mm correspond to hours and minutes respectively. The mm and the preceding colon may be omitted if the minutes are zero.

Canonical representation: The time zone must be omitted or must be UTC (as indicated by the following Z).

Applicable facets: enumeration, maxExclusive, maxInclusive, minExclusive, minInclusive, pattern, and whiteSpace.

Examples

An instant in time

```
<instant>2001-02-13T22:20:00</instant>
```

10:20pm on February 13th 2001

An instant in time with negative time zone modifier

```
<instant>2001-02-13T17:20:00-05:00</instant>
```

5:20pm on February 13th 2001, Eastern Standard Time

An instant in time with positive time zone modifier

```
<instant>2001-02-13T23:20:00+01:00</instant>
```

11:20pm on February 13th 2001, Central European Time

8.2.7 decimal

The decimal datatype represents arbitrary precision decimal numbers.

Value space: The infinite set of all decimal numbers.

Lexical space: A finite sequence of decimal digits with a period as the decimal point indicator and an optional leading sign character (+ or –). The default sign is positive. Leading and trailing zeros may appear. If the digits following the decimal point are all zero, those digits and the decimal point may be omitted.

Canonical representation: The decimal point is required and there must be at least one digit to the left and to the right of the decimal point. Otherwise, preceding or trailing zeros are prohibited, as is the preceding + sign.

Applicable facets: enumeration, fractionDigits, maxExclusive, maxInclusive, minExclusive, minInclusive, pattern, totalDigits, and whiteSpace.

Derived type: integer.

Schema I

Examples

decimal values

```
<num>123456</num>
<num>1.23456</num>
<num>+12.3456</num>
<num>0000123456.0000</num>
<num>0012.345600</num>
<num>-123456</num>
<num>0</num>
```

Various decimal values as element content

Canonical decimal values

```
<num>123456.0</num>
<num>1.23456</num>
<num>12.3456</num>
<num>123456.0</num>
<num>12.3456</num>
<num>-123456.0</num>
<num>0.0</num>
```

Canonical representation of the decimal values in the previous example.

8.2.8 double

The double datatype represents IEEE double-precision 64-bit floating point numbers (IEEE 754-1985).

Value space: $+2^{53} \times 2^{970}$ to $-2^{53} \times 2^{970}$. Smallest representable value is $\pm 1 \times 2^{-1075}$. Other values in value space are, in value order, NaN, positive infinity, positive zero, negative zero, negative infinity.

Lexical space: A decimal mantissa optionally followed by 'E' or 'e' followed by an integer exponent. The lexical representation of the mantissa follows the rules for the decimal datatype. The lexical representation of the exponent follows the rules for the integer datatype. The other values in the value space are represented as NaN, INF, 0, -0, -INF.

Canonical representation: In the mantissa the decimal point is required and there must be exactly one digit to the left and at least one digit to the right of the decimal point. Otherwise, preceding and trailing zeros are prohibited in the mantissa, as is the preceding + sign. The exponent, if any, must be indicated by 'E'.

Applicable facets: enumeration, maxExclusive, maxInclusive, minExclusive, minInclusive, pattern, and whiteSpace.

Examples

double values

```
<num>123456</num>
<num>1.23456E5</num>
<num>+12.3456E72</num>
<num>0000123456.0000</num>
<num>0012.345600e-10</num>
<num>-123456E-5</num>
<num>0</num>
```

Various **double** values as element content

Canonical double values

```
<num>1.23456E5</num>
<num>1.23456E5</num>
<num>1.23456E73</num>
<num>1.23456E5</num>
<num>1.23456E-9</num>
<num>-1.23456</num>
<num>0</num>
```

Canonical representation of the **double** values in the previous example

---

8.2.9 duration

The **duration** datatype represents a duration of time in Gregorian years, months, days, hours, minutes, and seconds according to ISO 8601. (See Reference section at end of chapter.)

Value space: Any duration of time per ISO 8601.

Lexical space: PnYnMnDTnHnMnS according to ISO 8601. T is the date/ time separator and nY, nM, nD, nH, nM, and nS correspond to the number of years, months, days, hours, minutes, and seconds respectively. The lowest order unit may use an arbitrary decimal for n whereas all higher order units must use an arbitrary integer for n. Any unit that has zero as its value may be omitted. If hour, minute, and seconds are omitted, the time separator, T, must be omitted. The P and at least one unit must always be present.

Applicable facets: enumeration, maxExclusive, maxInclusive, minExclusive, minInclusive, pattern, and whiteSpace.

Examples

A *duration* with days as the smallest unit

```
<duration>P1Y2M4D</duration>
<duration>P1Y2M4DT0H0M0S</duration>
```

One year, two months, four days

A *duration* with hours as the largest unit

```
<duration>P0Y0M0DT1H2M4S</duration>
<duration>PT1H2M4S</duration>
```

One hour, two minutes, four seconds

A *duration* with various units

```
<duration>P1M2DT5M</duration>
<duration>P0Y1M2DT0H5M0S</duration>
```

One month, two days, five minutes

8.2.10 ENTITIES

The ENTITIES datatype represents the XML 1.0 ENTITIES type, a list of ENTITY names separated by whitespace. This type should only be used for attribute values. A given ENTITY value in the list must match the name of an unparsed entity declared elsewhere in the XML document.

Base type: ENTITY

Derived by: list

Value space: The set of finite, nonzero-length sequences of ENTITY values that have been used in an XML document.

Lexical space: The set of whitespace-separated lists of ENTITY values that have been used in an XML document.

Applicable facets: `enumeration`, `length`, `maxLength`, `minLength`, and `whiteSpace`.

Example

ENTITIES attributes

```
<reference sound='bgsound fgsound' />
<reference pic='mymugshot carpic flower' />
<reference data='mystuff yourstuff somestuff' />
```

ENTITIES attributes on various elements

8.2.11 ENTITY

The ENTITY datatype represents an XML 1.0 ENTITY type. This type should only be used for attribute values. A given ENTITY value must match the name of an unparsed entity declared elsewhere in the XML document.

Base type: NCName.

Value space: All strings that match the NCName production of Namespaces in XML and have been declared as an unparsed entity elsewhere in the XML document.

Lexical space: All strings that match the NCName production of namespaces in XML.

Applicable facets: `enumeration`, `length`, `maxLength`, `minLength`, `pattern`, and `whiteSpace`.

Derived type: ENTITIES.

Schema I

Example

ENTITY attributes

```
<reference sound='bgsound' />
<reference pic='mymugshot' />
<reference data='mystuff' />
```

ENTITY attributes that refer to unparsed entities

8.2.12 float

The float datatype represents IEEE single-precision 32-bit floating point numbers (IEEE 754-1985).

Value space: $+2^{24}$ x 2^{104} to -2^{24} x 2^{104}. Smallest representable value is ± 1 x 2^{-149}. Other values in value space are in value order, NaN, positive infinity, positive zero, negative zero, negative infinity.

Lexical space: A decimal mantissa optionally followed by 'E' or 'e' followed by an integer exponent. The lexical representation of the mantissa follows the rules for the decimal datatype. The lexical representation of the exponent follows the rules for the integer datatype. The other values in the value space are represented as NaN, INF, 0, -0, -INF.

Canonical representation: In the mantissa the decimal point is required and there must be exactly one digit to the left and at least one digit to the right of the decimal point. Otherwise, preceding and trailing zeros are prohibited in the mantissa, as is the preceding + sign. The exponent, if any, must be indicated by 'E'.

Applicable facets: enumeration, maxExclusive, maxInclusive, minExclusive, minInclusive, pattern, and whiteSpace.

Examples

float values

```
<num>123456</num>
<num>1.23456E5</num>
<num>+12.3456E4</num>
<num>0000123456.0000</num>
<num>0012.345600e-10</num>
```

```
<num>-123456E-5</num>
<num>0</num>
```

Various float values as element content

Canonical float values

```
<num>1.23456E5</num>
<num>1.23456E5</num>
<num>1.23456E5</num>
<num>1.23456E5</num>
<num>1.23456E-9</num>
<num>-1.23456</num>
<num>0</num>
```

Canonical representation of the float values in the preceding example

8.2.13 gDay

The gDay datatype represents a Gregorian day that recurs, specifically a one-day-long, monthly recurring period.

Value space: Any day-long, monthly recurring period.

Lexical space: ---DD where DD corresponds to the day. An optional following Z indicates the gDay is specified in Coordinated Universal Time. Alternatively a time zone may be indicated by providing a following + or − sign followed by the offset from UTC as hh:mm where hh and mm correspond to hours and minutes respectively. The mm and the preceding colon may be omitted if the minutes are zero.

Applicable facets: enumeration, maxExclusive, maxInclusive, minExclusive, minInclusive, pattern, and whiteSpace.

Example

A recurring Gregorian day

```
<day>---13</day>
```

13th of every month

8.2.14 gMonth

The gMonth datatype represents a Gregorian month that recurs every year.

Value space: Any month-long, annually recurring period.

Lexical space: --MM-- where MM corresponds to the month. An optional following Z indicates the gMonth is specified in Coordinated Universal Time. Alternatively a time zone may be indicated by providing a following + or – sign followed by the offset from UTC as hh:mm where **hh** and **mm** correspond to hours and minutes respectively. The mm and the preceding colon may be omitted if the minutes are zero.

Applicable facets: enumeration, maxExclusive, maxInclusive, minExclusive, minInclusive, pattern, and whiteSpace.

Examples

A recurring Gregorian month

```
<monthDay>--02--</monthDay>
```

February

A recurring Gregorian month with a negative time zone modifier

```
<monthDay>--02---05:00</monthDay>
```

February, Eastern Standard Time

A recurring Gregorian month with a positive time zone modifier

```
<monthDay>--02--+01:00</monthDay>
```

February, Central European Time

8.2.15 gMonthDay

The gMonthDay datatype represents a Gregorian date that recurs, specifically, a day of the year.

Value space: Any day-long, annually recurring period.

Lexical space: --MM-DD where MM and DD correspond to the month and day respectively. An optional following Z indicates that the gMonthDay is specified in Coordinated Universal Time. Alternatively a time zone may be indicated by providing a following + or – sign followed by the offset from UTC as hh:mm where **hh** and **mm** correspond to hours and minutes respectively. The mm and the preceding colon may be omitted if the minutes are zero.

Applicable facets: enumeration, maxExclusive, maxInclusive, minExclusive, minInclusive, pattern, and whiteSpace.

Examples
A recurring Gregorian date

```
<monthDay>--02-13</monthDay>
```

February 13th

A recurring Gregorian date with a negative time zone modifier

```
<monthDay>--02-13-05:00</monthDay>
```

February 13th, Eastern Standard Time

A recurring Gregorian date with a positive time zone modifier

```
<monthDay>--02-13+01:00</monthDay>
```

February 13th, Central European Time

8.2.16 gYear

The gYear datatype represents a Gregorian calendar year.

Value space: Any Gregorian calendar year.

Lexical space: CCYY where CC and YY correspond to the century and year respectively. Additional digits may appear to the left of CC to indicate years greater than 9999. A preceding – sign is allowed.

Applicable facets: enumeration, maxExclusive, maxInclusive, minExclusive, minInclusive, pattern, and whiteSpace.

Example

A Gregorian year

```
<year>2001</year>
```

The year 2001.

8.2.17 gYearMonth

The gYearMonth datatype represents a particular Gregorian month in a particular Gregorian year.

Value space: Gregorian calendar months; any month-long nonrecurring period.

Lexical space: CCYY–MM where CC, YY, and MM correspond to century, year, and month respectively. An optional following Z indicates that the gYearMonth is specified in Coordinated Universal Time. Alternatively, a time zone may be indicated by providing a following + or – sign followed by the offset from UTC as hh:mm where hh and mm correspond to hours and minutes respectively. The mm and the preceding colon may be omitted if the minutes are zero.

Applicable facets: enumeration, maxExclusive, maxInclusive, minExclusive, minInclusive, pattern, and whiteSpace.

Examples

A Gregorian calendar month

```
<month>2001-02</month>
```

February 2001

A Gregorian calendar month with a negative time zone modifier

```
<month>2001-02-05:00</month>
```

February 2001, Eastern Standard Time

A Gregorian calendar month with a positive time zone modifier

```
<month>2001-02+01:00</month>
```

February 2001, Central European Time

8.2.18 hexBinary

The hexBinary datatype represents hex-encoded binary data.

Value space: Any finite sequence of binary octets.

Lexical space: Any finite sequence of binary octets where each octet is encoded using two hexadecimal digits.

Applicable facets: enumeration, length, maxLength, minLength, pattern, and whiteSpace.

Example

Hex-encoded data

```
<data>0102030507090B0D1113</data>
```

A prime number sequence for the numbers 1, 2, 3, 5, 7, 9, 11, 13, 17, and 19.

8.2.19 ID

The ID datatype represents the XML 1.0 ID type. This type should only be used for attribute values. A given ID value can only appear once in a given XML document.

Base type: NCName.

Value space: All strings that match the NCName production of namespaces in XML.

Lexical space: As value space.

Applicable facets: enumeration, length, maxLength, minLength, pattern, and whiteSpace.

Example

ID attributes

```
<name id='id1' />
<name id='apple' />
<name id='x1' />
```

ID attributes on various elements

Schema I

8.2.20 IDREF

The IDREF datatype represents an XML 1.0 IDREF type. This type should only be used for attribute values. A given IDREF value must match an ID value elsewhere in the XML document.

Base type: NCName

Value space: All strings that match the NCName production of namespaces in XML.

Lexical space: As value space.

Applicable facets: enumeration, length, maxLength, minLength, pattern, and whiteSpace.

Derived type: IDREFS.

Examples

IDREF attributes

```
<reference ref='id1' />
<reference ref='x1' />
<reference ref='apple' />
```

IDREF attributes on various elements

8.2.21 IDREFS

The IDREFS datatype represents the XML 1.0 IDREFS type—a list of ID values separated by whitespace. This type should only be used for attribute values. A given token in an IDREFS value must match an ID value elsewhere in the XML document.

Base type: IDREF.

Value space: Set of finite, nonzero-length sequences of ID values that have been used in an XML document.

Lexical space: The set of whitespace-separated lists of ID values that have been used in an XML document.

Applicable facets: enumeration, length, maxLength, minLength, and whiteSpace.

Example

IDREFS attributes

```
<references ref='id1 id3 id5 ' />
<references ref='x1 x2 x3' />
<references ref='apple orange pear' />
```

IDREFS attributes on various elements

8.2.22 int

The int datatype represents the range of integer values that can be stored in a 32-bit signed field.

Base type: long.

Value space: +2,147,483,647 to –2,147,483,648.

Lexical space: A finite sequence of decimal digits with an optional leading sign character (+ or –). The default sign is positive. Leading zeros may appear.

Canonical representation: Leading zeros are prohibited, as is the preceding + sign.

Applicable facets: enumeration, fractionDigits, maxExclusive, maxInclusive, minExclusive, minInclusive, pattern, totalDigits, and whiteSpace.

Derived type: short.

Examples

int values

```
<num>1234567890</num>
<num>42</num>
<num>+12</num>
<num>-273</num>
<num>0000056</num>
<num>0</num>
```

Various int values as element content

Canonical int values

```
<num>1234567890</num>
<num>42</num>
<num>12</num>
<num>-273</num>
<num>56</num>
<num>0</num>
```

Canonical representation of the int values in the preceding example

---

8.2.23 integer

The integer datatype represents arbitrary integer values.

Base type: decimal.

Value space: The infinite set of all integers.

Lexical space: A finite sequence of decimal digits with an optional leading sign character (+ or −). The default sign is positive. Leading zeros may appear.

Canonical representation: Leading zeros are prohibited, as is the preceding + sign.

Applicable facets: enumeration, fractionDigits, maxExclusive, maxInclusive, minExclusive, minInclusive, pattern, totalDigits, and whiteSpace.

Derived types: long, nonNegativeInteger, and nonPositiveInteger.

Examples

integer values

```
<num>123456</num>
<num>42</num>
<num>+12</num>
<num>-273</num>
<num>0000056</num>
<num>0</num>
```

Various integer values as element content

Canonical integer values

```
<num>123456</num>
<num>42</num>
<num>12</num>
<num>-273</num>
<num>56</num>
<num>0</num>
```

Canonical representation of the integer values in the previous example

8.2.24 language

The language datatype represents natural language identifiers according to RFC 1766.

Base type: token.

Value space: The set of all strings that are language identifiers according to Section 2.12 of XML 1.0 Recommendation (second edition).

Lexical space: As value space.

Applicable facets: enumeration, length, maxLength, minLength, pattern, and whiteSpace.

Example

language identifier attributes

```
<text xml:lang='en'>a man a plan a canal panama</text>
<text xml:lang='en-GB'>Do me a favour!</text>
<text xml:lang='en-US'>Do me a favor</text>
<town xml:lang='de'>Unterschleißheim</town>
<language xml:lang='fr'>Français</language>
<language xml:lang='es'>Español</language>
```

Several language identifiers in attribute values

Schema I

8.2.25 long

The long datatype represents the range of integer values that can be stored in a 64-bit signed field.

Base type: integer.

Value space: +9,223,372,036,854,775,807 to −9,223,372,036,854,775,808.

Lexical space: A finite sequence of decimal digits with an optional leading sign character (+ or −). The default sign is positive. Leading zeros may appear.

Canonical representation: Leading zeros are prohibited, as is the preceding + sign.

Applicable facets: enumeration, fractionDigits, maxExclusive, maxInclusive, minExclusive, minInclusive, pattern, totalDigits, and whiteSpace.

Derived type: int.

Examples

long values

```
<num>1000000000000</num>
<num>1234567890</num>
<num>42</num>
<num>+12</num>
<num>-273</num>
<num>0000056</num>
<num>0</num>
```

Various long values as element content

Canonical long values

```
<num>1000000000000</num>
<num>1234567890</num>
<num>42</num>
<num>12</num>
<num>-273</num>
<num>56</num>
<num>0</num>
```

Canonical representation of the long values in the previous example

8.2.26 Name

The Name datatype represents XML Names, typically used for names of elements and attributes.

Base type: token.

Value space: The set of all strings that match the Name production in XML 1.0 Recommendation (second edition).

Lexical space: As value space.

Applicable facets: enumeration, length, maxLength, minLength, pattern, and whiteSpace.

Derived type: NCName.

Example

XML Names

```
<name val='Person'/>
<name val='age'/>
<name val='height.units'/>
<name val='_uuidof'/>
<name val='www.develop.com'/>
<name val='Chumley-Warner'/>
```

Various XML Names as attribute values

8.2.27 NCName

The NCName datatype represents XML noncolonized names, typically used for the local names of namespace-qualified elements and attributes; that is, the part after the prefix and the colon.

Base type: Name.

Value space: The set of all strings that match NCName production in XML 1.0 Recommendation (second edition).

Lexical space: As value space.

Applicable facets: enumeration, length, maxLength, minLength, pattern, and whiteSpace.

Derived types: ENTITY, ID, and IDREF.

Example

XML NCNames

```
<name val='Person'/>
<name val='age'/>
<name val='height.units'/>
<name val='_uuidof'/>
<name val='www.develop.com'/>
<name val='Chumley-Warner'/>
```

Various XML NCNames as attribute values

8.2.28 negativeInteger

The negativeInteger datatype represents integer values of −1 or less.

Base type: nonPositiveInteger.

Value space: The infinite set of all integers with values of −1 or less.

Lexical space: A finite sequence of decimal digits with a preceding minus sign character (-). Leading zeros may appear.

Canonical representation: Leading zeros are prohibited.

Applicable facets: enumeration, fractionDigits, maxExclusive, maxInclusive, minExclusive, minInclusive, pattern, totalDigits, and whiteSpace.

Derived type: negativeInteger.

Examples

negativeInteger values

```
<num>-42</num>
<num>-273</num>
<num>-0000056</num>
```

Various negativeInteger values as element content

Canonical negativeInteger values

```
<num>-42</num>
<num>-273</num>
<num>-56</num>
```

Canonical representation of the negativeInteger values in the preceding example

---

8.2.29 NMTOKEN

The NMTOKEN datatype represents the XML 1.0 NMTOKEN type. This type should only be used for attribute values.

Base type: token.

Value space: The set of strings that match NMTOKEN production in *XML 1.0 Recommendation* (second edition).

Lexical space: As value space.

Applicable facets: enumeration, length, maxLength, minLength, pattern, and whiteSpace.

Derived type: NMTOKENS.

Example

NMTOKEN attributes

```
<stuff name='hayley' />
<stuff name='porsche' />
<stuff name='.com' />
<stuff name='Name_With_Underscores' />
```

NMTOKEN as attribute values

8.2.30 NMTOKENS

The NMTOKENS datatype represents the XML 1.0 NMTOKENS type, a list of NMTOKEN values separated by whitespace. This type should only be used for attribute values.

Base type: NMTOKEN.

Derived by: List.

Value space: The set of finite, nonzero-length sequences of NMTOKEN values

Lexical space: The set of whitespace-separated lists of NMTOKEN values.

Applicable facets: enumeration, length, maxLength, minLength, and whiteSpace.

Example

NMTOKENS attributes

```
<stuff name='hayley barbara sarah' />
<stuff name='porsche bmw audi volkswagen' />
<stuff name='.com .net .org .edu' />
<stuff name='Name_With_Underscores Another_Name' />
```

NMTOKENS as attribute values

8.2.31 nonNegativeInteger

The nonNegativeInteger datatype represents the integer values zero or more.

Base type: integer.

Value space: The infinite set of all integers with values of zero or more.

Lexical space: A finite sequence of decimal digits with an optional preceding plus sign character (+). Leading zeros may appear.

Canonical representation: Leading zeros are prohibited, as is the preceding + sign.

Applicable facets: enumeration, fractionDigits, maxExclusive, maxInclusive, minExclusive, minInclusive, pattern, totalDigits, and whiteSpace.

Derived types: positiveInteger and unsignedLong.

Examples

nonNegativeInteger values

```
<num>42</num>
<num>+273</num>
<num>0000056</num>
<num>0</num>
<num>0000</num>
```

Various **nonNegativeInteger** values as element content

Canonical nonNegativeInteger values

```
<num>42</num>
<num>273</num>
<num>56</num>
<num>0</num>
<num>0</num>
```

Canonical representation of the **nonNegativeInteger** values in the preceding example

---

8.2.32 nonPositiveInteger

The **nonPositiveInteger** datatype represents the integer values zero or lower.

Base type: integer.

Value space: The infinite set of all integers with values of zero or less.

Lexical space: A finite sequence of decimal digits with a preceding minus sign character (-). If the digits are all zeros then the preceding sign character may be omitted. Leading zeros may appear.

Canonical representation: Leading zeros are prohibited. The preceding minus sign is mandatory in all cases.

Applicable facets: enumeration, fractionDigits, maxExclusive, maxInclusive, minExclusive, minInclusive, pattern, totalDigits, and whiteSpace.

Derived type: negativeInteger.

Examples

nonPositiveInteger values

```
<num>-42</num>
<num>-273</num>
<num>-0000056</num>
<num>0</num>
```

Various nonPositiveInteger values as element content

Canonical nonPositiveInteger values

```
<num>-42</num>
<num>-273</num>
<num>-56</num>
<num>-0</num>
```

Canonical representation of the nonPositiveInteger values in the preceding example

---

8.2.33 normalizedString

The normalizedString datatype represents strings that have been normalized with respect to whitespace; that is, all carriage return (#xD), line feed (#xA), and tab (#x9) characters have been converted to space (#x20) characters.

Base type: string.

Value space: The set of strings that do not contain carriage return (#xD), line feed (#xA), or tab (#x9) characters.

Lexical space: As value space.

Applicable facets: enumeration, length, maxLength, minLength, pattern, and whiteSpace.

Derived type: token.

Examples

A normalized string with preceding and trailing whitespace

```
<speech>   Now is the winter   of our discontent   </speech>
```

A string where a carriage return and two tab characters between "winter" and "of" have been converted into three spaces (see the corresponding example under the `string` and `token` datatypes).

A normalized string

```
<cities>London Paris Munich</cities>
```

A string in which a tab character between each item in the list has been replaced with a space. (See the corresponding example under the `string` datatype).

8.2.34 NOTATION

The NOTATION datatype represents the XML 1.0 NOTATION type. This type cannot be used directly but must be derived from using the enumeration facet to list all the names of NOTATIONs declared in the current scheme. Types derived from NOTATION should only be used for attribute values.

Value space: The set of QNames.

Lexical space: The set of NOTATION names declared in the current schema.

Applicable facets: `enumeration`, `length`, `maxExclusive`, `maxInclusive`, `maxLength`, `minExclusive`, `minInclusive`, `minLength`, `pattern`, and `whiteSpace`.

Example

A type derived from NOTATION

```
<xs:schema xmlns:xs='http://www.w3.org/2001/XMLSchema'
           targetNamespace='http://example.org/Pictures'
           xmlns:tns='http://example.org/Pictures' >

  <xs:notation name='jpg' public='image/jpeg'
    system='display.exe' />
  <xs:notation name='png' public='image/png'
    system='display.exe' />
  <xs:notation name='gif' public='image/gif'
    system='display.exe' />

  <xs:simpleType name='myNotations'>
    <xs:restriction base='xs:NOTATION'>
```

Schema I

```
      <xs:enumeration value='jpg' />
      <xs:enumeration value='png' />
      <xs:enumeration value='gif' />
    </xs:restriction>
  </xs:simpleType>

  <xs:complexType name='picture' >
    <xs:attribute name='width' type='xs:short' />
    <xs:attribute name='height' type='xs:short' />
    <xs:attribute name='format' type='xs:myNotations' />
  </xs:complexType>

</xs:schema>
```

A schema containing NOTATION declarations and a simple type derived from the NOTATION type

---

8.2.35 positiveInteger

The positiveInteger datatype represents integer values of 1 or more.

Base type: nonNegativeInteger.

Value space: The infinite set of all integers with values of 1 or more.

Lexical space: A finite sequence of decimal digits with an optional preceding plus sign character (+). Leading zeros may appear.

Canonical representation: Leading zeros are prohibited, as is the preceding + sign.

Applicable facets: enumeration, fractionDigits, maxExclusive, maxInclusive, minExclusive, minInclusive, pattern, totalDigits, and whiteSpace.

Examples

positiveInteger values

```
<num>42</num>
<num>+273</num>
<num>0000056</num>
```

Various positiveInteger values as element content

Canonical `positiveInteger` *values*

```
<num>42</num>
<num>273</num>
<num>56</num>
```

Canonical representation of the `positiveInteger` values in the preceding example

8.2.36 QName

The QName datatype represents qualified names in XML according to Namespace in XML.

Value space: The set of pairs of a namespace name and a local name where a namespace name is a URI reference and a local name is an NCName.

Lexical space: The set of strings that match QName production in Namespace in XML.

Applicable facets: `enumeration`, `length`, `maxLength`, `minLength`, `pattern`, and `whiteSpace`.

Example

QName attributes

```
<elem attr='p:syntax' />
<elem attr='xsd:schema' />
```

Example QNames as attribute values

8.2.37 short

The `short` datatype represents the range of integer values that can be stored in a 16-bit signed field.

Base type: `int`.

Value space: +32,767 to –32,768.

Lexical space: A finite sequence of decimal digits with an optional leading sign character (+ or –). The default sign is positive. Leading zeros may appear.

Canonical representation: Leading zeros are prohibited, as is the preceding + sign.

Applicable facets: enumeration, fractionDigits, maxExclusive, maxInclusive, minExclusive, minInclusive, pattern, totalDigits, and whiteSpace.

Derived type: byte.

Examples

short values

```
<num>4242</num>
<num>+12</num>
<num>-273</num>
<num>0000056</num>
<num>0</num>
```

Various short values as element content

Canonical short values

```
<num>4242</num>
<num>12</num>
<num>-273</num>
<num>56</num>
<num>0</num>
```

Canonical representation of the short values in the preceding example

8.2.38 string

The string datatype represents Unicode character strings (strictly finite sequences of ISO-10646 character values that match the Char production specified in *XML 1.0 Recommendation* [second edition]).

Value space: All finite-length sequences of ISO-10646 characters as specified by the Char production in *XML 1.0 Recommendation* (second edition).

Lexical space: As value space.

Applicable facets: enumeration, length, maxLength, minLength and whiteSpace.

Derived type: normalizedString.

Examples

Elements containing strings

```
<greeting>Hello World!</greeting>
<price>$9.95</price>
<price>£9.95</price>
<town>Unterschleißheim</town>
<language>Français</language>
<language>Español</language>
```

Element containing strings. The strings are made up of various Unicode characters.

Attributes containing strings

```
<root name='Martin' language='Français'
    town='Unterschleißheim' />
```

Attributes containing strings. The strings are made up of various Unicode characters.

A string with various whitespace characters

```
<speech>    Now is the winter
        of our discontent    </speech>
```

A string containing carriage return, line feed, and tab characters along with preceding and trailing spaces (see the corresponding examples under the `normalizedString` and `token` datatypes).

A string with tab characters

```
<cities>London    Paris    Munich</cities>
```

A string containing tab characters (see the corresponding example under the `normalizedString` datatype).

8.2.39 time

The `time` datatype represents an instant in time that recurs each day.

Value space: Any zero-duration daily instant in time.

Lexical space: `hh:mm:ss.sss` where `hh`, `mm,` and `ss.sss` correspond to the hour, minute, and second (with fractions) respectively. An optional following

Z indicates the time is specified in Coordinated Universal Time. Alternatively a time zone may be indicated by providing a following + or − sign followed by the offset from UTC as hh:mm where hh and mm correspond to hours and minutes respectively. The mm and the preceding colon may be omitted if the minutes are zero.

Canonical representation: The time zone must be omitted or must be UTC (as indicated by the following Z).

Applicable facets: enumeration, maxExclusive, maxInclusive, minExclusive, minInclusive, pattern, and whiteSpace.

Examples

A time

```
<time>22:20:00</time>
```

10:20 PM

A time with a negative time zone modifier

```
<time>17:20:00-05:00</time>
```

5:20 PM, Eastern Standard Time

A time with a positive time zone modifier

```
<time>23:20:00+01:00</time>
```

11:20 PM, Central European Time

8.2.40 token

The token datatype represents "tokenized" strings. These are strings in which all preceding or trailing space (#x20) characters have been removed, all carriage return (#xD), line feed (#xA), and tab (#x9) characters have been converted to space characters, and all sequences of two or more space characters have been converted to a single space character.

Base type: normalizedString.

Value space: The set of strings that do not contain carriage return (#xD), line feed (#xA) or tab (#x9) characters.

Lexical space: As value space.

Applicable facets: enumeration, length, maxLength, minLength, pattern, and whiteSpace.

Derived types: language, Name, and NMTOKEN.

Example

A token *value*

```
<speech>Now is the winter of our discontent</speech>
```

A string in which preceding and trailing whitespaces have been removed, and multiple whitespace characters between "winter" and "of" have been converted to a single space. (See the corresponding examples under the string and normalizedString datatypes.)

8.2.41 unsignedByte

The unsignedByte datatype represents the range of integer values that can be stored in an 8-bit unsigned field.

Base type: unsignedShort.

Value space: +255 to zero.

Lexical space: A finite sequence of decimal digits with an optional leading plus sign character (+). Leading zeros may appear.

Canonical representation: Leading zeros are prohibited, as is the preceding + sign.

Applicable facets: enumeration, fractionDigits, maxExclusive, maxInclusive, minExclusive, minInclusive, pattern, totalDigits, and whiteSpace.

Examples

unsignedByte values

```
<num>255</num>
<num>+12</num>
<num>0000056</num>
<num>0</num>
```

Various unsignedByte values as element content

Canonical *unsignedByte* values

```
<num>255</num>
<num>12</num>
<num>56</num>
<num>0</num>
```

Canonical representation of the unsignedByte values in the preceding example

---

8.2.42 unsignedInt

The unsignedInt datatype represents the range of integer values that can be stored in a 32-bit unsigned field.

Base type: unsignedLong.

Value space: +4,294,967,295 to zero.

Lexical space: A finite sequence of decimal digits with an optional leading plus sign character (+). Leading zeros may appear.

Canonical representation: Leading zeros are prohibited, as is the preceding + sign.

Applicable facets: enumeration, fractionDigits, maxExclusive, maxInclusive, minExclusive, minInclusive, pattern, totalDigits, and whiteSpace.

Derived type: unsignedShort.

Examples
unsignedInt values

```
<num>1234567890</num>
<num>42</num>
<num>+12</num>
<num>0000056</num>
<num>0</num>
```

Various unsignedInt values as element content

Canonical *unsignedInt values*

```
<num>1234567890</num>
<num>42</num>
```

```
<num>12</num>
<num>56</num>
<num>0</num>
```

Canonical representation of the `unsignedInt` values in the preceding example

---

8.2.43 `unsignedLong`

The `unsignedLong` datatype represents the range of integer values that can be stored in a 64-bit unsigned field.

Base type: `nonNegativeInteger`.

Value space: 18,446,744,073,709,551,615 to zero.

Lexical space: A finite sequence of decimal digits with an optional leading plus sign character (+). Leading zeros may appear.

Canonical representation: Leading zeros are prohibited, as is the preceding + sign.

Applicable facets: `enumeration`, `fractionDigits`, `maxExclusive`, `maxInclusive`, `minExclusive`, `minInclusive`, `pattern`, `totalDigits`, and `whiteSpace`.

Derived type: `unsignedInt`.

Examples

`long` values

```
<num>1000000000000</num>
<num>1234567890</num>
<num>42</num>
<num>+12</num>
<num>0000056</num>
<num>0</num>
```

Various `unsignedLong` values as element content

Canonical `long` values

```
<num>1000000000000</num>
<num>1234567890</num>
<num>42</num>
```

```
<num>12</num>
<num>56</num>
<num>0</num>
```

Canonical representation of the unsignedLong values in the preceding example

8.2.44 unsignedShort

The unsignedShort datatype represents the range of integer values that can be stored in a 16-bit unsigned field.

Base type: unsignedInt.

Value space: +65,535 to zero.

Lexical space: A finite sequence of decimal digits with an optional leading plus sign character (+). Leading zeros may appear.

Canonical representation: Leading zeros are prohibited, as is the preceding + sign.

Applicable facets: enumeration, fractionDigits, maxExclusive, maxInclusive, minExclusive, minInclusive, pattern, totalDigits, and whiteSpace.

Derived type: unsignedByte.

Examples

unsignedShort values

```
<num>4242</num>
<num>+12</num>
<num>0000056</num>
<num>0</num>
```

Various unsignedShort values as element content

Canonical unsignedShort values

```
<num>4242</num>
<num>12</num>
<num>56</num>
<num>0</num>
```

Canonical representation of the unsignedShort values in the preceding example

8.3   Facets

Facets are used to restrict the set of values a datatype can contain, thus allowing types with different value ranges to be derived from other types. The new value range must be equal to or narrower than the value range of the base type. It is not possible to expand the value space of a type using facets.

Multiple facets can be specified in a single type definition, in which case the value space of the type is constrained by all the facets listed. Any values appearing in the instance must conform to all the listed facets.

There are 12 facet elements, all of which share a common syntax. They each have a mandatory `value` attribute that specifies the value for the facet. Although this attribute is of type `xs:string`, the value must typically be a valid value of the type to which the facet is applied. For example, if a `minExclusive` facet is being used to constrain the `decimal` datatype then the value must be numerical. Facets also have an optional `fixed` attribute of type `boolean`. If the value of this attribute is `true`, then the facet cannot be respecified in a derived type. Lastly, facets have an optional `id` attribute of type ID that is for application use.

In this section the facets are listed in alphabetical order, each with a description, valid values for the value attribute, a list of datatypes to which the facet applies, and examples.

8.3.1 enumeration

```
<xs:enumeration value='string' fixed='boolean' id='ID'  />
```

Defines a fixed value that the type must match. Multiple `enumeration` facets can be used to specify multiple legal values. Thus, multiple `enumeration` facets have a cumulative effect, allowing multiple possible values.

Values: Any value that matches the type of the base type

Applies to: anyURI, base64Binary, byte, date, dateTime, decimal, double, duration, ENTITIES, ENTITY, float, gDay, gMonth, gMonthDay, gYear, gYearMonth, hexBinary, ID, IDREF, IDREFS, int, integer, language, long, Name, NCName, negativeInteger, NMTOKEN, NMTOKENS, nonNegativeInteger, nonPositiveInteger, normalizedString, NOTATION, positiveInteger, QName, short, string, time, token, unsignedByte, unsignedInt, unsignedLong, and unsignedShort

Examples

An enumerated string type

```
<xs:simpleType name='sizes'>
  <xs:restriction base='xs:string' >
    <xs:enumeration value='small' />
    <xs:enumeration value='medium' />
    <xs:enumeration value='large' />
  </xs:restriction>
</xs:simpleType>
```

An enumerated string type allowing three values: small, medium, and large

An enumerated integer type

```
<xs:simpleType name='smallprimes' >
  <xs:restriction base='xs:integer' >
    <xs:enumeration value='2' />
    <xs:enumeration value='3' />
    <xs:enumeration value='5' />
    <xs:enumeration value='7' />
    <xs:enumeration value='11' />
    <xs:enumeration value='13' />
  </xs:restriction>
</xs:simpleType>
```

An enumerated integer type allowing prime numbers less than 15

8.3.2 fractionDigits

```
<xs:fractionDigits value='positiveInteger' fixed='boolean'
                   id='ID'  />
```

Specifies the maximum number of decimal digits to the right of the decimal point for types derived from number. If totalDigits and fractionDigits facets both appear, the value of the fractionDigits facet must be less than or equal to the value of the totalDigits facet.

Values: positiveInteger

Applies to: byte, decimal, int, integer, long, negativeInteger, nonNegativeInteger, nonPositiveInteger, positiveInteger, short, unsignedByte, unsignedInt, unsignedLong, and unsignedShort

Example

A decimal type

```
<xs:simpleType name='frac5' >
  <xs:restriction base='xs:decimal' >
    <xs:fractionDigits value='5' />
  </xs:restriction>
</xs:simpleType>
```

A decimal type with at most five digits to the right of the decimal point

8.3.3 length

```
<xs:length value='nonNegativeInteger' fixed='boolean'
          id='ID'  />
```

Defines the number of characters in a string-based type, the number of octets in a binary-based type, or the number of items in a list-based type. The length facet may not appear with either the minLength or maxLength facets.

Values: nonNegativeInteger

Applies to: anyURI, base64Binary, ENTITIES, ENTITY, hexBinary, ID, IDREF, IDREFS, language, Name, NCName, NMTOKEN, NMTOKENS, normalizedString, NOTATION, QName, string, and token

Examples

Fixed-length types

```
<xs:simpleType name='String10' >
  <xs:restriction base='xs:string' >
    <xs:length value='10' />
  </xs:restriction>
</xs:simpleType>
```

Schema I

```
<xs:simpleType name='uri50' >
  <xs:restriction base='xs:anyURI' >
    <xs:length value='50' />
  </xs:restriction>
</xs:simpleType>
```

Two types, both with a fixed number of characters

A fixed-length list type

```
<xs:simpleType name='idrefs10' >
  <xs:restriction base='xs:IDREFS' >
    <xs:length value='10' />
  </xs:restriction>
</xs:simpleType>
```

A type based on a built-in list type with a fixed number of list items

A fixed-length list type

```
<xs:simpleType name='double10' >
  <xs:restriction>
    <xs:simpleType>
      <xs:list itemType='xs:double' />
    </xs:simpleType>
    <xs:length value='10' />
  </xs:restriction>
</xs:simpleType>
```

A list of ten doubles based on restriction of an anonymous list of doubles

8.3.4 maxExclusive

```
<xs:maxExclusive value='number' fixed='boolean' id='ID'  />
```

Specifies an exclusive upper bound on the value space of the type. The value specified by the facet is not part of the value space of the new type. The maxExclusive facet may not be combined with the maxInclusive facet. If the maxExclusive facet appears with either the minInclusive or minExclusive facets, then the value of the maxExclusive facet must be greater than or equal to the value of the minInclusive or minExclusive facet.

Values: A value in the value space of the base type

Applies to: `byte`, `date`, `dateTime`, `decimal`, `double`, `duration`, `float`, `gDay`, `gMonth`, `gMonthDay`, `gYear`, `gYearMonth`, `int`, `integer`, `long`, `negativeInteger`, `nonNegativeInteger`, `nonPositiveInteger`, `positiveInteger`, `short`, `time`, `unsignedByte`, `unsignedInt`, `unsignedLong` and `unsignedShort`

Examples

A numerical type with an exclusive upper bound

```
<xs:simpleType name='notquiteagrand' >
  <xs:restriction base='xs:decimal' >
    <xs:maxExclusive value='1000' />
  </xs:restriction>
</xs:simpleType>
```

A numerical type with an exclusive upper bound of 1,000. Values up to but not including 1,000 are in the value space

A gMonth type with an exclusive upper bound

```
<xs:simpleType name='notNovemberOrDecember' >
  <xs:restriction base='xs:gMonth' >
    <xs:maxExclusive value='--11--' />
  </xs:restriction>
</xs:simpleType>
```

A `gMonth` type with an upper bound of October, specified as an exclusive upper bound for November; that is, November is not in the value space

8.3.5 `maxInclusive`

```
<xs:maxInclusive value='number' fixed='boolean' id='ID' />
```

Specifies an inclusive upper bound on the value space of the type. The value specified by the facet is part of the value space of the new type. The `maxInclusive` facet may not be combined with the `maxExclusive` facet. If the `maxInclusive` facet appears with either the `minInclusive` or `minExclusive` facets, then the value of the `maxInclusive` facet must be

Schema I

greater than or equal to the value of the `minInclusive` or `minExclusive` facet.

Values: A value in the value space of the base type

Applies to: `byte`, `date`, `dateTime`, `decimal`, `double`, `duration`, `float`, `gDay`, `gMonth`, `gMonthDay`, `gYear`, `gYearMonth`, `int`, `integer`, `long`, `negativeInteger`, `nonNegativeInteger`, `nonPositiveInteger`, `positiveInteger`, `short`, `time`, `unsignedByte`, `unsignedInt`, `unsignedLong`, and `unsignedShort`

Examples

A numerical type with an inclusive upper bound

```
<xs:simpleType name='notquiteagrand' >
  <xs:restriction base='xs:decimal' >
    <xs:maxInclusive value='999.99' />
  </xs:restriction>
</xs:simpleType>
```

A numerical type with an inclusive upper bound of 999.99. Values of up to and including 999.99 are in the value space.

A gMonth type with an inclusive upper bound

```
<xs:simpleType name='notNovemberOrDecember' >
  <xs:restriction base='xs:gMonth' >
    <xs:maxInclusive value='--10--' />
  </xs:restriction>
</xs:simpleType>
```

A gMonth type with an upper bound of ten (October)

8.3.6 maxLength

```
<xs:maxLength value='nonNegativeInteger' fixed='boolean'
              id='ID' />
```

Defines the maximum number of characters in a string-based type, the maximum number of octets in a binary-based type, or the maximum number of items in a list-based type. The maxLength facet may not be combined with the `length`

facet. If both maxLength and minLength facets appear, the value of
maxLength must be greater than or equal to the value of minLength.

Values: nonNegativeInteger

Applies to: anyURI, base64Binary, ENTITIES, ENTITY, hexBinary,
ID, IDREF, IDREFS, language, Name, NCName, NMTOKEN, NMTOKENS,
normalizedString, NOTATION, QName, string, and token

Examples

Length-restricted types

```
<xs:simpleType name='String10orless' >
  <xs:restriction base='xs:string' >
    <xs:maxLength value='10' />
  </xs:restriction>
</xs:simpleType>
<xs:simpleType name='uri50orless' >
  <xs:restriction base='xs:anyURI' >
    <xs:maxLength value='50' />
  </xs:restriction>
</xs:simpleType>
```

Two types, both with a maximum number of characters

A length-restricted list type

```
<xs:simpleType name='idrefs10orless' >
  <xs:restriction base='xs:IDREFS' >
    <xs:maxLength value='10' />
  </xs:restriction>
</xs:simpleType>
```

A type based on a built-in list type with a maximum number of list items

A length-restricted list type

```
<xs:simpleType name='double10orless' >
  <xs:restriction>
    <xs:simpleType>
      <xs:list itemType='xs:double' />
    </xs:simpleType>
    <xs:maxLength value='10' />
```

Schema I

```
    </xs:restriction>
  </xs:simpleType>
```

A list of at most ten doubles based on restriction of an anonymous list of doubles

---

8.3.7 minExclusive

```
<xs:minExclusive value='number' fixed='boolean' id='ID' />
```

Specifies an exclusive lower bound on the value space of the type. The value specified by the facet is not part of the value space of the new type. The minExclusive facet may not be combined with the minInclusive facet. If the minExclusive facet appears with either the maxInclusive or maxExclusive facets, then the value of the minExclusive facet must be less than or equal to the value of the maxInclusive or maxExclusive facet.

Values: A value in the value space of the base type

Applies to: byte, date, dateTime, decimal, double, duration, float, gDay, gMonth, gMonthDay, gYear, gYearMonth, int, integer, long, negativeInteger, nonNegativeInteger, nonPositiveInteger, positiveInteger, short, time, unsignedByte, unsignedInt, unsignedLong, and unsignedShort

Examples

A numerical type with an exclusive lower bound

```
<xs:simpleType name='morethanagrand' >
  <xs:restriction base='xs:decimal' >
    <xs:minExclusive value='1000.00' />
  </xs:restriction>
</xs:simpleType>
```

A numerical type with an exclusive lower bound of 1,000. Values more than 1,000 are in the value space.

A gMonth type with an exclusive lower bound

```
<xs:simpleType name='H2' >
  <xs:restriction base='xs:gMonth' >
```

```
      <xs:minExclusive value='--06--' />
    </xs:restriction>
</xs:simpleType>
```

A gMonth type representing months in the second half of the year

---

8.3.8 minInclusive

```
<xs:minInclusive value='number' fixed='boolean' id='ID'  />
```

Specifies an inclusive lower bound on the value space of the type. The value specified by the facet is part of the value space of the new type. The minInclusive facet may not be combined with the minExclusive facet. If the minInclusive facet appears with either the maxInclusive or maxExclusive facets, then the value of the minInclusive facet must be less than or equal to the value of the maxInclusive or maxExclusive facet.

Values: A value in the value space of the base type

Applies to: byte, date, dateTime, decimal, double, duration, float, gDay, gMonth, gMonthDay, gYear, gYearMonth, int, integer, long, negativeInteger, nonNegativeInteger, nonPositiveInteger, positiveInteger, short, time, unsignedByte, unsignedInt, unsignedLong, and unsignedShort

Examples

A numerical type with an inclusive lower bound

```
<xs:simpleType name='atleastagrand' >
  <xs:restriction base='xs:decimal' >
    <xs:minInclusive value='1000.00' />
  </xs:restriction>
</xs:simpleType>
```

A numerical type with an inclusive lower bound of 1,000. Values of 1,000 and more are in the value space.

A gMonth type with an inclusive lower bound

```
<xs:simpleType name='H2' >
  <xs:restriction base='xs:gMonth' >
```

```
   <xs:minInclusive value='--07--' />
  </xs:restriction>
</xs:simpleType>
```

A gMonth type representing months in the second half of the year

---

8.3.9 minLength

```
<xs:minLength value='nonNegativeInteger' fixed='boolean'
              id='ID' />
```

Defines the minimum number of characters in a string-based type, the minimum number of octets in a binary-based type, or the minimum number of items in a list-based type. The minLength facet may not be combined with the maxLength facet. If both minLength and maxLength facets appear, the value of min-Length must be less than or equal to the value of maxLength.

Values: nonNegativeInteger

Applies to: anyURI, base64Binary, ENTITIES, ENTITY, hexBinary, ID, IDREF, IDREFS, language, Name, NCName, NMTOKEN, NMTOKENS, normalizedString, NOTATION, QName, string, and token

Examples

Length-restricted types

```
<xs:simpleType name='String10ormore' >
  <xs:restriction base='xs:string' >
    <xs:minLength value='10' />
  </xs:restriction>
</xs:simpleType>

<xs:simpleType name='uri50ormore' >
  <xs:restriction base='xs:anyURI' >
    <xs:minLength value='50' />
  </xs:restriction>
</xs:simpleType>
```

Two types, both with a minimum number of characters

A *length-restricted list type*

```
<xs:simpleType name='idrefs10ormore' >
  <xs:restriction base='xs:IDREFS' >
    <xs:minLength value='10' />
  </xs:restriction>
</xs:simpleType>
```

A type based on a built-in list type with a minimum number of list items

A *length-restricted list type*

```
<xs:simpleType name='double10ormore' >
  <xs:restriction>
    <xs:simpleType>
      <xs:list itemType='xs:double' />
    </xs:simpleType>
    <xs:minLength value='10' />
  </xs:restriction>
</xs:simpleType>
```

A list of at least ten doubles based on restriction of an anonymous list of doubles

---

8.3.10 pattern

```
<xs:pattern value='string' fixed='boolean' id='ID' />
```

Defines a pattern that the type must match based on a regular expression.

Values: A regular expression

Applies to: anyURI, base64Binary, boolean, byte, date, dateTime, decimal, double, duration, ENTITIES, ENTITY, float, gDay, gMonth, gMonthDay, gYear, gYearMonth, hexBinary, ID, IDREF, IDREFS, int, integer, language, long, Name, NCName, negativeInteger, NMTOKEN, NMTOKENS, nonNegativeInteger, nonPositiveInteger, normalizedString, NOTATION, positiveInteger, QName, short, string, time, token, unsignedByte, unsignedInt, unsignedLong, and unsignedShort

Schema I

Examples

A patterned string type

```
<xs:simpleType name='code' >
  <xs:restriction base='string' >
    <xs:pattern value='[A-Z]{2}\d{4}' />
  </xs:restriction>
</xs:simpleType>
```

A string type that requires two uppercase characters between A and Z followed by four decimal digits

A patterned numerical type

```
<xs:simpleType name='fourbyfour' >
  <xs:restriction base='xs:decimal' >
    <xs:pattern value='\d{4}\.\d{4}' />
  </xs:restriction>
</xs:simpleType>
```

A numerical type that requires four decimal digits on both sides of the decimal point

A patterned string type

```
<xs:simpleType name='temperature' >
  <xs:restriction base='xs:string' >
    <xs:pattern value='\d+\u00B0' />
  </xs:restriction>
</xs:simpleType>
```

A string type that requires any number of decimal digits followed by the degree character

---

8.3.11 totalDigits

```
<xs:totalDigits value='positiveInteger' fixed='boolean'
                id='ID' />
```

Specifies the maximum number of decimal digits for types derived from number. If totalDigits and fractionDigits facets both appear, the value of the `totalDigits` facet must be greater than or equal to the value of the `fractionDigits>` facet.

Values: `positiveInteger`

Applies to: `byte`, `decimal`, `int`, `integer`, `long`, `negativeInteger`, `nonNegativeInteger`, `nonPositiveInteger`, `positiveInteger`, `short`, `unsignedByte`, `unsignedInt`, `unsignedLong`, and `unsignedShort`

Example

A numerical type

```
<xs:simpleType name='dig10' >
  <xs:restriction base='xs:decimal' >
    <xs:totalDigits value='10' />
  </xs:restriction>
</xs:simpleType>
```

A numerical type with at most 10 digits

8.3.12 whiteSpace

```
<xs:whiteSpace value='preserve|replace|collapse'
               fixed='boolean' id='ID'  />
```

Defines rules for whiteSpace normalization. A value of `preserve` specifies that whitespace should be left unchanged. A value of `replace` specifies that all occurrences of carriage return (#xD), line feed (#xA), and tab (#x9) characters be converted to space (#x20) characters. A value of `collapse` specifies that all preceding or trailing space (#x20) characters be removed; all carriage return (#xD), line feed (#xA), and tab (#x9) characters be converted to space characters; and all sequences of two or more space characters be converted to a single space character.

Although strictly speaking the `whiteSpace` facet can be applied to any datatype for list types and restricted datatypes with a base that is other than `string` or `normalizedString` the `whiteSpace` facet has a value of `collapse` and may not be changed. For types derived from `string` any of the three possible values may be used. For types derived from `normalizedString`, either `replace` or `collapse` may be used. Because of these limitations on the use of the facet it is not generally used in schema documents because any derived type that required particular whitespace normalization would be derived from `string`, `normalizedString`, or `token` as appropriate.

Values: `preserve`, `replace`, or `collapse`

Applies to: `anyURI`, `base64Binary`, `byte`, `date`, `dateTime`, `decimal`, `double`, `duration`, `ENTITIES`, `ENTITY`, `float`, `gDay`, `gMonth`, `gMonthDay`, `gYear`, `gYearMonth`, `hexBinary`, `ID`, `IDREF`, `IDREFS`, `int`, `integer`, `language`, `long`, `Name`, `NCName`, `negativeInteger`, `NMTOKEN`, `NMTOKENS`, `nonNegativeInteger`, `nonPositiveInteger`, `normalizedString`, `NOTATION`, `positiveInteger`, `QName`, `short`, `string`, `time`, `token`, `unsignedByte`, `unsignedInt`, `unsignedLong`, and `unsignedShort`

8.4 Language constructs

The XML Schema language provides support for defining simple datatypes based on existing simple datatypes. New types can be defined to be a restriction of a type, a list of a type, or a union of two or more types.

In this section the language constructs for defining simple types—the `simpleType`, `restriction`, `list`, and `union` elements—are listed each with syntax, description, list of attributes, list of children, and, in the case of the latter three, examples. The syntax shows the attributes the elements can have along with their type. It also lists the names of the valid children of the element. More detail on attributes and children can be found in the attribute and children tables respectively. Each entry in the attributes table shows the name, type, default value, and description of the attribute. The description includes details on possible values and occurrence constraints with respect to other attributes or element children. Qualified attributes from namespaces other than `http://www.w3.org/2001/XMLSchema` may also appear on all four elements. Each entry in the children table gives the name of valid children in the order they must appear. When there is a choice between two or more elements, the set of such elements is listed as a single entry. Whether an element or set of elements is optional or mandatory and how many times the element or an element from a set can occur are also detailed.

8.4.1 `simpleType`

```
<xs:simpleType id='ID' final='list of token' name='NCName' >
  <!-- annotation list restriction union -->
</xs:simpleType>
```

The `simpleType` element is used to define new types based on existing simple types. Simple type definitions appearing as children of a `schema` element are named types available for use elsewhere in the schema and in other schemas. Simple types may also appear as the children of element or attribute declarations or of other simple type definitions, in which case they are anonymous types local to the context in which they appear.

Attributes

Name	Type	Default	Description
`id`	ID	None	An attribute for application use
`final`	List of token	None	Specifies which derivation mechanisms are prohibited for type definitions that reference this type as their base type. The setting specified by this attribute overrides any schemawide default specified by a `finalDefault` attribute on the `schema` element.

		Value	Description
		`restriction`	Simple types derived by restriction may not use this type as their base type.
		`list`	Simple types derived by list may not use this type as their item type.
		`union`	Simple types derived by union may not use this type as part of their member types list.
		`#all`	All of the above

Name	Type	Default	Description
`name`	NCName	None	The local part of the name of the type. No two complex or simple types in the same namespace may have the same local name.

Schema I

Child elements

Name	Occurrence
annotation	Optional, once
list *or* restriction *or* union	Mandatory, once

8.4.2 restriction

```
<xs:restriction id='ID' base='QName' >
  <!-- annotation enumeration fractionDigits length
       maxExclusive maxInclusive maxLength minExclusive
       minInclusive minLength pattern simpleType
       totalDigits whiteSpace  -->
</xs:restriction>
```

The restriction element appears as a child of the simpleType element and denotes that the simple type is a restriction of some other simple type; that is, it has a narrower set of legal values than the base type. The simple type on which the restricted type is based may be referred to using the base attribute or provided as an inline anonymous type in a simpleType child element.

Attributes

Name	Type	Default	Description
id	ID	None	An attribute for application use
base	QName	None	Specifies the base type from which the new type is derived. The base type must be a simple type and may be in the same schema document as the derived type, or it may be in a different schema document, potentially in a different namespace.

Child elements

Name	Occurrence
annotation	Optional, once
simpleType	Optional, once
enumeration *or* fractionDigits *or* length *or* maxExclusive *or* maxInclusive *or* maxLength *or* minExclusive *or* minInclusive *or* minLength *or* pattern *or* totalDigits *or* whiteSpace	Optional, unlimited

Example

Simple type restriction

```
<xs:simpleType name='Celcius' >
  <xs:restriction base='xs:decimal'>
    <xs:minExclusive value='-273' />
  </xs:restriction>
</xs:simpleType>
```

A simple type, `Celcius`, derived by restriction from the built-in `decimal` type

8.4.3 list

```
<xs:list id='ID' itemType='QName'>
  <!-- annotation simpleType  -->
</xs:list>
```

The `list` element appears as a child of the `simpleType` element and denotes that the simple type is a whitespace-delimited list of some other, atomic simple type. The simple type on which the list is based may be referred to using the `itemType` attribute or may be provided as an inline anonymous type in a `simpleType` child element.

Attributes

Name	Type	Default	Description
id	ID	None	An attribute for application use
itemType	QName	None	The simple type on which the list is based. The `list` element must either have this attribute or a `simpleType` child element.

Child elements

Name	Occurrence
annotation	Optional, once
simpleType	Optional, once

Examples

A list type

```
<xs:simpleType name='listOfNumbers' >
  <xs:list itemType='xs:decimal' />
</xs:simpleType>
```

A list type based on a built-in simple type

A list type

```
<xs:simpleType name='listOfQuarks' >
  <xs:list>
    <xs:simpleType>
      <xs:restriction base='xs:string' >
        <xs:enumeration value='up' />
        <xs:enumeration value='down' />
        <xs:enumeration value='strange' />
        <xs:enumeration value='beauty' />
        <xs:enumeration value='truth' />
      </xs:restriction>
    </xs:simpleType>
  </xs:list>
</xs:simpleType>
```

A list type based on an anonymous inline type

8.4.4 union

```
<xs:union id='ID' memberTypes='List of QName' >
  <!-- annotation simpleType  -->
</xs:union>
```

The union element appears as a child of the simpleType element and denotes that the simple type is a union of two or more other simple types. The simple types on which the union is based may be referred to using the memberTypes attribute and/or may be provided as inline anonymous types in simpleType child elements.

Attributes

Name	Type	Default	Description
id	ID	None	An attribute for application use
memberTypes	List of QName	None	A list of simple types on which the union is based. The ordering of types in the list is important because the values of elements or attributes of the union type will be compared against each of the types in the list in turn, then against any simpleType children. The first type that the value matches against will be the type of the value.

Child elements

Name	Occurrence
annotation	Optional, once
simpleType	Optional, unlimited

Examples

A numerical union

```
<xs:simpleType name='numbers' >
  <xs:union memberTypes='xs:byte xs:short xs:int xs:long' />
</xs:simpleType>
```

A union based on the built-in types byte, short, int, and long

A numerical/string union

```
<xs:simpleType name='sizes' >
  <xs:union>
    <xs:simpleType>
      <xs:restriction base='xs:integer' >
        <xs:minInclusive value='1' />
        <xs:maxInclusive value='10' />
      </xs:restriction>
    </xs:simpleType>
    <xs:simpleType>
      <xs:restriction base='xs:string' >
        <xs:enumeration value='small' />
```

Schema I

```
      <xs:enumeration value='medium' />
      <xs:enumeration value='large' />
   </xs:restriction>
  </xs:simpleType>
 </xs:union>
</xs:simpleType>
```

A union of the integers one through ten and the strings `'small'`, `'medium'`, and `'large'` created using two anonymous inline types

---

8.5   References

Biron, Paul V., Ashok, Malhotra, XML Schema Part 2: Datatypes.
http://www.w3.org./TR/xmlschema-2, 2001

Fallside, David C., XML Schema Part 0: Primer.
http://www.w3.org/TR/xmlschema-0, 2001

For more information on RFC 2396, please see
http://www.ietf.org/rfc/rfc2396.txt

For more information on RFC 2732, please see
http://www.ietf.org/rfc/rfc2732.txt

For more information on IEEE 754-1985, please see
http://standards.ieee.org/reading/ieee/stdpublic/description/busarch/754-1985_desc.html

For more information on ISO 8601, please see
www.iso.ch/markete/8601.pdf

For more information on RFC 1766, please see
http://www.ietf.org/rfc/rfc1766.txt

Chapter 9
XML Schema Structures

XML Schema provides a language for describing types in XML. The language is itself expressed in XML and includes facilities for defining structured and textual types, including types derived from other types. Structured types are used to describe elements that have child elements or attributes associated with them. Textual types are used for elements with text-only content and for attribute values. The language provides facilities for binding types to elements and, in the case of textual types, attributes.

This chapter provides a reference for all the parts of the Schema language related to defining complex (structured) types, including extensions and restrictions, model groups, wildcards, element and attribute declarations, and annotations. Parts of the language related to simple types can be found in Chapter 8.

9.1   Schema element groupings

Top-level elements
Elements appearing at the top level of a schema document; that is, as children of a schema element

Element name	Description
annotation	Annotation containing human- or machine-readable information
attribute	A global attribute declaration
attributeGroup	A named attribute group definition
complexType	A complex type definition
element	A global element declaration
group	A named model group definition
import	Brings in components in a different namespace
include	Brings in components in the same namespace
notation	A notation declaration

Schema II

Element name	Description
redefine	Redefines components in the same namespace
simpleType	A simple type definition

Particles

Elements that can have minOccurs and maxOccurs attributes. Such elements always appear as part of a complex type definition or as part of a named model group. Elements appearing at the top level of a schema never have minOccurs or maxOccurs attributes.

Element name	Description
all	A model group that allows elements in any order
any	An element wildcard
choice	A model group that allows one of the particles contained within it
element	An element declaration or reference
group	A reference to a named model group
sequence	A model group that allows particles in a fixed order

Elements related to constructing a schema from multiple documents and/or namespaces

Element name	Description
import	Brings in components in a different namespace.
include	Brings in components in the same namespace.
redefine	Redefines components in the same namespace.

Elements related to identity constraints

Element name	Description
field	A field in a uniqueness or key constraint
key	A key constraint
keyref	A reference to a key constraint
selector	A selector in a uniqueness or key constraint
unique	A uniqueness constraint

Elements related to attributes

Element name	Description
anyAttribute	An attribute wildcard
attribute	An attribute declaration or reference
attributeGroup	A named attribute group or reference to a named attribute group

Elements that have a name attribute

Named constructs can be referred to by QName from other schema constructs.

Element name	Description
attribute	An attribute declaration
attributeGroup	A named attribute group definition
complexType	A complex type definition
element	An element declaration
group	A named model group definition
key	A key constraint
keyref	A reference to a key constraint
notation	A notation declaration
simpleType	A simple type defintion
unique	A uniqueness constraint

Elements that appear as part of complex type definitions

Element name	Description
all	A model group that allows elements in any order
annotation	Annotation containing human- or machine-readable information
any	An element wildcard
anyAttribute	An attribute wildcard
appinfo	Machine-readable information
attribute	A local attribute declaration or reference
attributeGroup	A reference to a named attribute group
choice	A model group that allows one of the particles contained within it
complexContent	A complex type derived from another complex type
documentation	Human-readable information
element	A local element declaration or reference

Element name	Description
extension	A complex type that is an extension of another type
group	A reference to a named model group
restriction	A complex type that is a restriction of another type
sequence	A model group that allows particles in a fixed order
simpleContent	A complex type derived from a simple type

9.2 Structures

In this section the XML Schema language constructs are listed in alphabetical order with syntax, description, list of attributes, list of children, and examples. The syntax shows the attributes the element can have along with their type. It also lists the names of the valid children of the element. More detail on attributes and children can be found in the attribute and children tables respectively. Each entry in the attributes table shows the name, type, default value, and description of the attribute. The description includes details on possible values and occurrence constraints with respect to other attributes or element children. The names of required attributes appear in bold in both the syntax section and the attribute table. Qualified attributes from namespaces other than http://www.w3.org/ 2001/XMLSchema may also appear on all schema elements. Each entry in the children table gives the name of valid children in the order they must appear. When there is a choice between two or more elements, the set of such elements is listed as a single entry. Whether an element or set of elements is optional or mandatory and how many times the element or an element from a set can occur is also detailed. All elements in the Schema language for use in schema documents are in the http://www.w3.org/2001/XMLSchema namespace.

For reasons of brevity, not all examples are full schemas. In all prose and examples, the xs namespace prefix is mapped to the namespace name of the XML Schema language http://www.w3.org/2001/XMLSchema, even if no such namespace declaration appears in the example. Similarly, the xsi namespace prefix is mapped to the namespace name of the XML Schema Instance namespace http://www.w3.org/2001/XMLSchema-instance. The tns namespace prefix is mapped to the same namespace name as the targetNamespace attribute of the schema element even if that element is not shown.

9.2.1 all

```
<xs:all id='ID' maxOccurs='nonNegativeInteger'
       minOccurs='nonNegativeInteger' >
  <!-- annotation element  -->
</xs:all>
```

The all element is used to denote a model group in which the elements defined by the element declarations inside the all element may appear in any order in an instance document. Any child element declaration of the all element can only have the values zero or 1 for its minOccurs attribute and a value of 1 for its maxOccurs attribute. The all element can appear as part of a complex type definition or as part of a named model group. However, it must always be the outer model group of the content of a complex type. It cannot be nested inside a sequence or choice element either directly or through use of group references.

Attributes

Name	Type	Default	Description
id	ID	None	An attribute for application use.
maxOccurs	nonNegativeInteger	1	Specifies the maximum number of times the all group can appear. This attribute may only have the value 1. If the all element is a child of a top-level group element then this attribute may not occur.
minOccurs	nonNegativeInteger	1	Specifies the minimum number of times the all group can appear. This attribute may only have zero or 1 as its value. If the all element is a child of a top-level group element then this attribute may not occur.

Child elements

Name	Occurrence
annotation	Optional, once
element	Optional, unlimited

Examples

An all group in a complex type

```
<xs:complexType name='Bag' >
  <xs:all>
    <xs:element name='hairbrush' minOccurs='0' />
    <xs:element name='makeup' />
    <xs:element name='purse' />
  </xs:all>
</xs:complexType>
```

Elements of type Bag must contain child makeup and purse elements and, optionally, a hairbrush element. These children can appear in any order.

An all group in a named model group

```
<xs:group name='Bag' >
  <xs:all>
    <xs:element name='hairbrush' minOccurs='0'/>
    <xs:element name='makeup' />
    <xs:element name='purse' />
  </xs:all>
</xs:group>
```

Any complex type that references this model group would have the same content model as described for the previous example.

9.2.2 annotation

```
<xs:annotation id='ID' >
  <!-- appinfo documentation  -->
</xs:annotation>
```

The annotation element provides a place for schema documents to be annotated with human-readable or machine-readable information through the documentation and appinfo elements respectively.

Attribute

Name	Type	Default	Description
id	ID	None	An attribute for application use

Child element

Name	Occurrence
appinfo or documentation	Optional, unlimited

Example

See the appinfo and documentation entries for examples.

9.2.3 any

```
<xs:any id='ID' maxOccurs='union'
        minOccurs='nonNegativeInteger'
        namespace='special' processContents='NMTOKEN' >
  <!-- annotation  -->
</xs:any>
```

The any element is used to denote an element wildcard in a model group. In an instance document the wildcard is replaced by any element that matches the namespace constraint specified by the namespace attribute. This allows the construction of open content models for complex types, allowing additional elements to appear that were not specified as part of the type definition. In addition, this element provides control of whether the additional elements should be validated or not.

Schema II

Attributes

Name	Type	Default	Description
id	ID	None	An attribute for application use.
maxOccurs	union	1	Specifies the maximum number of times elements that satisfy this wildcard may appear in the instance document in this context. The value of this attribute may be any nonNegativeInteger or the string unbounded.
minOccurs	nonNegative-Integer	1	Specifies the minimum number of times elements that satisfy this wildcard must appear in the instance document in this context.
namespace	special	##any	Specifies which namespace or namespaces elements that satisfy this wildcard in the instance document must be drawn from. It is also possible to specify that replacement elements may be unqualified (in no namespace). The value of this attribute is either the string ##any, the string ##other, or a list of namespace URIs, and/or the string ##targetNamespace and/or the string ##local.

		Value	Description
		##any	Elements from any namespace including the target namespace of the schema document and unqualified elements (elements in no namespace) may appear in place of the wildcard.
		##other	Elements that are qualified but are not in the target namespace of the schema document may appear in place of the wildcard. Unqualified element may not appear in place of the wildcard.

Name	Type	Default	Description
		##target-Namespace	Elements in the target namespace of the schema document may appear in place of the wildcard.
		##local	Unqualified elements (elements in no namespace) may appear in place of the wildcard.
		namespace URI	Elements from the namespace may appear in place of the wildcard.
process-Contents	NMTOKEN	strict	Specifies whether a schema processor should find schema information and validate the elements appearing in place of the wildcard.
		Value	**Description**
		lax	The schema processor should validate the elements appearing in place of the wildcard if schema information for those elements is available.
		skip	The schema processor should not validate the elements appearing in place of the wildcard.
		strict	The schema processor must validate the elements appearing in place of the wildcard.

Child elements

Name	Occurrence
annotation	Optional, once

Examples

A complex type containing a wildcard allowing any element

```
<xs:complexType name='OpenPerson' >
  <xs:sequence>
    <xs:element name='name' />
    <xs:any namespace='##any' />
```

```
    </xs:sequence>
  </xs:complexType>
```

Elements of type OpenPerson must have a child name element followed by any qualified or unqualified element. This element must be validated.

A complex type containing a wildcard allowing elements in the target namespace

```
<xs:complexType name='OpenPerson' >
  <xs:sequence>
    <xs:element name='name' />
    <xs:any namespace='##targetNamespace' />
  </xs:sequence>
</xs:complexType>
```

Elements of type OpenPerson must have a child name element followed by an element qualified by the target namespace. This element must be validated.

A complex type containing a wildcard allowing unqualified elements

```
<xs:complexType name='OpenPerson' >
  <xs:sequence>
    <xs:element name='name' />
    <xs:any namespace='##local'
            processContents='skip' />
  </xs:sequence>
</xs:complexType>
```

Elements of type OpenPerson must have a child name element followed by an unqualified element. This element must not be validated.

A complex type containing a wildcard allowing qualified elements from namespaces other than the target namespace of the schema

```
<xs:complexType name='OpenPerson' >
  <xs:sequence>
    <xs:element name='name' />
    <xs:any namespace='##other' />
  </xs:sequence>
</xs:complexType>
```

Elements of type `OpenPerson` must have a child `name` element followed by a qualified element from a namespace other than the target namespace of the schema. This element must be validated.

A complex type containing two wildcards

```
<xs:complexType name='AjarPerson' >
  <xs:sequence>
    <xs:any namespace='http://example.org/People/extras
            http://example.org/Notes ##local'
            processContents='lax' />
    <xs:element name='name' />
    <xs:any maxOccurs='unbounded' namespace='##other'
        processContents='lax' />
  </xs:sequence>
</xs:complexType>
```

Elements of type `AjarPerson` must have a child element that is either in one of the two namespaces listed or an unqualified element, followed by a `name` element, followed by any number of qualified elements in namespaces other than the target namespace. Elements appearing in place of either wildcard may be validated if schema information for them is available.

9.2.4 anyAttribute

```
<xs:anyAttribute id='ID' namespace='special'
                processContents='NMTOKEN' >
  <!-- annotation -->
</xs:anyAttribute>
```

The `anyAttribute` element is used to denote an attribute wildcard for a complex type. In an instance document the wildcard is replaced by any number of attributes that match the namespace constraint specified by the namespace attribute. This allows additional attributes to appear that were not specified as part of the type definition.

Schema II

Attributes

Name	Type	Default	Description
id	ID	None	An attribute for application use.
namespace	special	##any	Specifies which namespace or namespaces attributes that replace this wildcard in the instance document must be drawn from. It is also possible to specify that replacement attributes may be unqualified (in no namespace). This value of this attribute is either the string ##any, the string ##other, or a list of namespace URIs, and/or the string ##targetNamespace and/or the string ##local.

		Value	Description
		##any	Attributes from any namespace including the target namespace of the schema document and unqualified elements (elements in no namespace) may appear.
		##other	Attributes that are qualified but are not in the target namespace of the schema document may appear.
		##target-Namespace	Attributes in the target namespace of the schema document may appear.
		##local	Unqualified attributes may appear.
		namespace URI	Attributes from the namespace may appear.
process-Contents	NMTOKEN	strict	Specifies whether a schema processor should find schema information and validate the attributes appearing in place of the wildcard.

		Value	Description
		lax	The schema processor should validate the attributes appearing in place of the wildcard if schema information is available.
		skip	The schema processor should not validate the attributes appearing in place of the wildcard.
		strict	The schema processor must validate the attributes appearing in place of the wildcard.

Child element

Name	Occurrence
annotation	Optional, once

Examples

An attribute wildcard allowing any attribute

```
<xs:complexType name='OpenPerson' >
  <xs:attribute name='name' use='required' />

  <xs:anyAttribute namespace='##any' />
</xs:complexType>
```

Elements of type `OpenPerson` must have a `name` attribute. In addition, attributes from any namespace or unqualified attributes may appear. Any additional attributes must be validated.

An attribute wildcard allowing attributes in the target namespace

```
<xs:complexType name='OpenPerson' >
  <xs:attribute name='name' use='required' />
  <xs:anyAttribute namespace='##targetNamespace' />
</xs:complexType>
```

Elements of type `OpenPerson` must have a `name` attribute. In addition, qualified attributes from the target namespace of the schema may appear. Any additional attributes must be validated.

An attribute wildcard allowing unqualified attributes

```
<xs:complexType name='OpenPerson' >
  <xs:attribute name='name' use='required' />
  <xs:anyAttribute namespace='##local' />
</xs:complexType>
```

Elements of type `OpenPerson` must have a `name` attribute. In addition, unqualified attributes may appear. Any additional attributes must be validated.

An attribute wildcard allowing attributes from namespaces other than the target namespace

```
<xs:complexType name='OpenPerson' >
  <xs:attribute name='name' use='required' />
  <xs:anyAttribute namespace='##other'
    processContents='skip' />
</xs:complexType>
```

Elements of type OpenPerson must have a name attribute. In addition, qualified attributes from namespaces other than the target namespace of the schema may appear. Any additional attributes are not validated.

An attribute wildcard allowing attributes from multiple namespaces

```
<xs:complexType name='AjarPerson' >
  <xs:attribute name='name' use='required' />
  <xs:anyAttribute namespace='http://example.org/People/
    extras http://example.org/Notes http://example.org/
    Annotations'
          processContents='lax' />
</xs:complexType>
```

Elements of type AjarPerson must have a name attribute. In addition, qualified attributes from any of the namespaces listed may appear. Any additional attributes may be validated if schema information for them is available.

9.2.5 appinfo

```
<xs:appinfo source='anyURI' >
  <!-- Any qualified or unqualified element  -->
</xs:appinfo>
```

The appinfo element denotes a machine-readable annotation to a schema. The machine-readable portion may be contained within the appinfo element as child elements or may be referenced from the URI reference provided by the source attribute, or both. The appinfo element provides a mechanism for application-level processors to augment schema processing with other processing tasks or information.

Attribute

Name	Type	Default	Description
source	anyURI	None	An attribute for supplementing the information provided in the appinfo element

Child element

Name	Occurrence
Any qualified or unqualified element	Optional, unlimited

Example

Use of appinfo

```
<xs:complexType name='Person' >
  <xs:annotation>
    <xs:appinfo source='http://www.apps.com/myapp'
          xmlns:app='urn:apps-com:myapps' >
      <app:process name='personprocess.exe' />
    </xs:appinfo>
  </xs:annotation>
  <xs:sequence>
    <xs:element name='name' />
  </xs:sequence>
</xs:complexType>
```

A complex type annotated with machine-readable information

9.2.6 attribute

```
<xs:attribute default='string' fixed='string'
          form='NMTOKEN' id='ID' name='NCName'
          ref='QName' type='QName' use='NMTOKEN' >
  <!-- annotation simpleType  -->
</xs:attribute>
```

The `attribute` element either denotes an attribute declaration, defining a named attribute and associating that attribute with a type, or it is a reference to such an attribute declaration. Attribute declarations appearing as children of a schema element are known as **global attribute declarations** and can be referenced from elsewhere in the schema or from other schemas. Attribute declarations appearing as part of a complex type definition, either directly or through an attribute group reference, are known as **local attribute declarations**. Such attribute declarations are local to the type in which they appear. Global attribute declarations describe attributes that are always part of the target namespace of the schema. Local attribute declarations describe attributes that may be part of the target namespace of the schema, depending on the values of the `form` attribute on the attribute declaration and the value of the `attributeFormDefault` attribute on the `schema` element.

Attributes

Name	Type	Default	Description
`default`	`string`	None	Specifies a default value for an attribute declaration with a `use` attribute that has the value `optional`. The `default` and `fixed` attributes are mutually exclusive.
`fixed`	`string`	None	Specifies a fixed value for an attribute declaration with a `use` attribute that has the value `required` or `optional`. The `fixed` and `default` attributes are mutually exclusive.
`form`	NMTOKEN	None	Specifies whether a local attribute declaration is qualified (in the target namespace for the schema) or unqualified (in no namespace). The value of this attribute overrides any schemawide default specified by an `attributeFormDefault` attribute on the `schema` element. This attribute may not appear on a global attribute declaration.
		Value	**Description**
		`qualified`	The local name of the attribute is qualified by the target namespace of the schema.
		`unqualified`	The attribute is unqualified.
`id`	ID	None	An attribute for application use.

Name	Type	Default	Description
name	NCName	None	Specifies the local name of the attribute being declared. The `name` and `ref` attributes are mutually exclusive
ref	QName	None	Specifies a reference to a global attribute declaration. The referenced attribute declaration may be in the same schema document as the referencing attribute declaration or it may be in a different schema document, potentially in a different namespace. This attribute may not appear on a global attribute declaration. The `ref` and `name` attributes are mutually exclusive.
type	QName	None	Specifies the type of the attribute being declared. This attribute is a reference to a simple type: either a built-in simple type or one defined in a schema. If the `type` and `ref` attributes are absent and the attribute declaration does not have a `simpleType` element as one of its children, then the attribute is of the type anySimpleType in the namespace http://www.w3.org/2001/XMLSchema. If a `simpleType` child element is present, then the attribute is of the type defined by that anonymous simple type definition.
use	NMTOKEN	optional	Specifies whether the attribute is optional, required, or prohibited.

Value	Description
optional	The attribute may appear in the instance document.
prohibited	The attribute must not appear in the instance document.
required	The attribute must appear in the instance document.

Schema II

Child elements

Name	Occurrence
annotation	Optional, once
simpleType	Optional, once

Examples

A global attribute declaration and an attribute reference

```
<xs:schema xmlns:xs='http://www.w3.org/2001/XMLSchema'
           targetNamespace='urn:example-org:Utilities'
           xmlns:tns='urn:example-org:Utilities' >

  <xs:attribute name='units' type='xs:string' />

  <xs:complexType name='HeightVector' >
    <xs:sequence>
      <xs:element name='height' type='xs:double' />
    </xs:sequence>
    <xs:attribute ref='tns:units' use='required' />
  </xs:complexType>

</xs:schema>
```

A global attribute declaration describing an attribute with a local name of `units`, a namespace name of `urn:example-org:Utilities`, and an attribute reference to that global attribute declaration. The attribute reference makes the attribute required in the instance document. The type of the attribute is the built-in `string` type. Elements of type `HeightVector` must have a `height` element. They must also have a `units` attribute in the `urn:examples-org:Utilities` namespace.

A local attribute declaration as part of a complex type

```
<xs:complexType name='Rowset'>
  <xs:sequence>
    <xs:element name='row' maxOccurs='unbounded' />
  </xs:sequence>
  <xs:attribute name='sortorder' type='xs:string'
    use='optional' default='ascending' />
</xs:complexType>
```

An attribute declaration describing an attribute with a local name of `sortorder`, which is based on the built-in `string` type, is optional in the instance and has a default value. Elements of type `Rowset` must have one or more `row` elements. They may also have a `sortorder` attribute. If such an attribute is not present, then one will be added with a value of `ascending`.

An attribute reference with a fixed value

```
<xs:schema xmlns:xs='http://www.w3.org/2001/XMLSchema'
           targetNamespace='urn:example-org:People'
           xmlns:tns='urn:example-org:People' >

  <xs:import namespace='http://www.w3.org/XML/1998/
     namespace' />

  <xs:complexType name='PersonName'>
    <xs:sequence>
      <xs:element name='givenName' />
      <xs:element name='familyName' />
    </xs:sequence>
    <xs:attribute ref='xml:lang' use='optional'
        fixed='EN-UK' />
  </xs:complexType>

</xs:schema>
```

An attribute reference to the `lang` attribute in the namespace `http://www.w3.org/XML/1998/namespace` from within a complex type in the namespace `urn:example-org:People`. The attribute reference specifies a fixed value for the `lang` attribute in this context. Elements of type `PersonName` must have a `givenName` element followed by a `familyName` element. They may also have a `lang` attribute in the `http://www.w3.org/XML/1998/namespace` namespace. If such an attribute appears, it must have the value EN–UK. If such an attribute does not appear, then one will be added with a value of EN–UK.

9.2.7 attributeGroup

```
<xs:attributeGroup id='ID' name='NCName' ref='QName' >
  <!-- annotation anyAttribute attribute
       attributeGroup -->
</xs:attributeGroup>
```

The `attributeGroup` element either denotes an attribute group definition, defining a named group of attribute declarations, other named attribute groups, and attribute wildcards, or it is a reference to such a group. The former appear as children of a `schema` element whereas the latter appear inside complex type definitions and other attribute group definitions. Attribute groups provide a convenient mechanism for using the same set of attributes in multiple complex type definitions.

Attributes

Name	Type	Default	Description
id	ID	None	An attribute for application use.
name	NCName	None	Specifies the local name of the attribute group being defined. This attribute can only appear if the `attributeGroup` element is a child of a `schema` element.
ref	QName	None	Specifies a reference to a named attribute group. The referenced attribute group may be in the same schema document as the referencing element declaration or it may be in a different schema document, potentially in a different namespace. This attribute can only appear if the `attributeGroup` element is not a child of a `schema` element.

Child elements

Name	Occurrence
annotation	Optional, once
attribute *or* attributeGroup	Optional, unlimited
anyAttribute	Optional, once

Example

A named attribute group and reference to that group from within a complex type

```
<xs:schema xmlns:xs='http://www.w3.org/2001/XMLSchema'
          targetNamespace='urn:example-org:Pictures'
          xmlns:tns='urn:example-org:Pictures' >

  <xs:attributeGroup name='WidthAndHeight'>
    <xs:attribute name='width' use='required' />
    <xs:attribute name='height' use='required' />
  </xs:attributeGroup>

  <xs:complexType name='Picture' >
    <xs:attributeGroup ref='tns:WidthAndHeight' />
  </xs:complexType>

</xs:schema>
```

Elements of type `Picture` must have a `width` attribute and a `height` attribute.

9.2.8 choice

```
<xs:choice id='ID' maxOccurs='union'
          minOccurs='nonNegativeInteger' >
  <!-- annotation any choice element
       group sequence  -->
</xs:choice>
```

The `choice` element denotes a model group in which one of the particles contained within the choice may appear in the instance document. The `choice` element can appear as part of a complex type definition or as part of a named model group. In both cases it may appear as the first child of the construct or as a more deeply nested descendant.

Attributes

Name	Type	Default	Description
id	ID		An attribute for application use.
maxOccurs	Union	1	Specifies the maximum number of times a particle from the choice may appear in the context the choice appears in. The value of this attribute may be any nonNegativeInteger or the string unbounded. If the choice element is a child of a top-level group element then this attribute may not occur.
minOccurs	nonNegativeInteger	1	Specifies the minimum number of times a particle from the choice must appear in the context the choice appears in. If the choice element is a child of a top-level group element then this attribute may not occur.

Child elements

Name	Occurrence
annotation	Optional, once
element *or* group *or* choice *or* sequence *or* any	Optional, unlimited

Examples

A choice group as part of a complex type

```
<xs:complexType name='MaleOrFemalePerson' >
  <xs:sequence>
    <xs:element name='name' type='xs:string' />
    <xs:choice>
      <xs:element name='boybits' />
      <xs:element name='girlbits' />
```

```
      </xs:choice>
    </xs:sequence>
  </xs:complexType>
```

Elements of type `MaleOrFemalePerson` must have a `name` element followed by either a `boybits` element or a `girlbits` element.

9.2.9 complexContent

```
<xs:complexContent id='ID' mixed='boolean' >
  <!-- annotation extension restriction  -->
</xs:complexContent>
```

The `complexContent` element appears as a child of the `complexType` element and indicates that the complex type is being explicitly derived from some other complex type. The `complexContent` element must have either an `extension` or a `restriction` element child according to whether the base type is being extended or restricted.

Attributes

Name	Type	Default	Description
id	ID		An attribute for application use.
mixed	boolean	false	If set to true, this attribute specifies that the content model of the complex type may contain text and element children. By default, the content model of a complex type derived from another complex type may not contain text children; that is, it may only contain elements. This is also the case for complex types with no explicit base.

Child elements

Name	Occurrence
annotation	Optional, once
extension or restriction	Mandatory, once

Example

See the `extension` and `restriction` entries for examples.

Schema II

9.2.10 complexType

```
<xs:complexType abstract='boolean' block='token'
                final='token' id='ID' mixed='boolean'
                name='NCName' >
  <!-- all annotation anyAttribute attribute
       attributeGroup choice complexContent
       group sequence simpleContent  -->
</xs:complexType>
```

The complexType element is used to define structured types. Complex types may have element content with or without attributes, text and element (mixed) content with or without attributes, or text content with attributes. Complex type definitions appearing as children of a schema element are named types and can be referenced from elsewhere in the schema and from other schemas. Complex types appearing as the children of element declarations define anonymous types local to the element declaration in which they appear. The complexType element has two possible content models as shown by the following two child element tables. The first set of children applies to complex types that have no explicit base type whereas the second applies to complex types derived from an explicit type. Complex types with no explicit base type are always restrictions of the anyType in the http://www.w3.org/2001/XMLSchema namespace.

Attributes

Name	Type	Default	Description
abstract	boolean	false	Specifies whether the type is abstract. An abstract type may not appear in an instance document; rather, a derived type must appear in its place either through use of xsi:type or substitution groups.
block	token	None	Specifies what substitution mechanisms are prohibited for this type. The value of this attribute overrides any schemawide default specified by a blockDefault attribute on the schema element.
		Value	**Description**
		extension	Types derived by extension may not appear in place of this type.

Name	Type	Default	Description
		`restriction`	Types derived by restriction may not appear in place of this type.
		`#all`	Both of the above
`final`	`token`	None	Specifies which derivation mechanisms are prohibited for type definitions that reference this type as their base type. The value of this attribute overrides any schemawide default specified by a `finalDefault` attribute on the `schema` element.
		Value	**Description**
		`extension`	This type cannot be extended. Types derived by extension may not use this type as their base type.
		`restriction`	This type cannot be restricted. Types derived by restriction may not use this type as their base type.
		`#all`	Both of the above
`id`	`ID`	None	An attribute for application use.
`mixed`	`boolean`	`false`	If set to `true`, this attribute specifies that the content model of the complex type may contain text and element children. If set to `false`, the content model of a complex type derived from another complex type may not contain text children; that is, it may only contain elements. This is also the case for complex types with no explicit base.
`name`	`NCName`	None	Specifies the local part of the name of the type. No two complex or simple types in the same schema may have the same local name. This attribute is required if the `complexType` element is a child of a `schema` element. If the `complexType` element is a child of an `element` element, then this attribute must not appear.

Child elements

Name	Occurrence
annotation	Optional, once
group or all or choice or sequence	Optional, once
attribute or attributeGroup	Optional, unlimited
anyAttribute	Optional, once

Name	Occurrence
annotation	Optional, once
simpleContent or complexContent	Mandatory, once

Examples

A complex type definition with no explicit base type containing only element declarations

```
<xs:complexType name='Person' >
  <xs:sequence>
    <xs:element name='name' />
    <xs:element name='height' />
  </xs:sequence>
</xs:complexType>
```

Elements of type Person must have child name and height elements, in that order.

An anonymous complex type definition appearing inside a global element declaration

```
<xs:element name='Person' >
  <xs:complexType>
    <xs:sequence>
      <xs:element name='name' />
      <xs:element name='height' />
    </xs:sequence>
  </xs:complexType>
</xs:element>
```

The Person element must have child name and height elements, in that order.

A complex type that cannot be derived either by restriction or extension

```
<xs:complexType name='Person' final='#all' >
  <xs:sequence>
    <xs:element name='name' type='xs:string' />
    <xs:element name='height' type='xs:double' />
  </xs:sequence>
</xs:complexType>
```

The `Person` type cannot be used as the base type for any other type.

For examples of complex types derived from simple types, see the `simpleContent` entry. For examples of types derived by extension or restriction, see the `extension` and `restriction` entries.

9.2.11 documentation

```
<xs:documentation source='anyURI' xml:lang='language' >
  <!-- Any qualified or unqualified element  -->
</xs:documentation>
```

The `documentation` element contains a human-readable annotation to a schema. The human-readable portion may be contained within the `documentation` element as child elements or may be referenced from the URI reference provided by the source attribute, or both.

Attributes

Name	Type	Default	Description
source	anyURI	None	Specifies an attribute for supplementing the information provided in the `documentation` element.
xml:lang	language	None	The `lang` attribute from the `http://www.w3.org/XML/1998/namespace` namespace specifies the human-readable language in which the information in the `documentation` element is written.

Child element

Name	Occurrence
Any qualified or unqualified element	Optional, unlimited

Example

Use of documentation

```
<xs:schema xmlns:xs='http://www.w3.org/2001/XMLSchema'
          targetNamespace='urn:example-org:People'
          xmlns:tns='urn:example-org:People' >

  <xs:annotation>
    <xs:documentation xml:lang='UK-ENG' >

    This schema is an example in a book. The colour of the
    book cover is green.

    </xs:documentation>
  </xs:annotation>

</xs:schema>
```

A schema annotated with human readable information

9.2.12 element

```
<xs:element abstract='boolean' block='token'
           default='string' final='token'
           fixed='string' form='NMTOKEN' id='ID'
           maxOccurs='union'
           minOccurs='nonNegativeInteger' name='NCName'
           nillable='boolean' ref='QName'
           substitutionGroup='QName' type='QName' >
  <!-- annotation complexType key keyref
       simpleType unique  -->
</xs:element>
```

The element element either denotes an element declaration, defining a named element and associating that element with a type, or it is a reference to such a declaration. Element declarations appearing as children of a schema element are known as **global element declarations** and can be referenced from elsewhere in the schema or from other schemas. Element declarations appearing as part of complex type definitions, either directly or through a group reference, are known as **local element declarations**. Such element declarations are local to the type in which they appear. Global element declarations describe elements that are always part of the target namespace of the schema. Local element declarations describe elements that may be part of the target namespace of the schema depending on the values of the `form` attribute on the element declaration and the value of the `elementFormDefault` attribute on the `schema` element.

Attributes

Name	Type	Default	Description
abstract	boolean	false	Specifies whether the element being declared is abstract. An abstract element may not appear in an instance document; rather, an element in this element's substitution group must appear instead.
block	token		Specifies what substitution mechanisms are prohibited for the element being declared. The value of this attribute can be a list of one or more of extension, restriction, and substitution or #all. The value of this attribute overrides any schemawide default specified by a blockDefault attribute on the schema element.

Value	Description
extension	Types derived by extension may not appear in place of this element either through use of xsi:type or substitution groups.
restriction	Types derived by restriction may not appear in place of this element either through use of xsi:type or substitution groups.
substitution	Elements in the substitution group for this element may not appear in place of this element.
#all	All of the above

Name	Type	Default	Description
default	string	None	Specifies a default value for an element whose type is a simple type or a complex type derived from a simple type. The default and fixed attributes are mutually exclusive.

Name	Type	Default	Description
final	token	None	Specifies which derivation mechanisms are prohibited for element declarations that are part of a substitution group with this element declaration as the head. The value of this attribute overrides any schemawide default specified by a finalDefault attribute on the schema element.
		Value	**Description**
		extension	Elements in the substitution group of this element may not be of a type derived by extension, either directly or indirectly, from the type of this element.
		restriction	Elements in the substitution group of this element may not be of a type derived by restriction, either directly or indirectly, from the type of this element.
		#all	Both of the above
fixed	string	None	Specifies a fixed value for an element with a type that is a simple type or a complex type derived from a simple type. The fixed and default attributes are mutually exclusive.
form	NMTOKEN	None	Specifies whether a local element declaration is qualified (in the target Namespace for the schema) or unqualified (in no namespace). The value of this attribute overrides any schemawide default specified by an elementFormDefault attribute on the schema element. This attribute may not appear on a global element declaration.
		Value	**Description**
		qualified	The local name of the element is qualified by the target namespace of the schema.
		unqualified	The element is unqualified.

Name	Type	Default	Description
id	ID	None	An attribute for application use.
maxOccurs	Union	1	Specifies the maximum number of times this element may appear in the context in which the declaration appears. The value of this attribute may be any nonNegativeInteger or the string unbounded. This attribute may not appear on a global element declaration.
minOccurs	nonNegative-Integer	1	Specifies the minimum number of times this element must appear in the context in which the declaration appears. This attribute may not appear on a global element declaration.
name	NCName	None	Specifies the local part of the name of the element being declared. The name and ref attributes are mutually exclusive.
nillable	boolean	false	If this attribute is set to true, then the element may have no content, provided it is annotated in the instance document with an xsi:nil attribute with a value of true.
ref	QName	None	Specifies a reference to a global element declaration. The referenced element declaration may be in the same schema document as the referencing element declaration or it may be in a different schema document, potentially in a different namespace. This attribute may not appear on a global element declaration. The ref and name attributes are mutually exclusive.

Name	Type	Default	Description
substitution-Group	QName	None	Specifies the element that serves as the head of the substitution group to which this element declaration belongs. This attribute can only appear on a global element declaration. The referenced element declaration may be in the same schema document as the referencing element declaration or it may be in a different schema document, potentially in a different namespace.
type	QName	None	Specifies the type of the element being declared. This attribute is a reference to a simple type or a complex type. If the `type` and `ref` attributes are both absent, then the element declaration may have a `simpleType` element or a `complexType` element as one of its children, in which case the type of the element is that anonymous inline type. If no such children are present, then the type of the element is the `anyType` in the namespace `http://www.w3.org/2001/XMLSchema`.

Child elements

Name	Occurrence
annotation	Optional, once
simpleType *or* complexType	Optional, once
key *or* keyref *or* unique	Optional, unlimited

Examples

A global element declaration

```
<xs:schema xmlns:xs='http://www.w3.org/2001/XMLSchema'
           targetNamespace='urn:example-org:People' >
```

```
    <xs:element name='description' type='xs:string' />

</xs:schema>
```

A global element declaration for an element with a local name of `description`
and a namespace name of `urn:example-org:People`. This element is
based on the built-in `string` type.

A global element declaration and several local element declarations

```
<xs:schema xmlns:xs='http://www.w3.org/2001/XMLSchema'
           targetNamespace='urn:example-org:People'
           xmlns:tns='urn:example-org:People' >

    <xs:element name='Person' type='tns:Person' />

    <xs:complexType name='person' >
      <xs:sequence>
        <xs:element name='name' type='xs:string' />
        <xs:element name='height' type='xs:double' />
      </xs:sequence>
    </xs:complexType>

</xs:schema>
```

A global element declaration for an element with a local name of `person` and a
namespace name of `urn:example-org:People`. This element is based on
the `Person` complex type in the same namespace that has several local element
declarations. A document conforming to this schema would have a document element with a local name of `person` in the `urn:example-org:People`
namespace. That element would have unqualified `name` and `height` children, in
that order. The `name` element would contain a string and the `height` element
would contain a double-precision floating point number.

A global element declaration and a reference to the declaration

```
<xs:schema xmlns:xs='http://www.w3.org/2001/XMLSchema'
           targetNamespace='urn:example-org:Utilities'
           xmlns:tns='urn:example-org:Utilities' >

    <xs:element name='height' type='xs:double' />
```

```
<xs:complexType name='HeightVector' >
  <xs:sequence>
    <xs:element ref='tns:height' />
  </xs:sequence>
</xs:complexType>
```

```
</xs:schema>
```

A global element declaration for an element with a local name of `height` and a namespace name of `urn:example-org:Utilities` and a reference to that global element declaration. The element is based on the built-in `double` type. Elements of type `HeightVector` must have a child element with a local name of `height` in the namespace `urn:example-org:Utilities`.

9.2.13 extension

```
<xs:extension base='QName' id='ID' >
  <!-- all annotation anyAttribute attribute
       attributeGroup choice group sequence
          -->
</xs:extension>
```

The `extension` element appears as part of a complex type definition and indicates that the complex type is being derived by extension from some base type. The base type may be either a simple type or a complex type. If the base type is a simple type, then the extended type may only add attributes. If the base type is a complex type, the extended type may add extra elements and/or attributes. When extra elements are added, these logically appear after the elements of the base type, the resulting content model being the content model of the base type followed by the content model of the derived type with both parts treated as if they were wrapped in a `sequence` element. Complex types with `all` as their top-level compositor cannot be extended by adding particles. Only attributes can be added to such types. Similarly, an `all` group can only be used to extend a type that has an empty content model.

Attributes

Name	Type	Default	Description
base	QName	None	Specifies the base type from which the new type is derived. If the parent of the `extension` element is a `simpleContent` element, then this attribute must refer to a simple type. If the parent of the `extension` element is a `complexContent` element, then this attribute must refer to a complex type. The base type may be in the same schema document as the derived type or it may be in a different schema document, potentially in a different namespace.
id	ID	None	An attribute for application use.

Child elements

Name	Occurrence
annotation	Optional, once
all or choice or group or sequence	Optional, once
attribute or attributeGroup	Optional, unlimited
anyAttribute	Optional, once

Examples

Extending a base type with a sequence compositor with another sequence

```
<xs:schema xmlns:xs='http://www.w3.org/2001/XMLSchema'
           targetNamespace='http://example.org/People'
           xmlns:tns='http://example.org/People' >

  <xs:complexType name='Person' >
    <xs:sequence>
      <xs:element name='name' />
      <xs:element name='height' />
    </xs:sequence>
  </xs:complexType>

  <xs:complexType name='Employee' >
    <xs:complexContent>
      <xs:extension base='tns:Person' >
        <xs:sequence>
          <xs:element name='salary' />
```

Schema II

```
      </xs:sequence>
      <xs:attribute name='employeeNumber' />
    </xs:extension>
  </xs:complexContent>
</xs:complexType>

</xs:schema>
```

Both types have `sequence` as their top-level model group. Elements of type `Employee` must have name, height, and salary children, in that order. They may also have an `employeeNumber` attribute.

Extending a base type with a sequence compositor with a choice

```
<xs:schema xmlns:xs='http://www.w3.org/2001/XMLSchema'
           targetNamespace='http://example.org/People'
           xmlns:tns='http://example.org/People' >

  <xs:complexType name='Person' >
    <xs:sequence>
      <xs:element name='name' />
      <xs:element name='height' />
    </xs:sequence>
  </xs:complexType>

  <xs:complexType name='MaleFemalePerson' >
    <xs:complexContent>
      <xs:extension base='tns:Person' >
        <xs:choice>
          <xs:element name='boybits' />
          <xs:element name='girlbits' />
        </xs:choice>
      </xs:extension>
    </xs:complexContent>
  </xs:complexType>

</xs:schema>
```

The base type has `sequence` as its top-level model group whereas the derived type has `choice`. Elements of type `MaleFemalePerson` must have **name** and **height** children, in that order, followed by either a **boybits** element or a **girlbits** element.

Extending a base type with an `all` compositor

```
<xs:schema xmlns:xs='http://www.w3.org/2001/XMLSchema'
           targetNamespace='http://example.org/People'
           xmlns:tns='http://example.org/People' >

  <xs:complexType name='Person' >
    <xs:all>
      <xs:element name='name' />
      <xs:element name='height' />
    </xs:all>
  </xs:complexType>

  <xs:complexType name='Employee' >
    <xs:complexContent>
      <xs:extension base='tns:Person' >
        <xs:attribute name='employeeNumber' />
      </xs:extension>
    </xs:complexContent>
  </xs:complexType>

</xs:schema>
```

The base type has an `all` compositor. The extended type adds an attribute to the base type. Elements of type `Employee` must have name and height children, in any order. They may also have an `employeeNumber` attribute.

Extending a simple type

```
<xs:schema xmlns:xs='http://www.w3.org/2001/XMLSchema'
           targetNamespace='http://example.org/People'
           xmlns:tns='http://example.org/People' >

  <xs:complexType name='Person' >
    <xs:simpleContent>
      <xs:extension base='xs:string'>
        <xs:attribute name='height' />
      </xs:extension>
    </xs:simpleContent>
  </xs:complexType>

</xs:schema>
```

Schema II

The extended type adds an attribute to the base type of `string`. Elements of type `Employee` may have a string of any length as their content. They may also have a `height` attribute.

9.2.14 `field`

```
<xs:field id='ID' xpath='string' >
  <!-- annotation  -->
</xs:field>
```

The `field` element identifies, via an XPath expression, an element or attribute relative to a context specified by a `selector` element. The element or attribute specified is part of a uniqueness or key constraint.

Attributes

Name	Type	Default	Description
id	ID	None	An attribute for application use.
xpath	string	None	Specifies the element or attribute for the field. This is always relative to the selector. This attribute uses a subset of XPath that allows forms shown in the following table where x, y, and z are element names that may be qualified or unqualified, and a is an attribute name that may be qualified or unqualified. The axis identifier `child::` may appear in front of x, y, and z, and the axis identifier `attribute::` may appear in place of the @ symbol.

XPath	Description
.	The selector itself
x	Child element
x/y	Grandchild element
x/y/z	Great-grandchild element, and so on
.//y	Descendant element
@a	Attribute
x/@a	Attribute of child element

Name	Type	Default	Description
		x/y/@a	Attribute of grandchild element
		x/y/z/@a	Attribute of great-grandchild element, and so on
		.//y/@a	Attribute of descendant element
		e | e*	Any combination of the above expressions

Note that the `//` notation can only appear immediately after the initial `.`; it cannot appear anywhere else in an expression.

Child element

Name	Occurrence
annotation	Optional, once

Example

See the `key` and `unique` entries for examples.

9.2.15 group

```
<xs:group id='ID' maxOccurs='union'
         minOccurs='nonNegativeInteger' name='NCName'
         ref='QName' >
  <!-- all annotation choice sequence -->
</xs:group>
```

The `group` element either denotes a model group definition, defining a named group of particles, or it is a reference to such a group. The former appear as children of a `schema` element whereas the latter appear inside complex type definitions and other model group definitions. Named model groups provide a convenient mechanism for using the same set of particles in multiple complex type definitions.

Schema II

Attributes

Name	Type	Default	Description
id	ID	None	An attribute for application use.
maxOccurs	Union	1	Specifies the maximum number of times the particles in a referenced model group can appear in the referencing context. The value of this attribute may be any nonNegativeInteger or the string unbounded. This attribute may not appear on a model group definition.
minOccurs	nonNegative Integer	1	Specifies the minimum number of times the particles in a referenced model group must appear in the referencing context. This attribute may not appear on a model group definition.
name	NCName	None	The local part of the name of the model group being defined. This attribute may only appear on a model group definition.
ref	QName	None	A reference to a named model group. The referenced model group may be in the same schema document as the referencing group element or it may be in a different schema document, potentially in a different namespace. This attribute may not appear on a model group definition.

Child elements

Name	Occurrence
annotation	Optional, once
all or choice or sequence	Optional, once

Example

A named model group

```
<xs:schema xmlns:xs='http://www.w3.org/2001/XMLSchema'
           targetNamespace='urn:example-org:People'
           xmlns:tns='urn:example-org:People' >

  <xs:group name='HeightAndWeightElems' >
    <xs:sequence>
      <xs:element name='height' />
```

```
        <xs:element name='weight' />
      </xs:sequence>
    </xs:group>

    <xs:complexType name='Person' >
      <xs:sequence>
        <xs:element name='name' />
        <xs:group ref='tns:HeightAndWeightElems' />
      </xs:sequence>
    </xs:complexType>

</xs:schema>
```

Elements of type **Person** must have name, height, and weight children, in that order.

9.2.16 import

```
<xs:import id='ID' namespace='anyURI'
          schemaLocation='anyURI' >
  <!-- annotation  -->
</xs:import>
```

The import element is used to bring schema constructs such as element declarations, complex and simple type definitions, and so forth in an external schema into the importing schema document. The target namespace of the imported schema must be different from the target namespace of the importing schema document. The imported schema may have no target namespace. In the latter case, the constructs in the imported schema document are available to be referenced through unqualified names. Such constructs do not become part of the target namespace of the importing schema document.

Attributes

Name	Type	Default	Description
id	ID	None	An attribute for application use.
namespace	anyURI	None	Specifies the namespace URI of the schema being imported. If this attribute is missing, then the schema being imported describes constructs that are unqualified.

Name	Type	Default	Description
schemaLocation	anyURI	None	Identifies the location of the schema to be imported. This attribute is just a hint. A schema processor may ignore the value of this attribute and retrieve a schema for the namespace specified by the namespace attribute by other means.

Child element

Name	Occurrence
annotation	Optional, once

Example

Use of import

```
<xs:schema xmlns:xs='http://www.w3.org/2001/XMLSchema'
           targetNamespace='urn:example-org:Base'
           xmlns:tns='urn:example-org:Base' >

  <xs:import namespace='http://www.w3.org/XML/1998/
  namespace' />

  <xs:complexType name='PersonName'>
    <xs:sequence>
      <xs:element name='givenName' />
      <xs:element name='familyName' />
    </xs:sequence>
    <xs:attribute ref='xml:lang' use='fixed' value='EN-UK'
    />
  </xs:complexType>

</xs:schema>
```

A schema document for the namespace urn:example-org:Base that imports another schema for the namespace http://www.w3.org/XML/1998/ namespace. The import element does not specify a schemaLocation attribute. The schema processor will locate a schema for the http:// www.w3.org/XML/1998/namespace by some out-of-band technique.

Use of import

```
<xs:schema xmlns:xs='http://www.w3.org/2001/XMLSchema'
           targetNamespace='urn:example-org:People'
           xmlns:tns='urn:example-org:People'
           xmlns:b='urn:example-org:Base' >

  <xs:import namespace='urn:example-org:Base'
      schemaLocation='http://example.org/schemas/
      base.xsd' />

  <xs:complexType name='Person'>
    <xs:sequence>
      <xs:element name='name' type='b:PersonName' />
      <xs:element name='height' />
    </xs:sequence>
  </xs:complexType>

</xs:schema>
```

A schema document for the namespace `urn:example-org:People` that imports another schema for the namespace `urn:example-org:Base`, as defined in the previous example. The `import` element specifies a `schemaLocation` attribute which the schema processor may or may not use to locate a schema for the `urn:example-org:Base` namespace. The `PersonName` type in the `urn:example-org:Base` namespace is used as the type of the `name` element in the type definition for `Person`.

9.2.17 include

```
<xs:include id='ID' schemaLocation='anyURI' >
  <!-- annotation  -->
</xs:include>
```

The `include` element is used to bring schema constructs such as element declarations, complex and simple type definitions, etc. in an external schema document into the including schema document. The target namespace of the included schema document must match the target namespace of the including schema or it must be empty (the included schema document describes constructs in no namespace). If the included schema document describes constructs in no namespace then those constructs become part of the target namespace of the including schema document.

Schema II

Attributes

Name	Type	Default	Description
id	ID	None	An attribute for application use.
schemaLocation	anyURI	None	Identifies the location of the schema document to be included.

Child element

Name	Occurrence
annotation	Optional, once

Example

Use of include

```
<xs:schema xmlns:xs='http://www.w3.org/2001/XMLSchema'
          targetNamespace='urn:example-org:People'
          xmlns:tns='urn:example-org:People' >

  <xs:include
    schemaLocation='http://example.org/schemas/
    PeopleBase.xsd' />

  <!-- element declarations, type definitions etc. go here
    -->

</xs:schema>
```

A schema document that includes another schema containing base types. Types, global element and attribute declarations, and attribute and model group definitions in PeopleBase.xsd are available for use in the including schema document.

9.2.18 key

```
<xs:key id='ID' name='NCName' >
  <!-- annotation field selector  -->
</xs:key>
```

The key element defines a named key made up of one or more element and/or attribute fields. A key requires that the combination of fields must be unique. Any element declaration referenced through a field child of a key element must not have a `nillable` attribute with a value of `true`. A key can be referenced, via its name, using the `refer` attribute of a `keyref` element, creating a referential constraint on the content of an instance document.

Attributes

Name	Type	Default	Description
id	ID	None	An attribute for application use.
name	NCName	None	Specifies the local part of the name of the key constraint.

Child elements

Name	Occurrence
annotation	Optional, once
selector	Mandatory, once
field	Mandatory, unlimited

Example

A key constraint

```
<xs:schema xmlns:xs='http://www.w3.org/2001/XMLSchema'
           targetNamespace='urn:example-org:Orders'
           xmlns:tns='urn:example-org:Orders' >

  <xs:complexType name='Customer' >
    <xs:sequence>
      <xs:element name='id' type='xs:short' />
      <xs:element name='name' type='xs:string' />
      <xs:element name='creditlimit' type='xs:short' />
    </xs:sequence>
  </xs:complexType>

  <xs:complexType name='WidgetOrder' >
    <xs:sequence>
      <xs:element name='id' type='xs:short' />
      <xs:element name='numwidgets' type='xs:short' />
      <xs:element name='customerid' type='xs:short' />
    </xs:sequence>
  </xs:complexType>

  <xs:element name='customersandorders' >
```

Schema II

```
      <xs:complexType>
        <xs:sequence>
          <xs:element name='customer' type='tns:Customer'
              minOccurs='1' maxOccurs='unbounded' />
          <xs:element name='order' type='tns:WidgetOrder'
              minOccurs='1' maxOccurs='unbounded' />
        </xs:sequence>
      </xs:complexType>

      <xs:key name='CustomerID' >
        <xs:selector xpath='customer' />
        <xs:field xpath='id' />
      </xs:key>

      <xs:keyref name='OrderToCustomer'
              refer='tns:CustomerID' >
        <xs:selector xpath='order' />
        <xs:field xpath='customerid' />
      </xs:keyref>
    </xs:element>

  </xs:schema>
```

The key element selects customer children of the customersandorders element through the xpath attribute of the selector element. The xpath attribute of the field element then specifies that the id children of those customer elements must be unique; that is, no two customer elements can have the same value for their id child. The key also has a name, CustomerID, so that it can be refered to from a keyref element.

The keyref element selects order children of the customersandorders element through the xpath attribute of the selector element. The refer attribute references the CustomerID key described earlier, and the xpath attribute of the field element then specifies that the customerid children of the order elements identified by the selector must have a corresponding value in the id elements identified by the key.

9.2.19 keyref

```
<xs:keyref id='ID' name='NCName' refer='QName' >
  <!-- annotation field selector  -->
</xs:keyref>
```

The keyref element defines a referential constraint made up of element and/or attribute fields that refer to a key that is similarly made up of element and/or attribute fields. The fields that make up the referential constraint are compared, in order, with the fields of the key to which the referential constraint refers.

Attributes

Name	Type	Default	Description
id	ID	None	An attribute for application use.
name	NCName	None	Specifies the local part of the name of the keyref constraint.
refer	QName	None	Specifies the QName of the key to which this keyref refers.

Child elements

Name	Occurrence
annotation	Optional, once
selector	Mandatory, once
field	Mandatory, unlimited

Example

See the key entry for an example.

9.2.20 notation

```
<xs:notation id='ID' name='NCName' public='token'
             system='anyURI' >
  <!-- annotation  -->
</xs:notation>
```

The notation element denotes a notation declaration associating a name with a public identifier and optionally a system identifier. Notation declarations are typically used to deal with out-of-band binary data.

Schema II

Attributes

Name	Type	Default	Description
id	ID	None	An attribute for application use.
name	NCName	None	Specifies the local name of the notation being declared.
public	token	None	Specifies the public identifier for the notation. The syntax for public identifiers is defined in ISO-8879.
system	anyURI	None	Specifies a system identifier for the notation, often an executable capable of dealing with resources of this notation type.

Child element

Name	Occurrence
annotation	Optional, once

Example

Use of notation

```
<xs:schema xmlns:xs='http://www.w3.org/2001/XMLSchema'
           targetNamespace='urn:example-org:Pictures'
           xmlns:tns='urn:example-org:Pictures' >

  <xs:notation name='jpg' public='image/jpeg'
    system='display.exe' />
  <xs:notation name='png' public='image/png' />
  <xs:notation name='gif' public='image/gif'
    system='display.exe' />

  <xs:simpleType name='myGraphicsFormats'>
    <xs:restriction base='xs:NOTATION'>
      <xs:enumeration value='jpg' />
      <xs:enumeration value='png' />
      <xs:enumeration value='gif' />
    </xs:restriction>
  </xs:simpleType>

  <xs:complexType name='picture' >
    <xs:attribute name='width' />
    <xs:attribute name='height' />
```

```
   <xs:attribute name='format'
       type='tns:myGraphicsFormats' />
  </xs:complexType>

</xs:schema>
```

A schema with notations for several graphic formats and a complex type containing a `format` attribute of type NOTATION. This attribute would have a QName value of `tns:jpg`, `tns:png`, or `tns:gif` in the instance document where the `tns` prefix was mapped to the `urn:example-org:Pictures` namespace URI.

9.2.21 redefine

```
<xs:redefine id='ID' schemaLocation='anyURI' >
  <!-- annotation attributeGroup complexType group
       simpleType  -->
</xs:redefine>
```

The `redefine` element is used to bring schema constructs such as element declarations, complex and simple type definitions, and so forth, in an external schema into a schema document and to redefine certain complex types, simple types, named model groups, and named attribute groups in the schema being brought in. Such redefinitions appear inside the `redefine` element and must be in terms of the type or group itself. That is to say, complex types and simple types must name themselves as the base type, and named model and attribute groups must contain exactly one reference to themselves. The redefined types and named groups effectively overwrite the definitions in the original schema such that any references to those types and model groups now reference the redefined versions. The target namespace of the redefined schema must match the target namespace of the including schema or it must be empty. If the target namespace of the redefined schema is empty, then the constructs in that schema become part of the target namespace of the redefining schema document.

Attributes

Name	Type	Default	Description
id	ID	None	An attribute for application use.
schemaLocation	anyURI	None	Identifies the location of the schema document to be redefined.

Child elements

Name	Occurrence
`annotation`	Optional, once
`simpleType` *or* `complexType` *or* group *or* `attributeGroup`	Optional, unlimited

Example

Use of `redefine`

```
<!-- person.v1.xsd -->
<xs:schema xmlns:xs='http://www.w3.org/2001/XMLSchema'
          targetNamespace='urn:example-org:People' >

  <xs:complexType name='Person' >
    <xs:sequence>
      <xs:element name='name' />
      <xs:element name='height' />
    </xs:sequence>
  </xs:complexType>
</xs:schema>


<!-- person.v2.xsd -->
<xs:schema xmlns:xs='http://www.w3.org/2001/XMLSchema'
          targetNamespace='urn:example-org:People'
          xmlns:tns='urn:example-org:People' >

  <xs:import namespace='http://www.w3.org/XML/1998/
    namespace' />
  <xs:redefine schemaLocation='person.v1.xsd' >
    <xs:complexType name='Person' >
      <xs:complexContent>
        <xs:extension base='tns:Person' >
          <xs:attribute ref='xml:lang' use='required' />
        </xs:extension>
      </xs:complexContent>
    </xs:complexType>
  </xs:redefine>

</xs:schema>
```

An example showing two schema documents, both with a `targetNamespace` attribute of `urn:example-org:People`. The second document, `person.v2.xsd`, uses `redefine` to add an `xml:lang` attribute to the `Person` type defined in `person.v1.xsd`.

9.2.22 `restriction`

```
<xs:restriction base='QName' id='ID' >
  <!-- all annotation anyAttribute attribute
       attributeGroup choice enumeration fractionDigits
       group length maxExclusive maxInclusive
       maxLength minExclusive minInclusive minLength
       pattern sequence simpleType totalDigits
       whitespace  -->
</xs:restriction>
```

The `restriction` element appears as part of a complex type definition and indicates that the complex type is being derived by restriction from a base type. The base type must be a complex type. If the base type has no particles, only text and/or attributes, then the derived type can specify a tighter value space for the text content using facets. The valid children for such use of the `restriction` element are shown in the first table under Child elements.

If the base type contains any particles, then the derived type may specify tighter occurrence constraints for those particles and/or narrower value spaces for the simple types used by elements in those particles. The derived type must list all the particles of the base type and the particles of the base type's ancestors. The derived type must be a valid instance of the base type; that is, it cannot remove any particles that were mandatory in the base type. The valid children for such use of the `restriction` element are shown in the second table under Child elements.

In both cases, if the base type contains attributes, then the derived type may specify tighter occurrence constraints for those attributes and/or narrower value spaces for the types of those attributes. The derived type cannot remove attributes that were required in the base type.

Attributes

Name	Type	Default	Description
base	QName	None	Specifies the base type from which the new type is derived. The base type must be a complex type. The type referred to may be in the same namespace as the derived type, a different namespace from the derived type, or may be unqualified (that is, in no namespace).
id	ID	None	An attribute for application use.

Child elements

Name	Occurrence
annotation	Optional, once
simpleType	Optional, once
minExclusive or minInclusive or maxExclusive or maxInclusive or totalDigits or fractionDigits or length or minLength or maxLength or enumeration or pattern or whiteSpace	Optional, unlimited
attribute or attributeGroup	Optional, unlimited
anyAttribute	Optional, once

Child elements

Name	Occurrence
annotation	Optional, once
all or choice or group or sequence	Optional, once
attribute or attributeGroup	Optional, unlimited
anyAttribute	Optional, once

Examples

Restriction of a complex type containing elements and attributes

```
<xs:schema xmlns:xs='http://www.w3.org/2001/XMLSchema'
           targetNamespace='urn:example-org:People'
           xmlns:tns='urn:example-org:People' >

  <xs:complexType name='MaleFemalePerson' >
    <xs:sequence>
      <xs:element name='name' />
```

```
    <xs:element name='weight' minOccurs='0' />
  </xs:sequence>
  <xs:attribute name='sex' />
</xs:complexType>

<xs:complexType name='WeightlessHermaphroditePerson' >
  <xs:complexContent>
    <xs:restriction base='tns:MaleFemalePerson' >
      <xs:sequence>
        <xs:element name='name' />
      </xs:sequence>
      <xs:attribute name='sex' use='prohibited' />
    </xs:restriction>
  </xs:complexContent>
</xs:complexType>

</xs:schema>
```

The base type is restricted by removing an element and an attribute. Elements of type `MaleFemalePerson` must have a name followed by an optional weight child. They may also have a `sex` attribute. Elements of type `WeightlessHermaphroditePerson` must have a name child only. They must not have a weight child or a `sex` attribute.

Restriction of a complex type containing text and attributes

```
<xs:schema xmlns:xs='http://www.w3.org/2001/XMLSchema'
           targetNamespace='urn:example-org:People'
           xmlns:tns='urn:example-org:People' >

  <xs:complexType name='MaleFemalePerson' >
    <xs:simpleContent>
      <xs:extension base='string'>
        <xs:attribute name='sex' />
      </xs:extension>
    </xs:simpleContent>
  </xs:complexType>

  <xs:complexType name='WeightlessHermaphroditePerson' >
    <xs:simpleContent>
      <xs:restriction base='tns:MaleFemalePerson' >
```

```
      <xs:minLength value='10' />
           <xs:maxLength value='100' />
        <xs:attribute name='sex' use='prohibited' />
      </xs:restriction>
    </xs:complexContent>
  </xs:complexType>

</xs:schema>
```

The base type is restricted by removing an attribute and applying facets to the simple type base. Elements of type MaleFemalePerson contain a string of any length and may also have a sex attribute. Elements of type WeightlessHermaphroditePerson must contain a string of at least ten characters and no more than 100 characters and must not have a sex attribute.

9.2.23 schema

```
<xs:schema attributeFormDefault='NMTOKEN'
         blockDefault='list of token'
         elementFormDefault='NMTOKEN'
         finalDefault='token' id='ID'
         targetNamespace='anyURI' version='string'
         xml:lang='language' >
  <!-- annotation attribute attributeGroup complexType
       element group import include notation redefine
       simpleType  -->
</xs:schema>
```

The schema element is always the top-level element of any XML Schema document. All type definitions, elements, declarations, and other constructs appear as descendants of the schema element. All the types, elements, attributes, and other items defined within a schema are either part of one particular namespace, as specified by the targetNamespace attribute, or are part of no namespace.

Attributes

Name	Type	Default	Description
attributeForm Default	NMTOKEN	Unqualified	Specifies whether local attribute declarations are qualified (in the target-Namespace for the schema) or unqualified by default. This setting specified by this attribute can be overridden on a per-attribute declaration basis by the `form` attribute.
blockDefault	list of token	Empty list	Specifies what substitution mechanisms are prohibited for elements. The setting specified by this attribute can be overridden on a per-type declaration basis by using the `block` attribute.
		Value	**Description**
		`extension`	Types derived by extension may not appear in place of a particular element either through the use of `xsi:type` or substitution groups.
		`restriction`	Types derived by restriction may not appear in place of a particular element either through use of `xsi:type` or substitution groups.
		`substitution`	Elements in the substitution group for a particular element may not appear in place of that element.
		`#all`	All of the above
elementForm Default	NMTOKEN	unqualified	Specifies whether local element declarations are `qualified` (in the targetNamespace for the schema) or `unqualified` by default. This setting specified by this attribute can be overridden on a per-element declaration basis by the `form` attribute.
finalDefault	token	Empty list	Specifies what derivation mechanisms are prohibited for type definitions defined in the schema document. The setting specified by this attribute can be overridden on a per-type definition basis by using the `final` attribute.

Name	Type	Default	Description
		Value	**Description**
		extension	Types cannot be extended by default.
		restriction	Types cannot be restricted by default.
		#all	Both of the above
id	ID		Specifies an attribute for application use.
target-Namespace	anyURI	None	Specifies the namespace that this schema document describes. All global element and attribute declarations along with all complex and simple type definitions, model group definitions and attribute group definitions, and uniqueness and key constraint defintions are part of the target namespace for a schema document. If this attribute is not present, then all schema constructs contained in the schema document describe constructs in no namespace. A schema document for a given namespace forms part of an overall schema that can be used to validate instance documents containing elements and/or attributes in that namespace. A schema document with no target namespace can be used to validate instance documents containing elements or attributes in no namespace. It can also become part of a schema with a target namespace through the include and/or redefine mechanisms.
version	string	None	Specifies an attribute for application use.
xml:lang	language	None	The lang attribute from the http://www.w3.org/XML/1998/namespace namespace denotes the human-readable language in which the schema element is written.

Child elements

Name	Occurrence
annotation *or* include *or* import *or* redefine	Optional, unlimited
annotation *or* attribute *or* attributeGroup *or* complexType *or* element *or* group *or* notation *or* simpleType	Optional, unlimited
annotation	Optional, unlimited

Examples

A schema document

```
<xs:schema xmlns:xs='http://www.w3.org/2001/XMLSchema'
           targetNamespace='urn:example-org:People'
           xmlns:t='urn:example-org:People' >

  <!-- type definitions, element attribute declarations
     etc. appear here -->

</xs:schema>
```

A schema document describing contructs in the namespace `urn:example-org:People`. Note the namespace declaration for `urn:example-org:People`. This is needed because various attributes in the schema language are of type `QName`, and it is common in a schema construct to want to refer to another schema construct. Having a namespace declaration for the target namespace makes this possible. The schema document uses default values for the `elementFormDefault` and `attributeFormDefault` attributes; therefore, local element declarations and local attribute declarations are not in the target namespace for the schema; that is, they are unqualified.

A schema document with no target namespace

```
<xs:schema xmlns:xs='http://www.w3.org/2001/XMLSchema' >

  <!-- type definitions, element attribute declarations
     etc. appear here -->

</xs:schema>
```

Schema II

A schema document describing constructs in no namespace. The schema document uses default values for the `elementFormDefault` and `attribute-FormDefault` attributes.

A schema document with qualified local element declarations

```
<xs:schema xmlns:xs='http://www.w3.org/2001/XMLSchema'
           targetNamespace='urn:example-org:Vehicles'
           xmlns:tns='urn:example-org:Vehicles'
           elementFormDefault='qualified' >

  <!-- type definitions, element attribute declarations
     etc. appear here -->

</xs:schema>
```

A schema document describing constructs in the namespace `urn:example-org:Vehicles`. Local element declarations are, by default, in the target namespace for the schema (`urn:example-org:Vehicles`); that is, they are qualified.

A schema document with several nondefault attribute values

```
<xs:schema xmlns:xs='http://www.w3.org/2001/XMLSchema'
           targetNamespace='urn:example-org:Utilities'
           xmlns:tns='urn:example-org:Utilities'
           finalDefault='#all'
           blockDefault='substitution' >

  <!-- type definitions, element attribute declarations
     etc. appear here -->

</xs:schema>
```

A schema document describing constructs in the namespace `urn:example-org:Utilities`. Complex types defined in this schema cannot, by default, be derived from either a extension or restriction as specified by the `finalDefault` attribute. Also, element substitution using substitution groups is disallowed by default as specified by the `blockDefault` attribute.

9.2.24 selector

```
<xs:selector id='ID' xpath='string' >
  <!-- annotation -->
</xs:selector>
```

The `selector` element identifies, via an XPath expression, an element relative to a context. The selected element provides the context for subsequent `field` elements.

Attributes

Name	Type	Default	Description
id	ID	None	An attribute for application use.
xpath	string	None	Specifies the element or attribute for the selector. This is always relative to the current context, typically an element declaration. This attribute uses a subset of XPath that allows the following forms, where x and y are element names that may be qualified or unqualified, and a is an attribute name that may be qualified or unqualified.

XPath	Description
.	The element itself
x	Child element
x/y	Grandchild element
x/y/z	Great-grandchild element, and so on
.//y	Descendant element
e | e*	Any combination of the above expressions

Child element

Name	Occurrence
annotation	Optional, once

Example

See the `key` and `unique` entries for examples.

Schema II

9.2.25 sequence

```
<xs:sequence id='ID' maxOccurs='union'
            minOccurs='nonNegativeInteger' >
  <!-- annotation any choice element
       group sequence  -->
</xs:sequence>
```

The sequence element is used to denote a model group in which all the particles contained within the sequence must appear in the instance document in the
order listed, or, if they are optional, be missing in the instance document. The
sequence element can appear as part of a complex type definition or as part of
a named model group. In both cases it may appear as the first child of the construct or as a more deeply nested descendant.

Attributes

Name	Type	Default	Description
id	ID		An attribute for application use.
maxOccurs	Union	1	Specifies the maximum number of times particles in the sequence group can appear in the context in which the sequence appears. The value of this attribute may be any nonNegativeInteger or the string unbounded. If the sequence element is a child of a top-level group element, then this attribute may not occur.
minOccurs	nonNegativeInteger	1	Specifies the minimum number of times the parti- cles in the sequence group must appear in the context in which the sequence appears. If the sequence element is a child of a top-level group element, then this attribute may not occur.

Child elements

Name	Occurrence
annotation	Optional, once
element *or* choice *or* group *or* sequence *or* any	Optional, unlimited

Examples

A sequence group as part of a complex type

```
<xs:schema xmlns:xs='http://www.w3.org/2001/XMLSchema'
           targetNamespace='urn:example-org:People'
           xmlns:tns='urn:example-org:People' >

  <xs:element name='Person' type='tns:Person' />

  <xs:complexType name='Person' >
    <xs:sequence>
      <xs:element name='name' />
      <xs:element name='height' />
    </xs:sequence>
  </xs:complexType>

</xs:schema>
```

Elements of type `Person` must have name and height children, in that order.

A repeating sequence and sequence as part of a named model group definition

```
<xs:schema xmlns:xs='http://www.w3.org/2001/XMLSchema'
           targetNamespace='urn:example-org:People'
           xmlns:tns='urn:example-org:People' >

  <xs:group name='GroceryElems' >
    <xs:sequence>
      <xs:element name='productname' />
      <xs:element name='price'   />
    </xs:sequence>
  </xs:group>

  <xs:complexType name='Groceries' >
    <xs:sequence>
      <xs:group ref='tns:GroceryElems' />
```

```
        <xs:sequence minOccurs='1' maxOccurs='50' >
        <xs:element name='state' />
            <xs:element name='taxable' />
        </xs:sequence>
    </xs:sequence>
  </xs:complexType>

</xs:schema>
```

Elements of type `Groceries` must have producename and price children, in that order, followed by between one and fifty pairs of `state` and `taxable` elements, in that order.

9.2.26 `simpleContent`

```
<xs:simpleContent id='ID' >
  <!-- annotation extension restriction  -->
</xs:simpleContent>
```

The `simpleContent` element appears as a child of the `complexType` element and indicates that the complex type is being explicitly derived from a simple type. The `simpleContent` element must have either an `extension` or a `restriction` element child according to whether the base type is being extended or restricted.

Attribute

Name	Type	Default	Description
id	ID	None	An attribute for application use.

Child elements

Name	Occurrence
annotation	Optional, once
extension *or* restriction	Mandatory, once

Example

See the `extension` and `restriction` entries for examples.

9.2.27 unique

```
<xs:unique id='ID' name='NCName' >
  <!-- annotation field selector  -->
</xs:unique>
```

The unique element is used to denote that an attribute or element value, or a combination thereof, must be unique within a particular context. The unique element appears inside an element declaration that provides the initial context. The context is then specified further by a selector. The field element is used to specify uniqueness constraints relative to the context specifed by the selector element.

Attributes

Name	Type	Default	Description
id	ID	None	An attribute for application use.
name	NCName	None	Specifies the local part of the name of the uniqueness constraint.

Child elements

Name	Occurrence
annotation	Optional, once
selector	Mandatory, once
field	Mandatory, unlimited

Example

An element-based uniqueness constraint

```
<xs:schema xmlns:xs='http://www.w3.org/2001/XMLSchema'
           targetNamespace='urn:example-org:Groceries'
           xmlns:tns='urn:example-org:Groceries' >

  <xs:complexType name='Grocery' >
    <xs:sequence>
      <xs:element name='produce' type='xs:string' />
      <xs:sequence minOccurs='1' maxOccurs='50' >
        <xs:element name='state' type='xs:string' />
        <xs:element name='taxable' type='xs:boolean' />
      </xs:sequence>
```

Schema II

```
      </xs:sequence>
    </xs:complexType>

    <xs:element name='grocery' type='tns:Grocery' >
      <xs:unique name='stateConstraint' >
        <xs:selector xpath='state' />
        <xs:field xpath='.' />
      </xs:unique>
    </xs:element>

  </xs:schema>
```

A uniqueness constraint that specifies that the `state` element children of a `grocery` element must have unique values.

9.3 XML Schema structures: instance attributes

The XML Schema language defines four attributes for use in XML instance documents (rather than schema documents). These attributes are all in the `http://www.w3.org/2001/XMLSchema-instance` namespace. This section lists the attributes in alphabetical order with syntax, a description, and examples. In all cases the `xsi` namespace prefix is mapped to the `http://www.w3.org/2001/XMLSchema-instance` namespace URI.

9.3.1 nil

`xsi:nil='boolean'`

The `nil` attribute is a boolean that when set to `true` marks an element as having missing content. Such an element must be empty and the element declaration in the schema must have been annotated with a `nillable` attribute with a value of `true`.

Example

Use of nil

```
<!-- person.xsd -->
<xs:schema xmlns:xs='http://www.w3.org/2001/XMLSchema'
```

```
              targetNamespace='urn:example-org:People'
              xmlns:tns='urn:example-org:People' >

  <xs:complexType name='Person' >
    <xs:sequence>
      <xs:element name='name' type='xs:string' />
      <xs:element name='height' type='xs:double'
    nillable='true' />
    </xs:sequence>
  </xs:complexType>

  <xs:element name='person' type='tns:Person' />
</xs:schema>

<!-- person.xml -->
<p:person xmlns:p='urn:example-org:People' >
  <name>Martin</name>
  <height xmlns:xsi='http://www.w3.org/2001/XMLSchema-
    instance' xsi:nil = 'true' />
</p:person>
```

A schema document, `person.xsd`, and an instance document, `person.xml`. The schema contains a type `Person` that has `name` and `height` element declarations; the latter being annotated with a `nillable` attribute with a value of `true`. It also contains an element declaration mapping the element `person` to the `Person` type. The instance contains a `person` element in the `urn:example-org:People` namespace with child `name` and `height` elements. An `xsi:nil` attribute is present on the `height` element and that element has no content.

9.3.2 noNamespaceSchemaLocation

`xsi:noNamespaceSchemaLocation='anyURI'`

The `noNamespaceSchemaLocation` attribute provides a way of associating a schema document that has no target namespace with an instance document. The value of the attribute is a location that contains a schema containing unqualified schema constructs; that is, constructs in "no namespace." This attribute is needed because the `schemaLocation` attribute provides no way of specifying locations for schemas with no target namespace. The information in a noNamespaceSchemaLocation attribute is only a hint to a processor. The processor is not required to use the information. It may locate schemas in any way it wishes.

Example

Use of noNamespaceSchemaLocation

```
<person xmlns:xsi='http://www.w3.org/2001/XMLSchema-
    instance'
        xsi:noNamespaceSchemaLocation='http://example.org/
    schemas/person.xsd'>
  <name>Martin</name>
  <height>64</height>
</person>
```

A noNamespaceSchemaLocation attribute on an instance document containing unqualified elements

9.3.3 schemaLocation

xsi:schemaLocation='list of anyURI'

The schemaLocation attribute provides a way of associating schema documents that have a target namespace with an instance document. The attribute is a list of pairs of URI references separated by whitespace. The first URI reference in each pair is a namespace name whereas the second is the location of a schema that describes that namespace. Multiple pairs of URI references can be listed, each with a different namespace name part. It is also legal to list the same namespace multiple times, thus providing multiple potential locations for a processor to locate a schema. The information in a schemaLocation attribute is only a hint to a processor. The processor is not required to use the information. It may locate schemas in any way it wishes.

Example

Use of schemaLocation

```
<p:Person xmlns:p='http://example.org/People'
          xmlns:v='http://example.org/Vehicles'
          xmlns:xsi='http://www.w3.org/2001/XMLSchema-
              instance'
```

```
              xsi:schemaLocation='http://example.org/People
                     http://example.org/schemas/people.xsd
                http://example.org/Vehicles http://
                     example.org/schemas/vehicles.xsd
                http://example.org/People http:
                     //example.org/schemas/people.xsd' >
  <name>Martin</name>
  <age>33</age>
  <height>64</height>
  <v:Vehicle>
    <colour>White</colour>
    <wheels>4</wheels>
    <seats>5</seats>
  </v:Vehicle>
</p:Person>
```

A `schemaLocation` attribute providing location information for several schema documents

---

9.3.4 type

```
xsi:type='QName'
```

The `type` attribute specifies the type of an element. The value of the attribute is a QName that refers to a type defined in a schema. This attribute allows an element to assert that it is of a particular type even though there may not be an element declaration in the schema binding that element to that type. It is also used when derived complex types are used in instance documents in place of the expected base type. In the latter case, the schema processor will ensure that the type specified in the `type` attribute is derived from the type specified in the element declaration in the schema.

Example

Use of type

```
<!-- person.xsd -->
<xs:schema xmlns:xs='http://www.w3.org/2001/XMLSchema'
           targetNamespace='urn:example-org:People'
           xmlns:tns='urn:example-org:People' >
  <xs:element name='person' type='tns:Person' />
```

```
<xs:complexType name='Person' >
  <xs:sequence>
    <xs:element name='name' type='xs:string' />
    <xs:element name='height' type='xs:double' />
  </xs:sequence>
</xs:complexType>

<xs:complexType name='Employee' >
  <xs:complexContent>
    <xs:extension base='tns:Person' >
      <xs:sequence>
        <xs:element name='salary' type='xs:double' />
      </xs:sequence>
    </xs:extension>
  </xs:complexContent>
</xs:complexType>

</xs:schema>

<!-- person.xml -->
<p:Person xmlns:p='urn:example-org:People'
          xmlns:xsi='http://www.w3.org/2001/XMLSchema-
              instance'
          xsi:type='p:Employee' >
  <name>Martin</name>
  <height>64</height>
  <salary>2.50</salary>
</p:Person>
```

A schema document, `person.xsd`, and an instance document, `person.xml`. The schema document contains a base type `Person`, derived type `Employee`, and an element declaration `person`. The instance shows the use of the `xsi:type` attribute to assert that the `person` element in the `urn:example-org:People` namespace is of type `Employee` in the same namespace.

9.4   References

Thompson, Henry S., et al. *XML Schema Part 1: Structures.*
Available at *http://www.w3.org/TR/xmlschema-1*. 2001.

Fallside, David C. *XML Schema Part Zero: Primer.*
Available at *http://www.w3.org/TR/xmlschema-0*. 2001.

Schema II

Chapter 10
SOAP 1.1

The Simple Object Access Protocol (SOAP) is an XML messaging specification that describes a message format along with a set of serialization rules for datatypes including structured types and arrays. In addition, it describes how to use the Hypertext Transfer Protocol (HTTP) as a transport for such messages. SOAP messages are effectively service requests sent to some end point on a network. That end point may be implemented in any number of ways—Remote Protocol Call (RPC) server, Component Object Model (COM) object, Java servlet, Perl script—and may be running on any platform. Thus, SOAP is about interoperability between applications running on potentially disparate platforms using various implementation technologies in various programming languages.

10.1 Introduction to SOAP messages

SOAP messages are transmitted between applications and may pass through a number of intermediaries as they travel from the initial sender to the ultimate recipient. SOAP messages are comprised of an `Envelope` element, with an optional `Header` and a mandatory `Body` child element. All three elements are in the namespace `http://schemas.xmlsoap.org/soap/envelope/`. The `Envelope` identifies the XML as being a SOAP message and must be the root element of the message. The `Body` element contains the message payload. The `Header` element provides an extension hook that allows SOAP to be extended in arbitrary ways. The following sections describe these elements, attributes that SOAP defines, the data encoding rules SOAP specifies, and the HTTP binding.

Example

Skeleton SOAP message

```
<soap:Envelope
    xmlns:soap='http://schemas.xmlsoap.org/soap/envelope/'
```

SOAP

357

```
    soap:encodingStyle='http://schemas.xmlsoap.org/soap/
       encoding/'>
 <soap:Header>
   <!-- extensions go here -->
 </soap:Header>
 <soap:Body>
   <!-- message payload goes here -->
 </soap:Body>
</soap:Envelope>
```

10.2 Elements in SOAP messages

SOAP defines four elements in the namespace `http://schemas.xmlsoap.org/soap/envelope/`. These elements are listed in the following sections in alphabetical order, with a description and details of child elements. All four elements can be annotated with any number of namespace-qualified attributes. Example SOAP request and response messages are shown for reference.

10.2.1 Body

```
<soap:Body
    xmlns:soap='http://schemas.xmlsoap.org/soap/envelope/' >
  <!-- message payload goes here -->
</soap:Body>
```

The Body element contains the message payload. In the case of a request message the payload of the message is processed by the receiver of the message and is typically a request to perform some service and, optionally, to return some results. In the case of a response message the payload is typically the results of some previous request or a fault.

Child elements

One or more namespace-qualified elements that are not in the `http://schemas.xmlsoap.org/soap/envelope/` namespace or, if a fault occurred, a Fault element in the `http://schemas.xmlsoap.org/soap/envelope/` namespace

Examples

A SOAP request

```
<soap:Envelope
      xmlns:soap="http://schemas.xmlsoap.org/soap/envelope/"
      soap:encodingStyle='http://schemas.xmlsoap.org/soap/
          encoding/'>
  <soap:Body>
    <m:Subtract
        xmlns:m="http://example.org/Calculator/Points">
        <pt1>
          <x>10</x>
          <y>20</y>
        </pt1>
        <pt2>
          <x>100</x>
          <y>200</y>
        </pt2>
    </m:Subtract>
  </soap:Body>
</soap:Envelope>
```

An example request message showing the Envelope and Body elements

A SOAP response

```
<soap:Envelope
      xmlns:soap="http://schemas.xmlsoap.org/soap/envelope/"
      soap:encodingStyle='http://schemas.xmlsoap.org/soap/
          encoding/'>
  <soap:Body>
    <method:SubtractResponse
        xmlns:method="http://example.org/Calculator/Points">
        <ptret>
          <x>-90</x>
          <y>-180</y>
        </ptret>
    </method:SubtractResponse>
  </soap:Body>
</soap:Envelope>
```

A message generated in response to the request message in the request example

10.2.2 Envelope

```
<soap:Envelope
      xmlns:soap='http://schemas.xmlsoap.org/soap/envelope/'
>
  <!-- header and body go here -->
</soap:Envelope>
```

The `Envelope` element is the root element for all SOAP messages, identifying the XML as a SOAP message.

Child elements

An optional `Header` element and a mandatory `Body` element. Both elements are in the `http://schemas.xmlsoap.org/soap/envelope/` namespace.

10.2.3 Fault

```
<soap:Fault
      xmlns:soap='http://schemas.xmlsoap.org/soap/envelope/'
>
  <!-- detail goes here -->
</soap:Fault>
```

The `Fault` element indicates that an error occurred while processing a SOAP request. This element only appears in response messages.

Child elements

A `faultcode` element followed by a `faultstring` element followed by an optional `faultactor` element and an optional `detail` element. Each of these children is described in the following:

Name	Syntax	Description
faultcode	`<faultcode xmlns=''>` `QName</faultcode>`	The `faultcode` element is of type QName and indicates what fault occurred. Several existing categories of fault code are defined, all in the `http://schemas.xmlsoap.org/soap/envelope/` namespace. `VersionMismatch` indicates that the recipient of a message did not recognize the namespace name of the `Envelope` element. `MustUnderstand` indicates that the recipient of an element child of the `Header` element had a `soap:mustUnderstand` attribute but that element was not understood by the recipient. `Client` indicates the SOAP message did not contain all the required information in order for the recipient to process it. This could mean that something was missing from inside the `Body` element. Equally, an expected extension inside the `Header` element could have been missing. In either case, the sender should not resend the message without correcting the problem. `Server` indicates that the recipient of the message was unable to process the message because of some server-side problem. The message contents were not at fault; rather, some resource was unavailable or some processing logic failed for a reason other than an error in the message. The sender may legitimately resend the message at a later time. All these fault codes may be followed by a period and a further string providing more detailed information about the error; for example, `Client.InvalidParameter`.

faultstring	`<faultstring`
	`xmlns=''>string`
	`</faultstring>`
		The `faultstring` element is of type `string` and provides a human-readable description of whatever fault occurred.

Name	Syntax	Description
faultactor	`<faultactor xmlns=''> uriReference </faultactor>`	The `faultactor` element is of type `uriReference` and indicates the source of the fault. This may be the ultimate recipient of the request message, in which case the element is optional. Alternatively, the source of the fault may be an intermediary somewhere in the path the message took to get from the sender to the ultimate recipient. In this case the element must be present.
detail	`<detail xmlns=''> any number of elements in any namespace </detail>`	The `detail` element is used to carry application-specific error information and may be annotated with any number of attributes from any namespace, and may have any number of namespace-qualified element children. The `detail` element must be present if the fault is the result of the recipient being unable to process the `Body` element. The `detail` element is not used to provide error information in the case of the recipient being unable to process an element child of the `Header` element. In such cases, error information is placed inside the `Header` element.

Example

A SOAP fault

```
<soap:Envelope
     xmlns:soap="http://schemas.xmlsoap.org/soap/envelope/"
     soap:encodingStyle='http://schemas.xmlsoap.org/soap/
         encoding/'>
  <soap:Body>
    <soap:Fault>
      <faultcode>soap:Client.InvalidRequest</faultcode>
      <faultstring>Invalid Request: Divide operation not
          supported</faultstring>
      <faultactor>http://marting.develop.com/soap/
          calcxslt.asp</faultactor>
      <detail>
        <m:MethodError
          xmlns:m='uuid:361C5CDE-FC66-4B17-A2C1-
          EB221DEFFD66'>
          <request>Divide</request>
```

```
            <reason>Operation not supported</reason>
          </m:MethodError>
        </detail>
      </soap:Fault>
    </soap:Body>
</soap:Envelope>
```

An example of a fault in which the request message contained an invalid operation request

10.2.4 Header

```
<soap:Header
      xmlns:soap='http://schemas.xmlsoap.org/soap/envelope/'
>
    <!-- extensions go here -->
</soap:Header>
```

The Header element namespace serves as a container for extensions to SOAP. No extensions are defined by the specification, but user-defined extension services such as transaction support, locale information, authentication, digital signatures, and so forth could all be implemented by placing some information inside the Header element. Children of the Header element may be annotated with the mustUnderstand and/or actor attributes.

Child elements

Any number of namespace-qualified elements that are not in the http:// schemas.xmlsoap.org/soap/envelope/ namespace

Example

A SOAP Header

```
<soap:Envelope
      xmlns:soap="http://schemas.xmlsoap.org/soap/envelope/"
      soap:encodingStyle='http://schemas.xmlsoap.org/soap/
          encoding/'>
  <soap:Header>
    <x:Locale
      xmlns:x='http://example.org/Extensions/Locale'>
      <language>en</language>
```

SOAP

```
        <sublang>uk</sublang>
      </x:Locale>
    </soap:Header>
    <soap:Body>
      <!-- message payload goes here -->
    </soap:Body>
  </soap:Envelope>
```

An example extension for locale information requesting that the recipient of the message send any responses localized for the specified locale; in this case, UK English.

10.3 Attributes in SOAP messages

SOAP defines three attributes in the namespace `http://schemas.xml-soap.org/soap/envelope/`. These attributes are listed in the following sections in alphabetical order with a description and examples.

10.3.1 actor

```
soap:actor='anyURI'
```

The `actor` attribute is used to annotate an extension element. It specifies a URI identifying the intermediary for which the annotated extension element is intended. If the value of the attribute is the URI `http://schemas.xml-soap.org/soap/actor/next`, then the extension is intended for the next intermediary in the chain, which in the case of the initial sender will be the first one. If the attribute is not present, then the extension element is intended for the ultimate recipient of the message.

Examples

Use of the `actor` *attribute*

```
<soap:Envelope
      xmlns:soap="http://schemas.xmlsoap.org/soap/envelope/"
      soap:encodingStyle='http://schemas.xmlsoap.org/soap/
          encoding/'>
  <soap:Header>
```

```
    <x:x
       xmlns:x='http://example.org/Extensions/'
       soap:actor='http://example.org/Nodes/Fireball/XL5'>
       <!-- extension detail goes here -->
    </x:x>
  </soap:Header>
  <soap:Body>
    <!-- message payload goes here -->
  </soap:Body>
</soap:Envelope>
```

An extension element intended for a specific intermediary in the chain

Use of the actor *attribute to target the first intermediary*

```
<soap:Envelope
      xmlns:soap="http://schemas.xmlsoap.org/soap/envelope/"
      soap:encodingStyle='http://schemas.xmlsoap.org/soap/
          encoding/'>
  <soap:Header>
    <x:x
xmlns:x='http://example.org/Extensions/'
soap:actor='http://schemas.xmlsoap.org/soap/actor/next'>
       <!-- extension detail goes here -->
    </x:x>
  </soap:Header>
  <soap:Body>
    <!-- message payload goes here -->
  </soap:Body>
</soap:Envelope>
```

An example extension intended for the first intermediary in the chain

10.3.2 encodingStyle

```
soap:encodingStyle='list of anyURI'
```

The encodingStyle attribute indicates to the recipient of a SOAP message which serialization format was used to encode a given element and its descendants. This attribute may appear on any element. Descendant elements may override

SOAP

the value of an encodingStyle attribute specified on an ancestor. Elements that use the encoding style described in Section 5 of the SOAP specification should use the URI http://schemas.xmlsoap.org/soapencoding/ as the value of this attribute. Several URIs may be provided, in which case the URIs identifying the more specific encoding rules should appear before those identifying less specific encoding rules.

Example

Use of encodingStyle attribute

```
<soap:Envelope
      xmlns:soap='http://schemas.xmlsoap.org/soap/envelope/'
      soap:encodingStyle='http://schemas.xmlsoap.org/soap/
          encoding/'>
  <!-- header and body go here -->
</soap:Envelope>
```

A message that uses the encoding rules described in Section 5 of the SOAP specification

10.3.3 mustUnderstand

soap:mustUnderstand='boolean'

The mustUnderstand attribute indicates to the recipient of a SOAP message whether processing of an extension element is mandatory. If the attribute has the value 1, then the recipient must recognize the extension element and process it accordingly. If the recipient does not recognize the element, it must report a fault. If the attribute has the value 0 (the default), then processing of the extension element is optional.

Examples

Use of mustUnderstand attribute

```
<soap:Envelope
      xmlns:soap="http://schemas.xmlsoap.org/soap/envelope/"
      soap:encodingStyle='http://schemas.xmlsoap.org/soap/
          encoding/'>
  <soap:Header>
    <x:x
```

```
         xmlns:x='http://example.org/Extensions/'
         soap:mustUnderstand='1' >
        <!-- extension detail goes here -->
      </x:x>
    </soap:Header>
    <soap:Body>
      <!-- message payload goes here -->
    </soap:Body>
  </soap:Envelope>
```

A mandatory extension as specified by the mustUnderstand attribute with a value of 1.

An optional extension

```
<soap:Envelope
      xmlns:soap="http://schemas.xmlsoap.org/soap/envelope/"
      soap:encodingStyle='http://schemas.xmlsoap.org/soap/
          encoding/'>
    <soap:Header>
      <x:x
         xmlns:x='http://example.org/Extensions/'
         soap:mustUnderstand='0' >
        <!-- extension detail goes here -->
      </x:x>
    </soap:Header>
    <soap:Body>
      <!-- message payload goes here -->
    </soap:Body>
  </soap:Envelope>
```

An optional extension as specified by the mustUnderstand attribute with a value of 0.

10.4 Introduction to SOAP serialization rules

SOAP defines a set of serialization rules for encoding datatypes in XML. All data is serialized as elements rather than attributes. Attributes are only used for structural metadata; for example, when references are needed. For simple types such as strings, numbers, dates, and so forth, the datatypes defined in XML Schema

SOAP

Part II—Datatypes are used. For types such as classes or structures, each field in the type is serialized using an element with the same name as the field. For array types, each array element is typically serialized using an element with the same name as the type, although other element names may be used. In both cases, if the field being serialized is itself a structure or an array, then nested elements are used. The top-level element in both the structure case and the array case is namespace qualified. Descendant elements should be unqualified.

The serialization rules apply to children of the **Header** element as well as children of the **Body** element. Such children are serialized types just like any other type. A request and any associated response are also treated as types, and are serialized according to the same rules.

Examples

Serialization of a structured Java or VB type

```
package example.org.People;
// Java class definition
class Person
{
  String name;
  float age;
  short height;
}

// VB Type definition
Public Type Person
  name As String
  age As Single
  height As Integer
End Type


<p:Person
   xmlns:p='urn:example-org:people'>
  <name>Martin</name>
  <age>33</age>
  <height>64</height>
</p:Person>
```

Serialization of a Java or VB array

```
package example.org.Num;
// Java class definition
class Numbers
{
  long[5] data;
}

// VB Type definition
Public Type Numbers
  data(5) As Long
End Type

<p:Numbers
   xmlns:p='urn:example-org:num'>
   <data enc:arrayType='xsd:long[5]'
xmlns:enc='http://schemas.xmlsoap.org/soap/encoding/'>
    <enc:long>2</enc:long>
    <enc:long>3</enc:long>
    <enc:long>5</enc:long>
    <enc:long>7</enc:long>
    <enc:long>9</enc:long>
   </data>
</p:Numbers>
```

10.4.1 Serialization of simple structured data

Serializing data structures, when each field is referred to exactly once, is straight-forward. Each field is serialized as an embedded element, a descendant element of the Body element, not as an immediate child. Such an element is called a *single-reference accessor*, and it provides access to the data in the field at a single location in the message. The element name used to contain the data is the same as the field name used in the programmatic type.

Example

Serializing structured data

```
package example.org.People;
// Java class definitions
class PersonName
{
  String givenName;
  String familyName;
}

class Person
{
  PersonName name;
  float age;
  short height;

  public static void AddPerson ( Person person );
}

// VB Type definitions
Public Type PersonName
  givenName As String
  familyName As String
End Type

Public Type Person
  name As PersonName
  age As Single
  height As Integer
End Type

Public Sub AddPerson ( ByRef person As Person )
End Sub


<soap:Envelope
     xmlns:soap="http://schemas.xmlsoap.org/soap/envelope/"
     soap:encodingStyle='http://schemas.xmlsoap.org/soap/
          encoding/'>
  <soap:Body>
    <p:AddPerson
```

```
     xmlns:p='urn:example-org:people'>
     <person>
       <name>
         <givenName>Martin</givenName>
         <familyName>Gudgin</familyName>
       </name>
       <age>33</age>
       <height>64</height>
     </person>
   </p:AddPerson>
  </soap:Body>
</soap:Envelope>
```

Java and VB definitions for a method call taking a structured type representing a Person as a single parameter, followed by the SOAP message representing a request to execute such a method.

10.4.2 Serialization of structured data with multiple references

In cases when a field in a data structure is referred to in several places in that data structure (for example, in a doubly linked list), then the field is serialized as an independent element, an immediate child element of Body, and must have an id attribute of type ID. Such elements are called *multireference accessors*. They provide access to the data in the field from multiple locations in the message. Each reference to the field in the data structure is serialized as an empty element with an href attribute of type IDREF, where the value of the attribute contains the identifier specified in the id attribute on the multireference accessor preceded by a fragment identifier, #.

Example

Multireference accessors

```
package example.org.People;
// Java class definition
class PersonName
{
  String givenName;
  String familyName;
}
```

SOAP

```
class Person
{
  PersonName name;
  float age;
  short height;

  public static boolean Compare ( Person p1, Person p2 );
}


<soap:Envelope
      xmlns:soap="http://schemas.xmlsoap.org/soap/envelope/"
      soap:encodingStyle='http://schemas.xmlsoap.org/soap/
          encoding/'>
  <soap:Body xmlns:p='urn:example-org:people'>
    <p:Compare>
      <p1 href='#pid1' />
      <p2 href='#pid1' />
    </p:Compare>
    <p:Person id='pid1' >
      <name>
        <givenName>Martin</givenName>
        <familyName>Gudgin</familyName>
      </name>
      <age>33</age>
      <height>64</height>
    </p:Person>
  </soap:Body>
</soap:Envelope>
```

Java definition for a method call taking two parameters both of type `Person`, followed by the SOAP message representing a request to execute such a method where both parameters refer to the same instance of `Person`.

10.4.3 Dealing with null references in complex data structures

In certain cases when reference types exist in a programmatic data structure there is a need to represent a null reference. Such references are modeled in

SOAP messages using the `nil` attribute in the `http://www.w3.org/2001/XMLSchema-instance` namespace. Setting the value of the attribute to 1 indicates that the accessor on which it appears represents a null reference.

Example

Null references

```
package example.org.Nodes;

// Java class definition
class Node
{
  String val;
  Node next;

  public static long ListLength ( Node node );
}


<soap:Envelope
    xmlns:soap="http://schemas.xmlsoap.org/soap/envelope/"
    soap:encodingStyle='http://schemas.xmlsoap.org/soap/
        encoding/'>
    <next xmlns:xsi='http://www.w3.org/2001/XMLSchema'
        -instance xsi:nil='1' />
  <soap:Body >
    <n:ListLength xmlns:n='urn:example-org:nodes'>
    <node>
      <val>New York</val>
        <next>
          <val>Paris</val>
            <next>
              <val>London</val>
            </next>
        </next>
    </node>
    </n:ListLength>
  </soap:Body>
</soap:Envelope>
```

Java class definition for a simple linked list. The end of the list is indicated by a null reference in the `next` field. A list of three items is passed in the request message.

10.4.4 Serializing dynamically typed data

SOAP provides for serialization of dynamically typed data; that is, data typed at run-time, through a polymorphic accessor. Such accessors look like normal accessors apart from the presence of a `type` in the `http://www.w3.org/2001/XMLSchema-instance'` namespace. This attribute indicates the type the accessor actually holds. The value of this attribute may well vary from message to message.

Example

Dynamically typed date

```
package example.org.Poly;

// Java definitions
class Poly
{
  public static void Execute ( Object param );
}

' Visual Basic Definition
Public Sub Execute ( param As Variant )
End Sub


<soap:Envelope
     xmlns:soap="http://schemas.xmlsoap.org/soap/envelope/"
     soap:encodingStyle='http://schemas.xmlsoap.org/soap/
          encoding/'>
  <soap:Body>
    <p:Execute
    xmlns:p='urn:example-org:poly'
    xmlns:xsi='http://www.w3.org/2001/XMLSchema-instance'
    xmlns:xsd='http://www.w3.org/2001/XMLSchema' >
      <param xsi:type='xsd:long' >2000</param>
```

```
    </p:Execute>
   </soap:Body>
 </soap:Envelope>

<soap:Envelope
     xmlns:soap="http://schemas.xmlsoap.org/soap/envelope/"
     soap:encodingStyle='http://schemas.xmlsoap.org/soap/
         encoding/'>
  <soap:Body>
   <p:Execute
   xmlns:p='urn:example-org:poly'
   xmlns:xsi='http://www.w3.org/2001/XMLSchema-instance'
   xmlns:pre='urn:example-org:people'>
     <param xsi:type='pre:Person' >
       <name>
         <givenName>Martin</givenName>
         <familyName>Gudgin</familyName>
       </name>
       <age>33</age>
       <height>64</height>
     </param>
   </p:Execute>
  </soap:Body>
 </soap:Envelope>
```

Java and VB definitions for a method call taking a dynamically typed parameter followed by several SOAP messages representing a request to execute such a method. The first SOAP message passes a parameter of type `long` whereas the second passes a parameter of type `Person`.

10.4.5 Arrays

SOAP provides comprehensive array support. Single and multidimensional arrays are supported, along with sparse and jagged arrays and partial transmission. Arrays in SOAP are always of type `Array` in the `http://schemas.xml-soap.org/soap/encoding/` namespace, or a type derived by restriction from that type. If they are of the `Array` type, they are encoded using an `Array` element also in the `http://schemas.xmlsoap.org/soap/encoding/` namespace. If they are of a derived type, then any element name may be used. In either case, an `arrayType` attribute in the `http://schemas.xmlsoap.org/soap/encoding/` namespace is mandatory. The type of this attribute is `string`, but it in fact indicates the type of the array along with dimension information. Each dimension appears in square brackets after the QName for the type, separated by commas. Each array item is serialized as an element. The name of this element can be the type name or some arbitrary name.

Example

Simple array example

```
<soap:Envelope
    xmlns:soap='http://schemas.xmlsoap.org/soap/envelope/'
    soap:encodingStyle='http://schemas.xmlsoap.org/soap/
        encoding/'>
  <soap:Body>
    <m:MethodResponse
      xmlns:m='urn:example-org:someuri' >
      <enc:Array
    xmlns:enc='http://schemas.xmlsoap.org/soap encoding/'
    xmlns:xsd='http://www.w3.org/2001/XMLSchema'
        enc:arrayType='xsd:long[5]' >
        <enc:long>2</enc:long>
        <enc:long>3</enc:long>
        <enc:long>5</enc:long>
        <enc:long>7</enc:long>
        <enc:long>9</enc:long>
      </enc:Array>
    </m:MethodResponse>
  </soap:Body>
</soap:Envelope>
```

A response message containing an array of five `long` values. Note the value of the `arrayType` attribute indicating the size of the array.

10.4.6 Multidimensional arrays

Multidimensional arrays can be encoded by specifying multiple dimensions separated by commas inside the square brackets in the `arrayType` attribute. Any number of dimensions may be specified.

Example

Multidimensional array example

```
<soap:Envelope
    xmlns:soap='http://schemas.xmlsoap.org/soap/envelope/'
    soap:encodingStyle='http://schemas.xmlsoap.org/soap/
        encoding/'>
  <soap:Body>
    <m:Method
        xmlns:m='urn:example-org:some-uri' >
      <enc:Array
    xmlns:enc='http://schemas.xmlsoap.org/soap/encoding/'
        xmlns:xsd='http://www.w3.org/2001/XMLSchema'
        enc:arrayType='xsd:string[2,3]' >
        <item>row 1 column 1</item>
        <item>row 1 column 2</item>
        <item>row 1 column 3</item>
        <item>row 2 column 1</item>
        <item>row 2 column 2</item>
        <item>row 2 column 3</item>
      </enc:Array>
    </m:Method>
  </soap:Body>
</soap:Envelope>
```

A request message containing a two-dimensional array of strings. Note the value of the `arrayType` attribute indicating the type and dimensions of the array.

10.4.7 Partial transmission of arrays

In certain scenarios an array of a certain size may need to be transmitted, but only a subset of the items needs to be sent. For such arrays the `array` element is annotated with an `offset` attribute in the `http://schemas.xml-soap.org/soap/encoding/` namespace. The value of the `offset` attribute indicates the zero-based offset of the first element. The value appears in square brackets. Listed items are assumed to appear at contiguous locations in the array. Items may be omitted from the end of the array.

Example

Partial array tranmission

```
<soap:Envelope
    xmlns:soap='http://schemas.xmlsoap.org/soap/envelope/'
    soap:encodingStyle='http://schemas.xmlsoap.org/soap/
        encoding/'>
  <soap:Body>
    <m:Method xmlns:m='urn:example-org:someuri' >
      <enc:Array
      xmlns:enc='http://schemas.xmlsoap.org/soap/encoding/'
      xmlns:xsd='http://www.w3.org/2001/XMLSchema'
          enc:arrayType='xsd:string[9]'
          enc:offset='[2]'>
        <item>Earth</item>
        <item>Mars</item>
        <item>Jupiter</item>
      </enc:Array>
    </m:Method>
  </soap:Body>
</soap:Envelope>
```

A request message that transmits the third, fourth, and fifth items in a nine-item array

10.4.8 Sparse arrays

Sparse arrays, those in which noncontiguous items need to be transmitted, are also supported. Each serialized array item is annotated with a `position` attribute in the `http://schemas.xmlsoap.org/soap/encoding/` namespace. The value of the `position` attribute is a zero-based offset of the position of the item in the array, enclosed in square brackets.

Example

Sparse arrays

```
<soap:Envelope
    xmlns:soap='http://schemas.xmlsoap.org/soap/envelope/'
    soap:encodingStyle='http://schemas.xmlsoap.org/soap/
        encoding/'>

  <soap:Body>
```

```
      <m:Method xmlns:m='urn:example-org:someuri' >
        <enc:Array
       xmlns:enc='http://schemas.xmlsoap.org/soap/encoding/'
       xmlns:xsd='http://www.w3.org/2001/XMLSchema'
            enc:arrayType='xsd:string[9]' >
          <item enc:position='[1]'>Venus</item>
          <item enc:position='[3]'>Mars</item>
          <item enc:position='[7]'>Neptune</item>
        </enc:Array>
      </m:Method>
    </soap:Body>
  </soap:Envelope>
```

A request message that transmits the second, fourth, and eighth items in a nine-
item array

10.4.9 Jagged arrays

SOAP supports jagged arrays, also known as *arrays of arrays*. The arrayType
attribute contains a type that includes empty square brackets, as many as necessary to indicate how many dimensions each array has, followed by the dimensions of the array of arrays in square brackets as normal. The inner array elements are also annotated with the appropriate arrayType attribute.

Examples

Jagged arrays with single-reference accessors

```
<soap:Envelope
     xmlns:soap='http://schemas.xmlsoap.org/soap/envelope/'
     soap:encodingStyle='http://schemas.xmlsoap.org/soap/
         encoding/'>
  <soap:Body>
    <enc:Array
   xmlns:enc='http://schemas.xmlsoap.org/soap/encoding/'
       xmlns:xsd='http://www.w3.org/2001/XMLSchema'
       enc:arrayType='xsd:string[][2]' >
      <enc:Array enc:arrayType='xsd:string[2]'>
        <item>Mercury</item>
        <item>Venus</item>
```

SOAP

```
        </enc:Array>
        <enc:Array enc:arrayType='xsd:string[6]'>
          <item>Mars</item>
          <item>Jupiter</item>
          <item>Saturn</item>
          <item>Uranus</item>
          <item>Neptune</item>
          <item>Pluto</item>
        </enc:Array>
      </enc:Array>
    </m:Method>
  </soap:Body>
</soap:Envelope>
```

A request message that transmits an array of arrays of strings. Each array is encoded using a single-reference accessor.

Jagged arrays with multireference accessors

```
<soap:Envelope
      xmlns:soap='http://schemas.xmlsoap.org/soap/envelope/'
      soap:encodingStyle='http://schemas.xmlsoap.org/soap/
          encoding/'>
  <soap:Body
    xmlns:enc='http://schemas.xmlsoap.org/soap/encoding/'
    xmlns:xsd='http://www.w3.org/2001/XMLSchema' >
    <m:Method xmlns:m='urn:some-uri' >
      <enc:Array enc:arrayType='xsd:string[][2]' >
        <item href='#id1' />
        <item href='#id2' />
      </enc:Array>
    </m:Method>
    <enc:Array id='id1' enc:arrayType='xsd:string[2]'>
      <item>Mercury</item>
      <item>Venus</item>
    </enc:Array>
    <enc:Array id='id2'
                enc:arrayType='xsd:string[6]'>
      <item>Mars</item>
      <item>Jupiter</item>
```

```
        <item>Saturn</item>
        <item>Uranus</item>
        <item>Neptune</item>
        <item>Pluto</item>
      </enc:Array>
    </soap:Body>
  </soap:Envelope>
```

A request message that transmits an array of arrays of strings. Each array is encoded using a multireference accessor.

10.5 Introduction to the SOAP HTTP binding

SOAP defines a binding to the HTTP protocol. This binding describes the relationship between parts of the SOAP request message and various HTTP headers. All SOAP requests use the HTTP POST method and specify at least three HTTP headers: `Content-Type`, `Content-Length`, and a custom header `SOAPAction`. The actual SOAP message is passed as the body of the request or response.

10.5.1 Content-Type

```
Content-Type: text/xml; charset=character encoding
```

The `Content-Type` header for SOAP requests and responses specifies the MIME type for the message and is always `text/xml`. It may also specify the character encoding used for the XML body of the HTTP request or response. This follows the `text/xml` part of the header values.

Example

Use of Content-Type

```
POST /endpoint.pl HTTP/1.1
Content-Type: text/xml
```

An example `Content-Type` header in an HTTP request

SOAP

10.5.2 Content-Length

The Content-Length header for SOAP requests and responses is set to the number of bytes in the body of the request or response.

Examples

Use of Content-Length

```
POST /endpoint.pl HTTP/1.1
Content-Type: text/xml
Content-Length: 167
SOAPAction: urn:example-org:demos#Method

<s:Envelope
   xmlns:s='http://schemas.xmlsoap.org/soap/envelope/' >
   <s:Body>
     <m:Method xmlns:m='urn:example-org:demos' />
   </s:Body>
</s:Envelope>
```

An example Content-Length header in an HTTP request. The request is encoding using an 8-bit encoding format.

Use of Content-Length with charset

```
POST /endpoint.pl HTTP/1.1
Content-Type: text/xml; charset=UTF-16
Content-Length: 167
SOAPAction: urn:example-org:demos#Method

<s:Envelope
   xmlns:s='http://schemas.xmlsoap.org/soap/envelope/' >
   <s:Body>
     <m:Method xmlns:m='urn:example-org:demos' />
   </s:Body>
</s:Envelope>
```

An example Content-Length header in an HTTP request. The request is encoding using a 16-bit encoding format.

10.5.3 SOAPAction

The SOAPAction header indicates to the HTTP server that the request is a SOAP request. The value of the header is a URI. Beyond that, its value is undefined.

Example

Use of SOAPAction

```
POST /endpoint.pl HTTP/1.1
Content-Type: text/xml; charset=UTF-16
Content-Length: 167
SOAPAction: urn:example-org:demos#Method

<s:Envelope
   xmlns:s='http://schemas.xmlsoap.org/soap/envelope/' >
  <s:Body>
    <m:Method xmlns:m='urn:example-org:demos' />
  </s:Body>
</s:Envelope>
```

An example SOAPAction header in an HTTP request. The string preceding the # is the namespace name of the first child of the Body element whereas the string following the # is the local name of that element.

10.6 References

For more on SOAP specification, please visit

http://www.w3.org/TR/SOAP/

Index

continued

continued

continued

continued

continued